D0077050

Moral Responsibility in Conflicts

Moral Responsibility in Conflicts

Essays on Nonviolence, War, and Conscience

James F. Childress

Louisiana State University Press
Baton Rouge and London

WILLIAM MADISON RANDALL LIBRARY UNC AT WILMINGTON

Copyright © 1982 by Louisiana State University Press
All rights reserved
Manufactured in the United States of America

Designer: Rod Parker
Typeface: Melior
Typesetter: Graphic Composition, Inc.
Printer Binder: Thomson-Shore, Inc.

Library of Congress Cataloging in Publication Data

Childress, James F.
  Moral responsibility in conflicts.

  Includes bibliographical references and index.
    1. Christianity and war—Addresses, essays, lectures.
  2. Christian ethics—Addresses, essays, lectures.
  3. Responsibility—Addresses, essays, lectures.
  I. Title.
  BT736.2.C53   261.8′73   82–15197
  ISBN 0–8071–1019–1   AACR2

BT 736
.2
.C53

To my twin sons
Albert Franklin and James Frederic
in the hope that their generation
may be spared wars and rumors of wars

226868

Contents

Acknowledgments

First drafts of parts of this book, especially Chapters 1, 2, and 5, originated while I was a Fellow in Law and Religion at the Harvard Law School with fellowship support from the American Council of Learned Societies and the Center for Advanced Studies at the University of Virginia. Most of Chapter 4 was researched and written at the Henry E. Huntington Library in San Marino, California, which provided a research award, a wonderful setting, and permission to quote from the Lieber Papers. The Milton S. Eisenhower Library of the Johns Hopkins University also granted permission to quote from their Lieber papers. Finally, the Kennedy Institute of Ethics provided a stimulating context for some of the research and writing, and the Small Grants Committee at the University of Virginia provided a grant to facilitate the preparation of the manuscript. I am grateful to all these institutions for their support.

Most of this book has appeared in a different form in articles. I am grateful to the several journals and publishers for permission to use earlier materials in substantially revised form. Chapter 1 appeared in a longer version in *Journal of Religious Ethics*, I (Fall, 1973), 87–112. Chapter 2 originally appeared in a shorter version as "Reinhold Niebuhr's Critique of Pacifism," *Review of Politics*, XXXVI, No. 4 (October, 1974), 467–91. Chapter 3 first appeared in *Theological Studies*, XXXIX (September, 1978), 427–45; its current revision incorporates some materials from my review essay in *Bulletin of the Atomic Scientists*, XXXIV (October, 1978), 44–48 (reprinted by permission of the *Bulletin of the Atomic Scientists*, a magazine of science and public affairs, copyright © 1978 by the Educational Foundation for Nuclear Science, Chicago, Ill.). Chapter 4 is an expanded version of an article that appeared in *American Journal of Jurisprudence*, XXI (1976), 34–70, while Chapter 5 appeared in *Ethics*, LXXXIX (July, 1979), and Chapter 6 appeared in a volume edited by Robert Fullinwider for the Center for Philosophy and Public Policy of the University of Maryland.

Several individuals generously contributed time, energy, and ideas to this project. In particular, I am indebted to Stanley Hauerwas, James Johnson, David Little, LeRoy Walters, and John Howard Yoder, with whom I have discussed many of the ideas in this book. They are not, of course, responsible for any defects that remain.

I am also indebted to several gracious and efficient secretaries who typed or retyped portions of this book: Wanda Proffitt, LaRea Frazier, and Doris Mays of the University of Virginia, and Mary Baker and Mary Ellen Timbol of the Kennedy Institute of Ethics. Three able graduate students—Steven Dalle-Mura, James Tubbs, and Dorle Vawter—also provided valuable assistance. I am also grateful to Mr. Tubbs for preparing the index.

As always, Georgia Childress helped in numerous ways, and I dedicate this book in faith, hope, and love to our twin sons, Albert Franklin and James Frederic.

Introduction

The term *responsibility* in the title encompasses both the general or formal responsibility of justifying actions, and particular responsibilities in conflicts. Under certain conditions, we expect moral agents to submit to a process of moral justification involving charges and rebuttals. This demand for moral justification emerges when there is some reason for thinking that an act is wrong. When an act appears to violate some moral principles or rules, the agent is answerable for it; he or she is expected to offer reasons in order to rebut the charges against it.

For example, Chapter 3 reconstructs the historical deposit of just-war criteria in terms of the *nature* of prima facie duties and the *content* of the prima facie duty not to injure or kill others. Two or more prima facie duties may come into conflict in particular cases. For example, the duty not to kill others may come into conflict with the duty to protect the innocent. In such conflicts, the agent is expected to engage in a process of moral deliberation and justification to determine which course of action is morally acceptable and even obligatory.[1]

One major task of this volume is to analyze and to appraise the reasons that are given to support some duties and to justify overriding some duties. Part of the debate is whether some du-

1 For a fuller discussion of deliberation and justification, see James F. Childress, "Scripture and Christian Ethics: Some Reflections on the Role of Scripture in Moral Deliberation and Justification," *Interpretation: A Journal of Bible and Theology,* XXXIV (October, 1980), 371–80, and Tom L. Beauchamp and James F. Childress, *Principles of Biomedical Ethics* (New York: Oxford University Press, 1979), esp. Chap. 1.

ties are absolute and not merely prima facie. For example, the pacifist may hold that the duty not to kill is absolute, while the proponent of just wars may hold that the duty not to kill innocent persons directly is absolute. Part of the debate is also whether some virtually absolute duties and prima facie duties can be overridden by an appeal to consequences.

Lines may be drawn and limits may be set in different places, but the arguments for crossing those lines or breaking those limits often appeal to ends and consequences of actions. Consider, for example, the following responses to perceived injustice: nonresistance, nonviolent resistance, violent resistance within limits, and violent resistance without limits. However the line or limit is justified, it is important to determine both its meaning and its strength.

The following chapters analyze the tension between limits and ends in conflicts. This tension is handled in very different ways by different theories of responsibility. Proponents of nonviolence such as the Quakers (see Chapter 1) frequently claim that nonviolent action is both right and effective. They hold that it is morally appropriate in conflict because it respects the opponent and effectively realizes the desired ends.

Defenders of justified armed conflict (see Chapters 2–4) contend that it is not possible in some settings to realize the end in view (e.g., preventing serious injustice) without armed force. They hold that responsibility as defined by necessity sometimes dictates violence.

But even among those who hold that some ends can justify armed force, there is serious disagreement about whether those ends can justify *all* uses of force which appear to be necessary to secure them. For example, can the threat of military defeat justify the direct bombing of civilian population centers? Or can it ever be responsible to lose a battle or even to lose a war rather than violate certain moral rules? These issues about the relation of means and ends, limits and purposes—which are frequently debated in terms of "necessity"—will appear at each stage of the argument, whether it regards resort to nonviolence or to violence or to particular forms of violence. Responsibility

involves both moral principles and rules, and ends and consequences.

Sometimes this last point appears to be disputed, especially
when a contrast is drawn between an ethic of absolute values
(*Gesinnungsethik*) and an ethic of responsibility (*Verantwort-
ungsethik*).[2] Such a contrast appears to put an ethic of responsibility on the side of consequentialist approaches which are
interested only or primarily in outcomes, not in moral principles and rules that are independently significant. Although
this distinction may be useful in some contexts, there are many
different types of ethics of responsibility in nonviolence, violence, and war. For example, it is plausible to construe George
Fox's pacifistic ethic as an ethic of responsibility, even though
it differs greatly from Reinhold Niebuhr's ethic of responsibility. There are different types of ethics of responsibility precisely because the questions "to whom" and "for what" one is
responsible can be answered in so many different ways. These
answers depend on various anthropological and theological
convictions as well as on various conceptions of morality. For
example, a conviction that God rather than man is in control of
history may lead Christians to set absolute limits at nonresistance, at nonviolent resistance, or at violence within limits. This
theological conviction may undergird respect for such limits
even when the probable historical effects appear to justify their
transgression. For example, John Howard Yoder contends that
the Christian is not responsible for using armed force to make
history come out right because God is in control, whereas Paul
Ramsey invokes God's responsibility for history to argue against
the violation of such moral rules as the prohibition of direct
attacks on civilians. Reinhold Niebuhr, however, sets no limits
except for proportionality.[3]

2 Max Weber, "Politics as a Vocation," in Hans Gerth and C. Wright Mills
(eds.), *From Max Weber: Essays in Sociology* (New York: Oxford University
Press, 1958), 118–28.
3 See John Howard Yoder, *The Original Revolution: Essays on Christian
Pacifism* (Scottdale, Pa.: Herald Press, 1971), 132–47 *passim*, as well as his
various other writings, and Paul Ramsey, *Deeds and Rules in Christian Ethics*

Some individuals refuse to cross the boundaries of nonresistance or nonviolence to participate in war. They frequently appeal to their consciences: "I could not live with myself if I did that." They claim a responsibility to and for themselves, as well as to others such as God and the state. When their claim conflicts with the state's claim of the necessity of war and conscription, how should the state respond to their requests for exemption from military service? In Chapter 5, I analyze the logic of appeals to conscience, and then in Chapter 6, I explore various considerations (such as the principles of fairness, respect for persons, and utility) for determining public policies toward conscientious objectors. Our government has exempted pacifists from military service, but it has not exempted those who draw lines elsewhere. Perhaps the most controversial of all are those who refuse to participate in what they take to be an unjust war, which may be unjust in terms of its ends and consequences or in terms of its conduct. I contend that such conscientious objectors should also be exempted from military service.

(New York: Charles Scribner's Sons, 1967), 108–109, and *The Just War: Force and Political Responsibility* (New York: Charles Scribner's Sons, 1968). See also Chapter 2.

Moral Responsibility in Conflicts

Chapter One

Nonviolence: Trust and Risk Taking

The Nature of Trust

Trust is pervasive in our existence as confidence in and reliance upon the structure of the everyday world. Without some trust, one simply would not be able to act at all. According to Erik Erikson, a child in the first year of life develops a fundamental orientation of trust or mistrust toward the world in general and people in particular—an orientation that may change because of other experiences.[1] A lack of trust can prevent personal development, as in the case of an autistic child. Of course, "basic trust" is compatible with distrust of some persons and objects in our world. Although there must be trust in some significant others and perhaps in the underlying structure of life itself, it does not have to be universal and unqualified. Indeed, universal and unqualified trust would reflect gullibility. While my analysis presupposes this general and pervasive phenomenon of trust, my attention is directed toward trust between persons and trust as an attitude of one person toward another, particularly as it is expressed in acts of reliance.

Let me start with a description and an example of trust that can serve as points of reference for this discussion. One of the best descriptions of trust appears in Knud Løgstrup's *The Ethical Demand*:

It is a characteristic of human life that we naturally trust one another. This is true not only in the case of persons who are well acquainted with one another but also in the case of utter strangers. Only because of some special circum-

1 Erik H. Erikson, *Childhood and Society* (2nd ed.; New York: W. W. Norton, 1963), 247–51.

1

stance do we ever distrust a stranger in advance. Perhaps some informer has destroyed the natural trust which people spontaneously have toward one another, so that their relationship becomes oppressive and strained. Perhaps because of strife in the land, where the land is ruled by men who have no respect for law and justice, people lose confidence in one another. Under normal circumstances, however, we accept the stranger's word and do not mistrust him until we have some particular reason to do so. We never suspect a person of falsehood until after we have caught him in a lie. If we enter into conversation on the train with a person whom we have never met before and about whom we know absolutely nothing, we assume that what he says is true and do not become suspicious of him unless he begins to indulge in wild exaggerations. Nor do we normally assume a person to be a thief; not until he conducts himself in a suspicious manner do we begin to suspect him. Initially we believe one another's word; initially we trust one another. This may indeed seem strange, but it is part of what it means to be human. Human life could hardly exist if it were otherwise. We would simply not be able to live, our life would be impaired and wither away if we were in advance to distrust one another, if we were to suspect the other of thievery and falsehood from the very outset.[2]

As another example, consider the case of a mother who entrusts her child to a sitter for a few hours.

In Løgstrup's description and in the trust exhibited by the mother several points are worthy of note. First, Løgstrup says that to trust is "to deliver oneself over into the hands of another," and he uses such metaphorical language as surrendering oneself, going out of oneself, placing something of one's life (or in the case of the baby-sitter, placing one's child) in the hands of another person. Whatever their final adequacy, such metaphors helpfully express the risks of trust. Although most actions obviously involve risks of some sort (for example, the uncertainty about anticipated consequences), actions expressing trust—at least in some of the forms I shall consider—are peculiarly risk filled, and the actors are especially vulnerable. Indeed, precisely this vulnerability leads the person whose trust is betrayed to express his resentment, for the other has demonstrated indifference to his vulnerability or has decided to take advantage of it.

Trust cannot exist where there is absolute control over the

2 Knud Løgstrup, *The Ethical Demand*, trans. Theodor I. Jensen (Philadelphia: Fortress Press, 1971), 8–9.

other person. Of course, the complexity of human relationships means that many acts will be mixtures of trust and control, but insofar as control is present, trust is to that extent excluded or rendered impossible. Trust requires the possibility of error and thus the possibility of rejection and betrayal. The trustee must have the freedom to respond in different ways than we expect him to respond. In Anthony Burgess' novel, *A Clockwork Orange*, Alex could not easily be trusted before his imprisonment and treatment because he refused to operate within the constraints and boundaries of morality, but he literally could not be trusted after his treatment because he had no freedom, no choice. Automata cannot be trusted. Attempts to impose controls are attempts to guarantee certain actions and to eliminate the necessity (and possibility) of trust. Such attempts stem in many instances from distrust or mistrust. In short, trust exists in situations of uncertainty (of varying degrees), where one cannot guarantee that the trustee will act in certain ways, although the truster expects him to do so or at least relies upon him to do so.

We must distinguish between situations in which the other person's actions are controlled or guaranteed and situations in which we have perfect or absolute confidence in him. The latter suggests that trust is sometimes less risky or risk filled than I have indicated. Although the trustee has the freedom to act in other ways, his character is thought to be such that he could not conceivably act in those ways. Thus, it is necessary to distinguish, as H. J. N. Horsburgh suggests, between two criteria of trust: "confidence" and "reliance." "A may be said to trust B to do x if B enjoys his confidence, that is, if A is sure that B has no defect of such a kind as to make it doubtful whether he will do x. A may also be said to trust B to do x if he is prepared to rely upon B's doing x, that is, if he is willing to run the risks of acting as if he felt certain that B will do x."[3] Although one can infer a willingness for reliance from confidence, one cannot in-

3 H. J. N. Horsburgh, "Trust and Social Objectives," *Ethics*, LXXII (1961), 28. See also Horsburgh, "The Ethics of Trust," *Philosophical Quarterly*, X (October, 1960), 343–54.

fer confidence from reliance. The mother who entrusts her child to a sitter can claim to trust the sitter (indeed her action indicates some reliance), and yet she can consistently say, "I do not fully trust her" (confidence and reliance).

Risks are present in both confidence and reliance although clearly in reliance a person is aware of greater risks or has less assurance about the fulfillment of his expectations than in confidence. Later I will examine a quite different and extreme situation in which one decides to rely upon another person even though one thinks that it is improbable that the trustee will meet the trust.

In the second place, while trust presupposes some degree of uncertainty about the other's actions—or at least the absence of control—it is nevertheless an attitude of expectation about those actions, particularly their limits and boundaries. Although there is general agreement that trust is an attitude of confidence in or a reliance upon another's disposition, there is some disagreement about what constitutes this disposition. Niklas Luhmann views trust as the generalized expectation that the trustee will handle his freedom and possibilities of action according to the disposition of the personality that he has publicly presented as his own. In this sense, it is possible to trust another person to tell a lie. In Joseph Heller's novel *Something Happened*, Slocum says, "He knows I drink and lie and whore around, and he therefore feels he can trust me." But trust has a narrower meaning of confidence in or reliance upon another's disposition "to act morally, to deal fairly with others, to live up to one's undertakings, and so on. Thus to trust another is first of all to expect him to accept the principle of morality in his dealings with you, to respect your status as a person, your personality."[4]

Even if we accept the narrower meaning of trust as counting on or expecting the trustee to act morally and not merely in harmony with his public face, several questions remain, espe-

4 Niklas Luhmann, *Vertrauen* (Stuttgart: Ferdinand Enke Verlag, 1968), 37; Joseph Heller, *Something Happened* (New York: Ballantine Books, 1975), 39; Charles Fried, "Privacy," in Graham Hughes (ed.), *Law, Reason, and Justice*

cially about the sort of morality that is relevant. In society at large, without further or additional commitments, trust refers to bedrock social morality rather than to attitudes and actions of heroes and saints. It stresses the boundaries within which action is expected. Thus, trust generally applies to the truster's expectation that the trustee will not murder or rob him, deceive him or lie to him, or the like. Previously indifferent acts may be drawn into the requirements of fulfilling trust when the trustee gives the truster reason (for example, by promises) to think that certain acts will be performed.

There is an important distinction "between what we can expect and demand from others and what we can merely hope for and receive with gratitude when we get it."[5] Trust generally applies to the former, but the line between expectation and demand, on the one hand, and hope, on the other, is not fixed. What is now merely hoped for may well become a matter of expectation, demand, and trust because of the other's acts and commitments. The mother's trust in the sitter commonly involves the expectation that the sitter will supervise the child's activities and meet the child's basic needs of safety and comfort. While the mother may hope that the sitter will love the child and perhaps even risk losing her life to keep the child from being killed in a fire, she cannot charge betrayal of trust if such attitudes and actions are not present, unless, of course, the sitter has given the mother reason to think that love and exceptional risk taking will be forthcoming.

When people voluntarily undertake certain activities with others, they may create expectations and others may rely on them. An example might be agreeing to join a group for a canoe trip in a dangerous area. But if dangers emerge, we cannot demand that a member of the expedition sacrifice himself in order to keep the trust placed in him, unless this demand had been clearly indicated at the outset. A person could, however, com-

(New York: New York University Press, 1969), 52; cf. Fried, *An Anatomy of Values* (Cambridge, Mass.: Harvard University Press, 1970).

5   J. O. Urmson, "Saints and Heroes," in A. I. Melden (ed.), *Essays in Moral Philosophy* (Seattle: University of Washington Press, 1958), 213.

plain that he was "let down," that his trust was betrayed, if his partners were unwilling to take some, perhaps even fairly great, risks on his behalf. Participation in some communities (e.g., churches or communes) may well engender great expectations, obligations, and trust, including self-sacrifice and "going the second mile." In such cases what was optional becomes obligatory (at least prima facie) because of explicit or implicit promises, consent, engendered expectations, and evoked trust. When the expected actions are not forthcoming other members of that community may rightly charge betrayal and unfaithfulness.

Even where the trustee's act violates moral principles such as fairness, the truster cannot always legitimately complain of a breach of trust. Such a complaint may not be acceptable, for example, if the trustee has given signals that he is not trustworthy. Thus, although the trustee's act could still be judged and criticized as unfair, he could perhaps rebut the charge of betrayal of trust by pointing to his prior signals of untrustworthiness and hence to the truster's naïveté and gullibility. While judgments of betrayal of trust and judgments of violations of principles of morality overlap, they are not identical; not all violations of moral principles and rules also involve a betrayal of trust.

Third—and this point is an implication of the two preceding ones—trust (now mainly confidence) is focused primarily on the person and only secondarily on his action and roles. A person expects certain actions because he discerns and trusts a certain disposition in the other person. Such an expectation does not stem from the trustee's situation (for example, the threat of sanction) or from his lack of choice, but rather from his being thought to be the sort of person who can be counted on to respect the limits of morality, who, in short, is trustworthy. One relies on this person's promises, not only because he made them, but because he is thought to be the sort of person who keeps promises.

Sometimes, however, we take account of the trustee's situation, for example, his fear of legal sanctions or social opprobrium if he betrays our trust (reliance), and this increases our confidence that certain acts will be performed although it does not increase our confidence in him. The defects of the trustee that make us wary of giving ourselves in trust are not eliminated, but other factors make it likely that he will perform the expected acts. Now we can predict and act with greater assurance that he will operate within the limits of morality, not because he respects those limits but perhaps because he fears the consequences of their violation. In the absence of (or presence of limited) confidence in another, we may try to substitute some form of control. Thus, the mother may try to make certain that the sitter will supervise her child by hinting that her husband will stop by sometime during the afternoon "to check on things." This mixture of trust and control is typical of many human actions, for we rely on various forms of control such as law and coercion to guard ourselves and to keep from having to rely solely on the trustee.

Several reasons for withholding trust have little to do with the other person's moral character. For example, we may attribute to him the best of intentions but refuse to express confidence and reliance because we think that he lacks the skills, intelligence, or imagination to fulfill the trust placed in him. Or perhaps we withhold confidence because of our doubts, while expressing a partial reliance and making sure that the sitter has precise instructions about what to do in every conceivable situation that might arise in our absence.

Fourth, the previous point might seem to indicate that attitudes and acts of trust are diffuse rather than specific because they are directed toward the person rather than toward definite acts. While absolute confidence is diffuse and implies general confidence in the other person regardless of the act in question, attitudes and acts of trust, especially reliance, can be delimited in quite definite ways in contrast, say, to love. When one person loves another, he cannot restrict that love to certain traits or to certain spheres of activity and relationship. But he may trust another person in most of their contacts, except in business deals where he has discovered the other person to be thoroughly unscrupulous or lacking in judgment. Or a mother may trust a young person in the neighborhood to purchase some groceries and bring back the correct change, but not to look after her child. When perfect confidence breaks down in one activity, it tends to dissolve in others as well, but reliance is based on the trustee's character traits that are directly relevant to the conduct in question. Thus, trust can be selective—directed toward persons in different ways and to different degrees according to the activities involved. Whether a person is willing to rely on another will depend not only on the degree of risk but also on the value of what is risked. Finally, a person may be trustworthy in one relationship but not in another, and there may even be greater variance in a person's trustworthiness from one relationship to another than from one activity to another within a relationship.[6]

Fifth, while trust refers to attitudes and actions of single agents, it also and perhaps primarily refers to relationships in which there is reciprocity or mutuality. Such relationships are treasured for themselves (often being viewed as at least partially constitutive of an ideal state of affairs), as conditions for other relationships (such as friendship), and also as instruments or means to accomplish certain ends (for example, the cooperation necessary for a business enterprise).

Sixth, with regard to the question of whether to trust or not to trust, neither alternative seems, at first glance, to raise fundamental moral questions. When a person enters relationships of trust, he creates certain expectations, and he therefore has certain prima facie obligations based on that relationship. But he is not bound to enter such relationships, although they are desirable and even, in some sense, morally ideal. Thus, from the standpoint of our experience and language, and most moral theories, trust does not seem to be the subject of ethical analysis. Being labeled in the abstract as neither a virtue nor a vice, trust seems to be ethically neutral.

Certainly trust is more pervasive than distrust, at least in normal times removed from systematic terrorism, increasing rates of crime, and so forth. But to show trust's depth and extent is not to show that distrust requires moral justification. Al-

6   See H. J. N. Horsburgh, "The Ethics of Trust," 343.

though we tend to trust strangers, and although our general trustworthiness usually makes such trust rational as well as normal, our moral standards do not demand it. That trust is natural and spontaneous in most societies most of the time, that it is generally well founded in experience and beliefs, and that it is generally rational—all of these points can be conceded without granting that trust has a prima facie claim upon us. Although trust may be naïve and distrust may be cynical in some situations, each attitude may be warranted in other situations.

It is not possible, then, to say that there is a general duty or obligation to express trust if the other person is utterly untrustworthy. A more important implication of this common view, however, is that no such obligation exists even if the other person is trustworthy. If one claims to have complete confidence in another person and yet is unwilling to rely on him, one is caught in some conceptual difficulties, which perhaps could be resolved by viewing confidence in relation to the other's moral disposition while refusing to express reliance because of the other's nonmoral inadequacies. But this is a conceptual, not a moral problem. Finally, even if one argues that the moral importance of relationships of trust derives from the fact that trust is necessary to the existence of human community, the argument does not establish that I have an obligation to trust any particular person I encounter.[7]

What I have stated in the last three paragraphs represents a common view of trust and morality that is generally but not fully and completely adequate. Although we may have good reasons for refusing to trust another person in particular situations, we cannot move to a generalized, systematic, absolute, and incorrigible distrust of that person without denying his nature as a moral agent or person.[8] Thus, recognition of the other as a moral agent precludes taking an attitude of absolute or incorrigible distrust toward him.

Another point, which will be discussed at greater length be-

7 See James M. Gustafson, *Christian Ethics and the Community* (Philadelphia: Pilgrim Press, 1971), 153–59.
8 Horsburgh, "The Ethics of Trust," 354.

low, also qualifies this common view of the relation of trust and morality. Even in the absence of a general duty or obligation to trust others, we sometimes ought to trust even those who are untrustworthy and who thus will probably betray our trust. Our attitudes and acts of trust and distrust have effects on the moral lives of others, and sometimes "therapeutic" or redemptive trust ought to be expressed, for as Milton Mayeroff suggests, "The realization that 'he trusts me' has its own way of motivating the person cared for to justify such trust and to trust himself to grow. My trust in him encourages him to trust himself and to be worthy of trust."[9] The most obvious examples of this "oughtness" of "therapeutic trust" depend on role relationships such as parent and child, teacher and pupil, and priest and church member. Although a parent may think that his son will disregard his instructions when he sends him to the corner store with some money, he may entrust him with this task in order to make him more trustworthy. Because the parent's trust provides an occasion for the child to perceive himself as one who is trusted and who can be trusted, the parent is willing to take the risk, perhaps small, for the child's sake. Such trust is reliance (although for effectiveness it may appear to the trustee as confidence), and despite the probability that the other person will betray it now, this trust is justified by the possible and probable long-term effects on the other person. It remains trust because the truster relies upon the trustee to respond appropriately and to respect moral limits in the future, if not this time. Even when such acts of trust occur within role relationships, their particular warrant depends on the probabilities of certain effects over time. And when reliance works successfully on a therapeutic level, it often is because of a significant and continuing relationship embodying elements of respect and the like. At any rate, its intention is to affect the moral life of the trustee so that he will come to respect moral limits in his dealings with others.

Apart from special relationships, increasing the trustworthiness of others may be one value among many to be considered

9   *Ibid.*; Milton Mayeroff, *On Caring* (New York: Harper and Row, 1971), 20, 44.

in determining the best act in particular circumstances. But how much weight such a value should have is not at all clear. Horsburgh maintains that "if moral agents can assist one another in a specifically moral way not only would there seem to be a clear duty to render such assistance but the duty to do so would seem to outweigh all other duties towards other individuals."[10] For him trust is one of the main ways one individual can assist another in his moral development. But his statement seems too strong, even in relation to the rest of his argument, and a rough analogy may suggest other aspects of "therapeutic trust" that merit consideration: the duty to take risks to rescue others or to render assistance to an injured person. Whether such a duty exists and how far it extends depend largely on the relationship between the parties. Thus, a lifeguard employed at a beach ought to take greater risks than a passerby to rescue a drowning person. Also, the one responsible for the person's being in the dangerous situation from which he needs rescue has a duty to take greater risks. The amount and probability of harm are also important: any passerby has the moral duty to try to rescue a drowning child from a shallow pool when the only apparent risk is wet clothes. Furthermore, as the law has recognized in Good Samaritan cases, when a person undertakes such rescue or assistance, he acquires special obligations of proper care. Similar points may apply to "therapeutic trust" also, but with the recognition that it is a more complicated matter because there is no easy determination of the precise difficulty from which a person needs to be rescued, or the goal toward which he is to be directed, and the strategies for accomplishing that end. Certain arguments for therapeutic trust appeal to general religious convictions about the breadth of role relationships (for example, the family or brotherhood of man), the significance of this value in relation to others (for example, a religious personalism may insist that we should take great risks with other values such as property), and the forces that make for long-term success (for example, the law of love). I

10 Horsburgh, "The Ethics of Trust," 354.

shall return to some of these convictions in the interpretation of nonviolent resistance and direct action.

Finally, the image of the human condition presupposed by this analysis is not that of individuals who must deliberate and choose whether they will come out of their isolated selves and insulated private spheres to trust perhaps because they discover that they need others. Humans are social beings who cannot escape trust, who have no choice but to trust if they are to live and act. But because I am concerned with situations of conflict, I shall emphasize individual and group decisions and acts of reliance. In such situations trust as confidence declines and its functional equivalents, such as law, become precarious; thus, reliance often becomes a matter of deliberate decisions and acts. Although decisions and acts do not exhaust trust, they are among its most important features in situations of serious social conflict. Nevertheless these decisions and acts belong to selves who have certain beliefs, loyalties, and moral values and principles and who have been formed in certain ways. I will pay less attention to some of the significant biographical and social psychological elements in trust in order to concentrate on decisions and acts.

Nonviolence as the Expression and Evocation of Trust

The Quaker notion of "answering that of God in every man" is a useful point of departure for an analysis of nonviolent resistance from the perspective of trust as I have sketched it. Emerging in the religious and political conflicts of mid-seventeenth-century England, Quakers (Friends) renounced carnal weapons in favor of spiritual weapons. It has been said that they admitted no weapons but their tongues, which they used unsparingly! One of their most important convictions was that their conduct should "answer that of God in every man." Conduct that corresponds to or is agreeable to the presence and action of God in other persons is also expected to reach that of God and hence to evoke a response, often conversion. As we have seen, at the heart of the concept of responsibility is the idea of answering, and early Quakers viewed their actions as "responsible" in a broad context of human and divine action. Just as H. R. Niebuhr used "responsibility" to try to transcend the alternatives of deontology and teleology in ethics, so George Fox, widely considered the founder of Quakerism, used "answering" to account for both the rightness and the effectiveness of actions. He advised Friends: "go not into the aggravating part to strive with it, lest ye do hurt to your souls and run into the same nature; for patience must get the victory, and [it] answers to that of God in everyone, and will bring everyone from the contrary. . . . That which joins to the aggravating part sets up the aggravating part, and breeds confusion, and reaches not to the witness of God in everyone." Friends sought a response, not merely a positive outcome; they wanted others to refrain from evil actions, not merely to be restrained from those actions. As Geoffrey Nuttall writes, "'Answering that of God' thus means *both* responding to God's seeking us and speaking to us through others *and* speaking to that of God in others, even when it is imprisoned, concealed, perhaps from their own eyes, still answering that of God which speaks in and through them, though their outer words may be in another tone and temper; and by answering it, drawing it out."[11]

Thus, Quakers emphasized not only the rightness of their

---

[11] For the controversy surrounding this phrase, see Henry J. Cadbury, "Answering That of God," *Journal of the Friends Historical Society*, XXXIX (1947), 3–14, and James F. Childress, " 'Answering That of God in Every Man': An Interpretation of Fox's Ethics," *Quaker Religious Thought*, XV (Spring, 1974), 2–41, in which I have also indicated some relations between Fox's conception of "answering that of God in every person" and Niebuhr's conception of "responsibility." On "responsibility" as a principle to unite themes that appear to be disparate and even irreconcilable, see Albert R. Jonsen, *Responsibility in Modern Religious Ethics* (Washington, D.C.: Corpus Books, 1968). George Fox quoted in A. Neave Brayshaw, *The Personality of George Fox* (London: Headley Brothers, 1919), 31, from Epistle #109; Geoffrey Nuttall, *Christian Pacifism in History* (Oxford: Blackwell, 1958), 64. For a good discussion of Fox's attitude toward violence and war, see T. Canby Jones, *George Fox's Attitude Toward War: A Documentary Study* (Annapolis, Md.: Academic Fellowship, 1972).

nonviolent resistance but also its effectiveness, for example, in
their relations with American Indians in the seventeenth and
eighteenth centuries. Nonviolent resistance can be right and effective because it answers that of God in all people. It is a mode
of "redemptive witness."[12] Nevertheless, early Quakers, in contrast to many contemporary Quakers, were quick to insist that
their actions served only as the *occasion* for God's action, not
as the *cause* of conversion.

Another way to state the Quaker point is to say that nonviolent resistance expresses and evokes (or attempts to evoke)
trust and trustworthiness. Although expression and evocation
are not fully separable, since expression is one basis of evocation, I will first analyze the way nonviolent resistance expresses
trust. In this chapter, the term nonviolent resistance refers to
action aimed at effecting or preventing social and political
changes either by doing what is unusual, unexpected, or prohibited or by failing to perform what is usual, expected, or required—all in a nonviolent way. *Nonviolence*, at least for purposes of this chapter, is more than the negation or absence of
violence defined as the intentional harming of another person
by physical force. My broader view focuses on a continuum of
risk imposition, including purposely, knowingly, recklessly,
and negligently imposing risks of bodily harm and death on
other persons. As Charles Fried suggests, we should not abstract the deliberate killing of another person from this continuum of risk imposition. Although we may acknowledge different degrees of culpability at different points on the continuum,
my contention is that nonviolent resistance—at least in the forms
identified with Mohandas K. Gandhi and Martin Luther King,
Jr.—is directed toward the whole continuum, assuming rather
than imposing risks of bodily harm and death.[13] I am concen-

12 See Theodor Sippell, *Werdendes Quäkertums* (Stuttgart: W. Kohlham-
mer, 1937), 109: "Denn das Quäkertum ist in erster Linie Zeugnis." The language and practice of testimony and witness are widespread. I am indebted
to Carroll Feagins for the phrase "redemptive witness."
13 Fried, *An Anatomy of Values*, 155–56. See James F. Childress, "Nonviolent Resistance and Direct Action: A Bibliographical Essay," *Journal of Re-*

trating on bodily harm and death here, though most theorists consider psychological effects as well.

The nonviolent resister puts his life in the hands of his opponent and entrusts him with it. While such a statement may have varying degrees of literal accuracy, in the most dramatic and demanding situations, the nonviolent resister makes himself vulnerable to physical assault, injury, and death, not to mention imprisonment. No doubt in some circumstances, a person who chooses to use violence may place his life in even greater jeopardy than the nonviolent resister, but I am emphasizing the choice to assume certain risks rather than to thrust them on others.

In typical instances, nonviolent resistance expresses and signifies trust that the opponent can control his actions and responses at least to the extent of refraining from physically assaulting or killing the resister and that he can and will respect certain moral limits in dealing with the resister. The nonviolent resister trusts that the opponent, if he initially responds in violence, will be moved to cease and desist and perhaps even to repent and make reparations and that the opponent can be brought to understand the reasons for the resistance and can even be persuaded to alter his own stance. In short, the nonviolent resister accepts only limited means of control such as public opinion and the legal process, and he expresses trust mainly as reliance, usually less as confidence, that the other person, regardless of his role and previous actions, will finally respond in appropriate ways and become more trustworthy.

Nonviolent resistance also attempts to evoke trust. When I put my life in my opponent's hands, while remaining nonvi-

---

ligion, LII (October, 1972), 376–96. One of the best analyses of nonviolence is Judith Stiehm, *Nonviolent Power: Active and Passive Resistance in America* (Lexington, Mass.: D. C. Heath, 1972). Much of what I am suggesting is expressed in the notions of love held by the early Quakers, Gandhi, and King. For a detailed discussion of the fascinating judgments that Gandhi, a lawyer, made in actual and hypothetical moral cases, some of which concern matters of acts and omissions and direct and indirect effects, see M. K. Gandhi, *Nonviolent Resistance* (New York: Schocken Books, 1961), 166–69, 161–62.

olent, I indicate that my intention is not to harm him or impose undue risks of harm on him. He is to understand that he
will not be excluded from the community and that his values
and interests, including his physical integrity, will be protected. Although a resister may stress the intention of including opponents in a broader and more comprehensive community of love and reconciliation, what is indispensable is the
drawing of limits and the setting of constraints on his actions:
"See," he says, "you can trust me! I will respect the limits of
morality in my dealings with you."

It is possible to draw suggestive analogies between games
and rituals, on the one hand, and nonviolent resistance, on the
other, in part because rules and principles in each activity set
certain boundaries for conduct, such as prescribed acts within
a definite time and space. Even pacific ritualization among animals constitutes an interesting parallel to nonviolent resistance, for many fights among animals of the same species are
simply ritualized tests of strength rather than mortal battles. In
such fights the weaker animal can finally avert the danger of
injury or death by turning its weapons such as teeth or claws
away from its opponent. Of course, this "appeasement gesture"
increases the weaker animal's vulnerability, but it thereby effectively inhibits further attack by the stronger animal. This remains only an analogy, albeit an interesting one, for Gandhi, as
Erik Erikson indicates, developed "a ritualization through
which men, equipped with both realism and spiritual strength,
can face each other with a mutual confidence analogous to
the instinctive safety built into the animals' pacific rituals." In
conflict situations mutual trust depends on "etiquettes or
rituals which all the parties understand and use."[14] Three features of nonviolent ritualization of conflict are especially
significant: (1) a recognition of sacred boundaries of action,

14   Anthony Storr, Human Aggression (New York: Bantam, 1968), 38; Erik
H. Erikson, Gandhi's Truth (New York: W. W. Norton, 1969), 433; H. B. Acton,
"Political Justification," in Hugo Bedau (ed.), Civil Disobedience: Theory and
Practice (New York: Pegasus, 1969). See also H. L. Nieburg, "Agonistics—
Rituals of Conflict," Annals of the American Academy of Political and Social
Science, CCCXCI (September, 1970), 56–73.

(2) a voluntary assumption of risk, and (3) a sense of equality.

(1) Although I have suggested the importance of the notion of sacred limits and boundaries, some additional points need explication. By emphasizing the ritualization of conflict as a basis of mutual trust, my position seems to contradict Richard Gregg's claim, in his very influential book, *The Power of Nonviolence*, that nonviolence is effective largely because it is so novel in a violent society.[15] For him it works by surprise and by the uncertainty it creates. While there is, no doubt, surprise that resisters would make themselves so vulnerable to physical attack or arrest and punishment and that they would express trust and invite mutual trust, their actions establish and take place within a framework that dispels much of the uncertainty about what they will do. Because nonviolence is the *ultima ratio*, the last resort, for many of them, their opponents can be confident of and rely upon their willingness to respect that limit even as they violate numerous other expectations short of it.

Examples from different social conflicts may illuminate the way this limit of nonviolence functions in the evocation of trust. In seventeenth-century England, Quakers waging the "Lamb's War" engaged in numerous nonviolent acts that violated social expectations, custom, and law in order to point to critical issues such as social inequality and to convert others to their religious perspective. Among their nonviolent acts were the disruption of worship, the stand against tithes, the refusal to render hat honor and to give salutes and greetings, the addressing of their social superiors by "thee" and "thou" rather than "you," and walking through the streets naked "for a sign." Although it is easy to see why their opponents viewed them as a threat to "turn the world upside down," the Quakers also set certain limits on their conduct as a basis for mutual trust. As Hugh Barbour writes in *The Quakers in Puritan England*:

Friends believed that the law was not made for righteous men like themselves. . . . To the men of seventeenth century England the Quaker theocracy was virtual anarchy, outwardly the same as Ranterism. . . . There could be no

15 Richard Gregg, *The Power of Nonviolence* (2nd rev. ed.; New York: Schocken Books, 1969).

guarantee of what a Quaker would do next, since he set no limit short of
world rule by Quaker Saints.

Such an impasse may develop whenever men are totally committed to an
ideal their opponents do not share, and no abstract theory can overcome
it. . . . Where ideals are irrevocably antagonistic . . . it is hard to achieve
enough mutual respect to remove the fear and hatred aroused by conflict. The
Friends' great contribution to statecraft was to realize that their own Peace
Testimony was not simply a response to actual war but an answer to the deadlock of consciences. . . . Friends saw that they could point to their attitude
toward violence and 'carnal' weapons as part of their commitment to love.
*Their opponents could know and trust that Friends, on principle, would
never use violence against them or cause them physical harm.* Their answer
to the deadlock did not require surrender of their claim to absolute authority
for the Light within their conscience, and yet it gave non-Friends a solid basis
for tolerating them.

In a dramatic trial at the Old Bailey in 1670, William Penn denied that he and three hundred followers had met in the streets
"with force and arms . . . unlawfully and tumultuously," creating disturbance and terror among the King's subjects. He argued, in part, "it is very well known that we are a peaceable
people, and cannot offer violence to any man." When the jury
found Penn guilty only of speaking in the streets, the court
fined and imprisoned the jury for contempt.[16]

For Gandhi, one's opponents should feel secure not because
of their superior strength, but because they discern an intention
of nonharm in the resisters; security through weapons is a matter of control, not trust. He insisted that if Indians could make
Englishmen feel that "their lives are protected against harm not
because of the matchless weapons of destruction which are at
their disposal, but because Indians refuse to take the lives even
of those whom they may consider to be utterly in the wrong,"
England's relationship to India would be completely trans-
formed. His conviction that Satyagraha should set one's opponents at ease had important consequences for his practice of
nonviolent resistance. For example, he emphasized the danger

16   Christopher Hill, *The World Turned Upside Down* (New York: Viking
Press, 1972); Hugh Barbour, *The Quakers in Puritan England* (New Haven:
Yale University Press, 1964), 220–21 (my italics); *State Trials* 6 (1670): 951.

of mass civil disobedience, which could appear as a threat of harm, and more important, he repudiated "secrecy" even to the extent of disclosing to the government every possible stage of the escalation of protest even if that stage were only a remote contingency. Such a repudiation of secrecy focused on clarifying the limits of resistance rather than revealing each particular tactic that might be employed, and even Gandhi's followers had to take much on faith (for example, the reasons for some decisions).[17]

Trust in the midst of conflict often presupposes procedural morality and secondary virtues. Ways and means of conducting disputes may provide the basis for trust even when there are serious conflicts about goals and purposes. Too often trust is construed in terms of ends rather than means, goals rather than procedures, and what is done rather than how it is done. Two sociologists contend that "short of brute force, people conduct their affairs because they trust each other, and trust implies a common acceptance of the higher aims toward which the activity is directed." But even when these higher aims are not accepted, procedural morality and secondary virtues may be sufficient for trust. For example, in periods of social conflict, secondary virtues such as conscientiousness, sincerity, and integrity, as well as nonviolence, may become very important. As Alasdair MacIntyre notes, such secondary virtues concern *how* we do what we do, while primary virtues establish our projects, that is, *what* we do.[18]

Thomas Hobbes suggested that "form is power, because, being a promise of good, it recommends men to the favor of women and strangers."[19] People estranged from each other be-

---

17 Gandhi, *Non-violent Resistance*, 154, 56, 306, 292, 294, 379, 116, 98–99, 302.

18 Nicholas Demerath and Phillip Hammond, *Religion in Social Context: Tradition and Transition* (New York: Random House, 1969), 204; Alasdair MacIntyre, *Secularization and Moral Change* (London: Oxford University Press, 1967), 24.

19 Thomas Hobbes, *Leviathan*, Pts. I, II (Indianapolis: Bobbs-Merrill, 1958), 79.

cause of their disputes about ends may nevertheless be able to trust each other. They may be *friendly strangers* because of their commitments to procedures and secondary virtues, which may be sufficient for trust even if not for harmony and reconciliation. By contrast to the nonviolent conduct of disputes, one aim of terrorist activity is to destroy mutual trust through random violent attacks that often repudiate all limits including, for example, the immunity of innocent persons from direct attack.

(2) So far I have suggested, but not developed, the voluntariness of the expression of trust through nonviolent resistance. Gandhi sharply distinguished the nonviolence of the strong from the nonviolence of the weak; true Satyagraha is the former, while "passive resistance" is the latter. Although this distinction was not very precise in his writings, it is important and suggestive. Despite having the personnel, weapons, and courage to engage in a campaign of violence, the strong choose, perhaps on both moral and political grounds, to renounce the use of physical force. The weak, on the other hand, have no choice but to be "unviolent."[20] Only the strong can be "trusted" (in a strict sense) because they have voluntarily renounced the use of violence, although such a renunciation may, of course, be only temporary. But the weak are unviolent because their situation precludes the use of violence; they are under control.

Everyone exposes himself and others to a variety of risks, including death, whenever he acts, or does not act. Stressing this point, Charles Fried goes on to discuss a "risk budget": in a person's life plan, the overall plan itself and "each end and life period will end up being 'worth' some risk of death." Because our choices and actions affect both our risks of death and the risks of death of other persons, it is important to ask how we use up our own lives and how we use up other lives. In much nonviolent resistance the resister chooses to impose greater risks on himself than on others, and he often borrows

20 Gandhi, *Non-violent Resistance*, 6, *et passim*; William Robert Miller, *Nonviolence: A Christian Interpretation* (New York: Association Press, 1964), 36.

on his life and suffering in order to try to effect or prevent change nonviolently. Life is a resource that may be spent in sundry ways, as Gandhi recognized when he described Satyagraha as "vindication of truth not by infliction of suffering on the opponent but on one's self" and when he claimed that "sacrifice of self even unto death is the final weapon in the hands of a nonviolent person." For the early Quakers, "suffering was a weapon in the Lamb's War." For King, "unmerited suffering is redemptive."[21]

Thus, the voluntary expression of trust is closely connected to the voluntary assumption of risks of suffering, and both are aimed not only at evoking trust but also at stimulating the opponents' trustworthiness. Following Gandhi's insistence that "success is the certain result of suffering of the extremest character, voluntarily undergone," others have understood the logic of nonviolence as voluntary suffering that enables the resister's opponents to perceive him as human. Not to be confused with passive suffering or nonresistance, nonviolent action involves suffering in resistance, in noncooperation, or in disobedience. Many examples could be given, including the alteration of the Massachusetts policy of excluding Quaker preachers after some had been jailed, whipped, and even executed when they refused to stay away; the impact of the brutal beatings of Indian protesters at Dharasana; and the struggle of freedom riders and sit-in participants in the United States in the early 1960s. Such nonviolent resistance is often effective because of the "sense of injustice" that is awakened by the resister's suffering. The sense of justice often works negatively.[22] Although it may not be strong enough to impel a group to alter unjust laws and policies initially, it may be strong enough to prevent that group from

21   Fried, *An Anatomy of Values*, 178; Gandhi, *Non-violent Resistance*, 6, 275; Barbour, *The Quakers in Puritan England*, 226; Martin Luther King, Jr., *Stride Toward Freedom* (New York: Harper and Row, 1964), 84.
22   Gandhi, *Non-violent Resistance*, 275; James Douglass, *The Nonviolent Cross* (New York: Macmillan, 1969), 71; John Rawls, "The Justification of Civil Disobedience," in Hugo Bedau (ed.), *Civil Disobedience: Theory and Practice* (New York: Pegasus, 1969), 253–54.

enforcing them by inflicting various penalties or by violating their own procedural standards.

Actually, nonviolent resistance that results in suffering often stimulates this sense of injustice in third parties, rather than in the direct oppressors. For example, public opinion in Britain would not indefinitely tolerate assaults on Indian resisters. Such nonviolent resistance appeals to public opinion for moral corroboration. A resister may not trust those officials in whose hands he places himself, but he may trust those persons and groups to whom the officials must explain and justify their acts, for unacceptable explanations may arouse moral indignation against the government. Many years ago E. A. Ross formulated this point: "Disobedience without violence wins, *if it wins*, not so much by touching the conscience of the masters as by exciting the sympathy of disinterested onlookers. The spectacle of men suffering for a principle *and not hitting back* is a moving one. It obliges the power holders to condescend to explain, to justify themselves. The weak get a change of venue from the will of the stronger to the court of public opinion, perhaps of world opinion."[23]

Often these third parties provide not only moral corroboration but also coercion. For example, a sit-in at the mayor's office may actually be directed at his reference groups who may force him through threats of withholding support and funds to make certain concessions to the protesters. In such cases we find a mixture of trust and control, partly because of the involvement of different audiences: one audience is trusted to coerce another audience. Gandhi sometimes recognized this element of coercion, but because his ideal was pure persuasion or, more accurately, conversion, he often failed to see the coercive elements in such nonviolent action as Swadeshi (using materials and products made in one's own country). He tended to obscure the actual mechanism of nonviolence by referring to the moral motives for engaging in it (for example, love) or by translating the

23   E. A. Ross, "Introduction," in Clarence Marsh Case, *Non-violent Coercion* (New York: Grove Press, 1968), 247 (Ross's italics).

logic of nonviolence into metaphysics or theology (for example, the law of love).[24]

Other difficulties plague the emphasis on voluntary suffering. Just as some zealous early Christians actively sought martyrdom—although some of their fellow Christians viewed this as complicity in murder—so some contemporary resisters court suffering on the grounds that it will be efficacious or redemptive. Occasionally a glorification of suffering for religious and other reasons, voluntary suffering in the contemporary context is more often an attempt to unmask the hypocrisy of the establishment by deliberately provoking retaliation. When policemen and public officials cannot control their responses or keep them within the limits of established procedures, the resisters claim that such overreactions disclose the true nature of the system. It is more consistent, however, with the fundamental principles of nonviolent resistance in the tradition of Gandhi and King—despite some of their own statements—to emphasize the assumption of risks of suffering. Gandhi insisted that "provoking lathi [a long club with a metal tip] charges or receiving lathi blows on your body in a spirit of bravado is not Satyagraha. True Satyagraha consists in the readiness to face blows if they come in the course of performing one's duty."[25]

The terms *trust* and *risk taking* appear to be inappropriate in many situations where one can be almost certain that his opponents will respond with physical violence. Faced with the possibility that an opponent would betray his trust, Gandhi insisted on trust: "A Satyagrahi bids goodby to fear. He is never

24 Michael Lipsky, *Protest in City Politics: Rent Strikes, Housing, and the Power of the Poor* (Chicago: Rand McNally, 1970). Obviously I refer only to a tendency in Gandhi's thought, for he did at times recognize coercion in particular instances of nonviolent resistance. See, for example, Gandhi, *Non-violent Resistance*, 291–93. In these reflections on voluntary suffering in relation to conversion and coercion, I have not tried to offer a comprehensive interpretation of the mechanisms of nonviolent resistance and direct action. For some of the literature on this topic, see Childress, "Nonviolent Resistance and Direct Action," 376–96. Nor have I indicated all of the elements and effects of the voluntary assumption of risk.

25 Gandhi, *Non-violent Resistance*, 294, *cf.* 280, 288.

afraid to trust the opponent. Even if the opponent plays him false twenty times, the Satyagrahi is ready to trust him the twenty-first time, for an implicit trust in human nature is the very essence of his creed."[26] Such trust obviously cannot be confidence, and even as reliance it seems inappropriate because there is certainty that his opponent will let him down again. But reliance, especially in the form of therapeutic trust, may not be directed at the opponent's immediate response but at his later responses, perhaps repentance and reparation, or at the responses of third parties. Gandhian trust does not imply that the mere act of trusting one's opponent will always be immediately sufficient; it is relinquishing the attempt to control the other through one's own physical force or violence.

(3) The analysis of nonviolent resistance in terms of trust also illuminates other distinctions drawn by many of its defenders such as between evil deeds or systems of evil and the evildoer. King maintained that he resisted the evil deed, not the evildoer, and that this was one reason for restricting his conduct to nonviolence. "The evil deed of the enemy-neighbor, the thing that hurts, never quite expresses all that he is." In a similar fashion, Gandhi maintained, "Man and his deed are two distinct things. Whereas a good deed should call forth approbation and a wicked deed, disapprobation, the doer of the deed, whether good or wicked, always deserves respect or pity as the case may be. 'Hate the sin but not the sinner' is a precept which, though easy enough to understand, is rarely practiced, and that is why the poison of hatred spreads in the world." It is tempting but finally impossible to dismiss such a distinction on the grounds that we simply do not encounter disembodied evil and that evil deeds are always committed by persons or that the distinction involves an untenable separation of body and soul. The distinction is fundamentally moral in intention, normative rather than descriptive, and it is connected with the attempt to hold together an act of resistance and a fundamental attitude of

26   Gandhi quoted in Louis Fischer, *Gandhi: His Life and Message for the World* (New York: New American Library, 1954), 36.

trust in the other person. Although the deed or conduct, law or policy is condemned, the person engaged in such actions is not condemned; he or she is treated as a moral agent with the capacity to respond appropriately. Rather than being viewed as an enemy, the evildoer is recognized as sharing some minimal moral capacity that can be awakened. For instance, Gandhi claimed that a criminal is different from others only in degree, not in kind, and that "even Nero is not devoid of a heart."[27]

Obviously, such claims raise difficult questions about the rationality of trust in particular instances. Reliance is rational if confidence is warranted, but it is necessary to inquire into the adequacy of the grounds of confidence in the other person. In particular situations, reliance apart from confidence may be rational, especially when combined with some form of control. "Therapeutic trust" presupposes that it is probable that the trustee will betray the reliance placed in him. Its adherents, nevertheless, take the view that providing another person with a moral opportunity to be worthy of trust, perhaps accompanied by the reasons for the risk taking, may well stimulate his long-term development. The rationality of such trust may depend on the value of what is risked, the degree of risk, and the probability of reaching this person over time.

Although the idea of therapeutic or redemptive trust is somewhat ambiguous in Gandhi's and King's writings, it usually refers more to the redemption of the other and his conversion than to the agent's own redemption. Most examples of therapeutic or redemptive trust come from interpersonal relations, such as a parent trusting his or her child in order to increase the child's trustworthiness. Indeed, many interpreters of nonviolence favor such interpersonal models, which form the basis of Gandhi's insistence that "every instance of public Satyagraha should be tested by imagining a parallel domestic case." In such models trust is seen as directed toward another

27 King, The Strength to Love (New York: Harper and Row, 1963), 36; Gandhi quoted in George Woodcock, Mohandas Gandhi (New York: Viking Press, 1971), 41; Gandhi, Non-violent Resistance, 350–52, 305, 386. See also King, Stride Toward Freedom, 84–85.

person for his own sake and in order to evoke a *response* rather than merely achieve a *result*. For example, although Gandhi recognized that punishing a robber for his crime would probably achieve a result—imprisonment obviously would prevent him from committing a robbery at least for a time—he denied that it would evoke a response, indeed, a conversion. Such a conversion, Gandhi suggested, could be brought about at least in some situations if people would simply leave their doors unlocked and express reliance in similar ways.[28] Also, his main concern was the realization of truth, which depends on response and recognition by both parties, particularly since no party has the complete truth.

It is far from clear, however, that such an interpersonal model can be strictly applied to institutions, especially the political order, without overlooking or distorting some unavoidable and important features of institutions in which coercion may be important, achieving some results may take precedence over evoking some responses, and the goods of several different parties may have to be considered. Most of the theorists of nonviolent resistance and direct action have failed to work out a satisfactory statement of the relations between doers and institutions. With the Social Gospel, King, who acknowledged his indebtedness to Walter Rauschenbusch, admitted that institutions are very significant in the determination of conduct, but he also insisted that change has to come through appeals to persons. This emphasis on persuading or converting persons diminished somewhat in the last years of King's life, especially as he increasingly emphasized coercion and moved from direct to indirect civil disobedience—both shifts being reflected in his legitimation of the massive dislocation of cities. His thought at this time also reflected an increased awareness of the structural or systemic basis of evil, as well as the interdependence of domestic and international levels and economics, politics, and law within the system.

While the model of therapeutic or redemptive trust is action

28   Gandhi, *Non-violent Resistance*, 179, 11–14.

undertaken for the trustee's own good, involving possible loss of some of the truster's own goods such as physical integrity and property, much social conflict includes action on behalf of third parties whose goods are at stake. Thus many defenders of justified violence contend that it is wrong to impose some risks on third parties when it is probable that the opponents/trustees will not respect the trust. Although Gandhi conceded that the costs of nonviolent resistance are high and that a nonviolent defense of India against Japan in the 1940s would risk the loss of several million lives, he claimed that the cost would be no greater than the cost of military action and that, furthermore, the ends brought about by different means would be quite different.[29]

Not only do theorists of nonviolence answer the charge of irrationality by pointing to comparative costs and by emphasizing the interdependence of means and ends, but they often appeal to general views of human nature and metaphysical or theological perspectives such as the Quaker view of "that of God in every man," or Gandhi's claim that "the law of suffering will work, just as the law of gravitation will work, whether we accept it or not," or King's belief that there is "some creative force that works for universal wholeness." Gandhi even suggested that nonviolence "means reliance on God" and that the first two requirements for a Satyagrahi are "a living faith in God" and a belief "in the inherent goodness of human nature"— matters of faith not susceptible to correction by empirical evidence.[30] Perhaps some such trust in human nature or a force in the universe is necessary to sustain nonviolent resistance, especially in the form of redemptive trust, but it may also prevent its adherents from looking realistically at evil.

Instead of offering a justification or defense of nonviolent resistance, I have tried to understand and to illuminate this way of conducting social conflict as seen by its practitioners and theoreticians, especially the early Quaker movement, Gandhi,

29 *Ibid.*, 377, 153.
30 *Ibid.*, 384, 58, 88, 387; King, *Stride Toward Freedom*, 88.

and King. They believed that nonviolent resistance is both right and effective. Because their nonviolent resistance represents a commitment to the moral limit of nonviolence in conflicts, it expresses and attempts to evoke trust and trustworthiness. Whether nonviolence has moral priority over violence, whether it can be effective, and in short, whether it is responsible are widely disputed. In the next chapter I will consider these issues, among others, by examining Reinhold Niebuhr's realistic critique of nonviolence and pacifism and his argument for responsible violence and war.

Chapter Two

Reinhold Niebuhr's Realistic Critique of Pacifism

Many recent attempts to demonstrate the shortcomings of political realism have accepted its interpretation of violence. Few of the political theologians, liberation theologians, and theologians of revolution who have tried to dismantle realism have reconsidered or modified this aspect of the realist perspective. Even Paul Ramsey's emphasis on *jus in bello* falls within a realist framework of thinking about violence and nonviolence, war and pacifism. It is now time to splash what Oliver Wendell Holmes called "cynical acid" on this assumed orthodoxy, especially but not only in Protestantism. The pacifist perspective on violence and war deserves a hearing, which this stacked jury of realists and their critics have refused to grant. Their refusal results in part from Reinhold Niebuhr's critique of pacifism, widely considered, even by pacifists, to be one of the most important of such critiques.[1]

I am aware of the dangers of trying to generalize about Niebuhr's ethics apart from its historical development in particular contexts, but I think that the *continuities* in his thought about violence from *Moral Man and Immoral Society* (1932) to the

1 Paul Ramsey, *War and the Christian Conscience: How Shall Modern War Be Conducted Justly?* (Durham, N.C.: Duke University Press, 1961); *The Just War: Force and Political Responsibility* (New York: Charles Scribner's Sons, 1968). For a recent view that war is wrong, but revolutionary violence is right, see *Christianity and Crisis*, XXXII (July 10, 1972). For pacifist critiques of Niebuhr, see John Howard Yoder, *Reinhold Niebuhr and Christian Pacifism* (Scottdale, Pa.: Herald Press, 1968); G. H. C. MacGregor, *The New Testament Basis of Pacifism and the Relevance of an Impossible Ideal* (Nyack, N.Y.: Fellowship Publications, 1954).

end of his career are more important than the discontinuities.[2]
And I am concerned with the general adequacy of his arguments rather than with their correlation with particular events,
although I will occasionally refer to their contexts. My stress on
the unity and continuity of Niebuhr's thought, at least in his
basic structure and framework for dealing with violence, results in a somewhat static rather than a developmental view.
But it offers an opportunity to examine some of the presuppositions and implications of Niebuhr's views on violence, many
of which are uncritically accepted by both realists and their
critics.

As partial compensation for this static view, I will sketch
briefly the major transitions in Niebuhr's defense of and subsequent attack on pacifism. Perhaps his critique of pacifism was
so vigorous and so effective in part because of his former pacifism. He was not a pacifist in World War I because of his desire,
as a German-American, to demonstrate his loyalty to the United
States and because of his support of Wilson's foreign policy. But
after the war, which, he said, made him "a child of the age of
disillusionment," disenchantment with liberal ideals and their
failure led him to revive his earlier pacifism. His Marxist critique of society and his identification with the proletariat during the depression led him to surrender his domestic pacifism
although he retained his international pacifism. In 1934 he finally left the Fellowship of Reconciliation, which he had
served as national chairman, because of his altered stance on
violence in domestic social change. He recognized that it was
probably more honest to disavow the pacifist label, even before
events rendered his international pacifism obsolete. He was a
vigorous supporter of the U.S. involvement in World War II. He
also emphasized the need to contain the Soviet Union. He sup-

2   Reinhold Niebuhr, *Moral Man and Immoral Society: A Study in Ethics
and Politics* (New York: Charles Scribner's Sons, 1960). See Ronald Stone,
Reinhold Niebuhr: Prophet to Politician (Nashville: Abingdon Press, 1972),
8, 177, *et passim*, for the dangers of abstracting Niebuhr's thought from its
context. But when Stone discusses Niebuhr's "ethic," he suggests this continuity too (p. 231).

ported our prompt military action in Korea, but he was critical on realistic grounds of the war in Vietnam.[3]

Niebuhr's Analysis of Human Acts

Internal Perspective	External Perspective—personal/social		
1. Motive	2. Policy:	→ 3. Ultimate	
	immediate	objectives	
	objectives	↓	
	and/or means	→ 4. Consequences	

This diagram, based largely on *Moral Man and Immoral Society*, indicates some of the elements in Niebuhr's analysis of acts most important for a discussion of violence, nonviolence, and pacifism. When we talk about "intrinsic" good or evil, Niebuhr contended that we should confine our attention to motive, for the only intrinsic good is goodwill, and the only intrinsic evil is ill will. He argued that it is wrong to say that violence, as policy, is intrinsically evil since only motives can be intrinsically evil. Against those who have held that violence is intrinsically evil because it is assumed to express ill will, he insisted that such an assumption does not hold in group relations where coercion may be necessary and may thus express benevolence.[4]

3   For a fuller treatment of these transitions, see Stone, *Reinhold Niebuhr*, from which some of this sketch is drawn; Donald B. Meyer, *The Protestant Search for Political Realism, 1919–1941* (Berkeley: University of California Press, 1961); and Paul Merkley, *Reinhold Niebuhr: A Political Account* (Montreal: McGill-Queen's University Press, 1975). See also William G. Chrystal (ed.), *Young Reinhold Niebuhr: His Early Writings, 1911–1931* (St. Louis: Eden, 1977), 95–100 (a 1918 defense of responsible force for peace); Reinhold Niebuhr, *Leaves from the Notebook of a Tamed Cynic* (New York: Willett, Clark, 1929); and D. B. Robertson (ed.), *Love and Justice: Selections from the Shorter Writings of Reinhold Niebuhr* (Cleveland: World, 1967), Pt. IV, esp. 254–59.
4   Niebuhr, *Moral Man and Immoral Society*, 172–73, *et passim*.

Particularly in social morality, the agent must be mainly concerned about policy, ultimate objectives and consequences, the area of pragmatic evaluation. We must regard "all problems of social morality in pragmatic rather than absolute terms." As Niebuhr insisted, "if the purpose of a social policy is morally and rationally approved, the choice of means in fulfilling the purpose raises pragmatic issues which are more political than they are ethical." Thus, "the realm of politics is a twilight zone where ethical and technical issues meet."[5]

This realism depends on an understanding of human nature that permits and requires the application of norms in complex ways to human acts. The notion of intrinsic good is applicable, from the internal perspective, only to motives, but values and principles affect the assessment of acts, ends, and consequences. In one sense, Niebuhr considered policy as the means to ends with certain actual results; the primary standards for their assessment as means would be technical and pragmatic. But in another sense, policy could be viewed as immediate objective (e.g., killing another person), which has a certain value or disvalue to be weighed against other immediate and ultimate objectives as well as probable consequences. From the internal perspective, which most religious positions assume, motives are critical. But from the external perspective, which is most appropriate for our acts in society, agents must look at policy, ultimate objectives, and consequences partly because motives are basically inaccessible. Thus, pragmatic reasoning enters and becomes dominant.

As an example of the application of norms to human action, what Niebuhr did with the "norm of love" is interesting. He maintained that love requires selflessness in motive, nonresistance as a policy, and voluntary brotherhood as an ultimate objective. But that ultimate or ideal objective cannot be realized in history. It remains an important standard of *indiscriminate* and *discriminate* criticism; that is, it not only discloses the evil in all acts and institutions (the expression of self-interest), but it also helps us discriminate between better and worse acts, pol-

5   *Ibid.*, 171, 237–38; Robertson (ed.), *Love and Justice*, 257.

icies, and institutions, especially through intermediate norms such as justice, liberty, and equality. But a policy of nonresistance is inconsistent with attempts to achieve better social institutions, for by definition a policy of nonresistance is inconsistent with the search for justice, especially if one's own "due" is involved. It would also end up on the cross. Thus, love as defined in the Sermon on the Mount would seem to require nonresistance and social irresponsibility. Of course, an agent's motives can express some goodwill even though he or she cannot eradicate egoism. In personal or interpersonal relations, such as in the family, love can often be expressed in actions that transcend justice, such as mutual love, but justice is the most we can expect in society under conditions of human finitude and sin. While justice always contradicts love, it also approximates love. This is the love-justice dialectic. Love is an "impossible possibility." It can never be fully embodied in motives, policies, and institutions, but it is possible to express it more fully than we do. Without some love, our actions and institutions will cease to be just.[6]

Niebuhr used the terms *law*, *ideals*, and *norms* very loosely and interchangeably, in part because of his polemical interests. For example, in his criticism of the Social Gospel, he used the language of ideals to show that some ideals are unattainable in history. But whatever his language, Niebuhr emphasized the limits of action—the impossibility of realizing certain ideals, the moral irresponsibility of obeying laws when obedience will have horrible consequences, and the conflicts between various norms. This is the crux of his realism: "the disposition to take all factors in a social and political situation, which offer resistance to established norms, into account, particularly the factors of self-interest and power."[7]

Although the language of internal and external perspectives

6   See Niebuhr's discussion of the love-justice dialectic in *An Interpretation of Christian Ethics* (New York: Meridian Books, 1956) and *The Nature and Destiny of Man* (2 vols. in one; New York: Charles Scribner's Sons, 1949), II, chap. 9.

7   Reinhold Niebuhr, *Christian Realism and Political Problems* (New York: Charles Scribner's Sons, 1953), 119. For an excellent discussion of the lan-

ceased to be important later in his career, Niebuhr made parallel points in other ways. For example, he distinguished between *religious* and *ethical* perspectives, the former accenting the equality of sin and the latter accenting the inequality of guilt (that is, the objective, historical consequences of sin). The former concentrates on the self before God, the latter on acts and their consequences in the world. The former is vertical, the latter horizontal.[8]

Niebuhr's Pacifism

In what sense was Niebuhr a pacifist? When he was an international pacifist, he viewed pacifists, in a general way, "as social idealists who are profoundly critical and skeptical of the use of physical force in the solution of social problems." The common belief of pacifists is that "the use of force is an evil," but the less consistent pacifists (including at that point Niebuhr himself) view it as a "necessary evil in some situations." To be a pacifist, he continued, one must express one's "critical attitude toward the use of force by disavowing it completely in at least one important situation." From his standpoint, "Armed international conflict stands in a category of its own because history has proved its *worthlessness* as a method of solving social problems so vividly that it has become practically impossible to justify it on any moral grounds." The disillusionment resulting from the dashed hopes of World War I is evident. Then, in explaining his departure from the Fellowship of Reconciliation in 1934, he identified himself with those "who are pacifists only in the sense that they will refuse to participate in an international armed conflict. Perhaps it would clear the issue if we admitted that we are not pacifists at all. We probably

guage of ideals, law, and norms, see James M. Gustafson, *Christ and the Moral Life* (New York: Harper and Row, 1968), which analyzes Niebuhr's position in terms of the logic of norms rather than ideals or laws.
8 Niebuhr, *Moral Man and Immoral Society*, 170, *Nature and Destiny*, I.

all recognize the terrible possibilities of violence. We regard an international armed conflict as *so suicidal* that we are certain that we will not participate in it."[9]

Niebuhr's definition of pacifism is not wholly unambiguous. It requires that the use of physical force must be viewed as an evil, and that force must be "disavowed" in at least one important situation. *Disavowal* is ambiguous. One must distinguish between justification of war and justification of participation in war, which, of course, are often associated in theory and in practice. A pacifist may say that war is never justified on moral (and perhaps other) grounds, or he may say that, although war is justified, say, by the moral standards available to the public order, the Christian's participation in war is not justified.[10] Thus, some early Christians gave the enterprise of war a relative justification although they refused to participate in it. Despite his language about participation, most of Niebuhr's arguments about violence concern the ethical justification of the activity itself.

Niebuhr defended his own pacifism on pragmatic grounds.[11] It is important to state this defense carefully, for his later attacks on pacifism were aimed primarily at certain pragmatic defenses, although he continued to offer pragmatic support for (relative) pacifism and nonviolent resistance. His pragmatic justification of international pacifism was negative. He did not claim that nonviolence would produce the best results or that it would work, but that international violence would be "worthless" and "suicidal." This difference between positive and negative pragmatism is more than semantic, for whether

9   Robertson (ed.), *Love and Justice*, 247 (from 1928), 256, my italics.
10   For a similar ambiguity, see Larry Rasmussen, *Dietrich Bonhoeffer: Reality and Resistance* (Nashville: Abingdon Press, 1972), 94–126. Jan Narveson contends that a person who says only that he ought not to meet force with force does not hold pacifism "as a *moral* principle or, indeed, as a principle at all," even if we continue to call him a pacifist in a loose sense. See Narveson, "Pacifism: A Philosophical Analysis," in Richard Wasserstrom (ed.), *War and Morality* (Belmont, Calif.: Wadsworth Press, 1970), 63–77.
11   See Charles W. Kegley and Robert W. Bretall (eds.), *Reinhold Niebuhr: His Religious, Social, and Political Thought* (New York: Macmillan, 1961), 8.

one or the other is chosen depends on certain assumptions about man, society, and coercion, among other factors. Furthermore, although Niebuhr's language seemed to be absolutistic, his argument was not. A genuinely pragmatic argument cannot be dogmatic and absolute; it must always be open to correction because it depends on an analysis and assessment of historical configurations and the relations of means and ends. When he finally surrendered his international pacifism, he simply directed the same argument against international pacifists that he had earlier leveled against domestic pacifists: when they offer pacifism as an absolute political alternative, their position is inconsistent, incoherent, and irresponsible.

Niebuhr continued to support some forms of nonviolent action on the domestic level on pragmatic grounds, although he had less hope for such actions on the international level. For example, in 1932 while stressing the similarities between violence and nonviolence (both coerce and destroy), he used an analysis of Gandhi's work and thought to indicate several pragmatic advantages of nonviolence in some situations. He continued, "non-violence is a particularly strategic instrument for an oppressed group which is hopelessly in the minority and has no possibility of developing sufficient power to set against its oppressors. The emancipation of the Negro race in America probably waits upon the adequate development of this kind of social and political strategy." In the 1960s he insisted that "Dr. King's conception of the non-violent resistance to evil is a real contribution to our civil, moral and political life."[12]

Religious and Pragmatic Pacifism

Although they purported to cover more territory, Niebuhr's analyses and criticisms were mainly limited to two types of pacifism: religious absolutism and pragmatic pacifism (offering

---

12　Niebuhr, *Moral Man and Immoral Society*, 252; Stone, *Reinhold Niebuhr*, 251 n.

a political alternative). It is important to recall the polemical contexts of his struggles against pacifism, first from the standpoint of the class struggle and then from the standpoint of World War II. These contexts shaped his attack, as did the specific arguments of his opponents. Nevertheless, here or elsewhere, he tended to set up positions in ideal-typical terms often limiting his opponents' possible options to two. He would describe his opponents' positions in general terms and try to offer them the horns of a dilemma. Such an approach ignored the subtlety of many types of pacifism.[13] Now I want to examine Niebuhr's arguments against the two types of pacifism that he identified and opposed.

We should not overlook Niebuhr's genuine appreciation for absolute religious pacifism, which concentrates mainly on the question of participation in violence. He viewed this type of pacifism as part of a general religious denial of the world and as perfectionist in orientation. It rightly presents a stringent interpretation of the norm of love expressed in the teachings of Jesus and the Cross; that norm requires nonresistance rather than nonviolent resistance. Furthermore, in accord with the teachings of Jesus, it does not offer this nonresistance as a political alternative: "In medieval ascetic perfectionism and in Protestant sectarian perfectionism (of the type of Menno Simons, for instance) the effort to achieve a standard of perfect love in individual life was not presented as a political alternative. On the contrary, the political problem and task were specifically disavowed."[14] Such a Christian pacifism is "a valuable asset for the Christian faith," for it reminds the Christian community of the distinction between what is normative or ideal and what is normal or real. It helps to keep alive an uneasy conscience about participation in war.

Niebuhr refused to quarrel with the pacifist's interpretation

13   For an indication of the range of pacifist positions and defenses, see John Howard Yoder, *Nevertheless: The Varieties of Religious Pacifism* (Scottdale, Pa.: Herald Press, 1972).

14   Reinhold Niebuhr, *Christianity and Power Politics* (New York: Charles Scribner's Sons, 1940), Chap. 1.

of Jesus' teachings and activities and conceded that they express and require nonresistance, but he contended that Christianity is more than a set of laws for obedience; it is a framework of interpretation of experience and a way to deal with failures to live up to demands. His other criticisms of this position derived largely from his understanding of responsibility (which I will examine in greater detail later). There is a responsibility to other people in the world (and not only to Christians) for what happens to the relative institutions of justice and order in the world (and not only in the Church). Religious absolutism, ascetic and perfectionist, denies the world and responsibility for it. In its drive for perfection, it ignores its dependence on the institutions of relative justice. Because it benefits from the world, its refusal to engage in world maintenance, for which coercion is a necessary instrument, can only be viewed as parasitical.[15] In moral terms, it is unfair. A related point is that, from Niebuhr's perspective, some religious pacifists draw the line of acceptable compromise at the use of force, thereby revealing their failure to see the general tension between the love commandment and the "necessities" of natural and social life.

At times Niebuhr lumped together several varieties of pacifism under the rubric "contemporary pacifism," whose features included religious absolutism, modern liberalism, and moral nausea over the brutalities and futilities of war. Sometimes he viewed moral nausea over or abhorrence toward violence as class-bound, but his position about "necessary evil" presupposed a general abhorrence. I will return to this issue later. The term *liberalism* designated Niebuhr's major political targets for many years even after he had reappropriated part of it in what Ronald Stone calls his "pragmatic-liberal" synthesis. Liberalism, which Niebuhr characterized as basically "faith in man," holds that coercion is not necessary in human communities, or

15   See Harry R. Davis and Robert C. Good (eds.), *Reinhold Niebuhr on Politics* (New York: Charles Scribner's Sons, 1960), 151. Much of Niebuhr's attack focused on the pacifist's alleged self-righteousness.

at least, that violent coercion is not necessary because persuasion is sufficient. When religious pacifism, usually after imbibing liberalism, ventures forth as a politically wise warrior, Niebuhr's counterattack is the most vigorous. Such a mixture of religious absolutism and political proposals can be found in some versions of Quakerism. As we saw in the last chapter, Quaker nonviolence can be characterized as "redemptive witness" because it combines a demand for witness with a hope in redemption of others through that witness. It is one thing to say that pacifism is right or mandatory because of religious convictions; it is another to say that it will work. When religious absolutism arrogates to itself this pragmatic judgment, it invites Niebuhr's scorn and invective. It dares to fight on his turf with his weapons of pragmatic judgment while having the fortress of religious absolutism for a safe retreat. Niebuhr recognized some value in both the religious and the political approaches to pacifism, especially religious pacifism, it is true, but he contended that their combination could only result in confusion.[16]

When such pacifism appears, it is tainted with "heresy" (a label that Niebuhr used somewhat loosely). It interprets the New Testament as endorsing nonviolent resistance instead of nonresistance, although the pragmatic distinction between violent and nonviolent resistance has nothing to do with the distinction between the ethics of the Kingdom of God and political strategies and tactics. Its heresy is mainly manifested in its faith in the goodness of man (Renaissance and Enlightenment) and its interpretation of the Cross as a symbol of the victories that love will gain in history. Its heresy is thus a rejection of Pauline elements for those of Jesus alone, as well as a misinterpretation of Jesus. Furthermore, it favors the spiritual over the physical. It is "equally heretical when judged by the facts of human existence." Niebuhr could make the last claim precisely because of his view that religious faith offers "prin-

16   Robertson (ed.), *Love and Justice*, 260; Kegley and Bretall (eds.), *Reinhold Niebuhr*, 8.

ciples of interpretation" for human experience. Faith and experience are dialectically related, with experience both corroborating and falsifying faith. Thus, Niebuhr's apologetic task was to a great extent the analysis of experience in order to indicate the weaknesses of competing world-views. After all, he could say that the doctrine of original sin is empirically verifiable.[17]

Niebuhr also charged "contemporary pacifism" with inconsistency. We violate the norm of nonresistance all our lives in our anxiety and self-assertion and even in our struggle for justice; we should feel the tension of violating our principles long before we reach physical coercion. For such pacifism to be consistent, it should seek withdrawal from the world.[18] Niebuhr's charge of inconsistency obviously rests on his understanding of society, especially his putatively empirical claims about evil and coercion. He conceded that such a pacifism could try to defend anarchism and thus regain its consistency by avoiding the problem of government and order altogether, but it would still be subject to his strictures about the nature of human community. Insofar as it refuses to accept martyrdom and political irresponsibility, it is inconsistent and confused.

Niebuhr's use of the criterion of consistency as a necessary condition of a satisfactory or admirable pacifism is extremely interesting because as a pacifist rejecting war between nations he was quite willing to sacrifice some consistency and because he abhorred "consistency as a matter of general principle." Despite his occasional polemical use of the demand for consistency, he tried to develop a dialectical logic to do justice to the facts of human experience. As Davis and Good have pointed

17   See Niebuhr, *Christianity and Power Politics*, Chap. 1, which charges that Richard Gregg's *The Power of Nonviolence* (2nd rev. ed.; New York: Schocken Books, 1969) favors the spiritual over the physical. See Niebuhr, *Nature and Destiny of Man*, I, Chap. 9, and Niebuhr, "Sin," in Marvin Halverson (ed.), *A Handbook of Christian Theology* (New York: Meridian Books, 1958), 342–45.
18   Niebuhr, *Christianity and Power Politics*, Chap. 1; Robertson (ed.), *Love and Justice*, 254, 263.

out, "the architecture of Niebuhr's political and ethical thought is anything but simple. It is full of dialectical cantilevers. The whole is suspended in marvellous [sic] tension like some Gothic cathedral that rises and is held fast only by the elaboration of opposing forces." A dialectical logic is necessary, Niebuhr contended, to take account of and to account for obdurate facts of human existence. For example, it is a dialectical truth that sin is inevitable but not necessary. As Niebuhr modified his realism toward the end of his life, he admitted that it had become "excessively consistent."[19]

Responsibility and Necessity

For Niebuhr, responsibility is both a key category and a test of an adequate social ethic. There are several affinities between his understanding of responsibility and Max Weber's classic statement of the ethics of responsibility, which emphasized the average deficiencies of man, concern for consequences of action, and willingness to use bad means for good ends. Certainly Niebuhr's idea of responsibility includes these elements among others. It embraces responsibility for the consequences of action, but also responsibility to others in the social and political order, as I have already suggested. In regard to the latter, Niebuhr often contrasted what a private individual may do and what a statesman may do. And he insisted that "a responsible relationship to the political order . . . makes an unqualified disavowal of violence impossible."[20]

Responsibility is defined only in the context of other themes,

19   Robertson (ed.), *Love and Justice*, 248. *Cf.* Niebuhr, *Nature and Destiny*, I, Chap. 9. Davis and Good (eds.), *Reinhold Niebuhr*, x; Reinhold Niebuhr, "Toward New Intra-Christian Endeavors," *Christian Century* LXXXVI (December 31, 1969), 1662.

20   See Reinhold Niebuhr, "The Problem of a Protestant Political Ethic," *Christian Century*, LXXVII (September 21, 1960), 1085; Max Weber, "Politics as a Vocation," in H. H. Gerth and C. Wright Mills (eds.), *From Max Weber: Essays in Sociology* (New York: Oxford University Press, 1958), 77–128; Niebuhr, *An Interpretation of Christian Ethics*, 170.

particularly those derived from an interpretation of human nature. Rejecting the idea of the orders of creation, as developed
by Emil Brunner among others, Niebuhr offered a dialectical
understanding of social and political life (e.g., man's capacity
for justice and inclination toward injustice) in order to take account of both freedom and necessity. In *Moral Man and Immoral Society* he found the constraints and limits of political life
mainly in the nature of the collectivity; in both *An Interpretation of Christian Ethics* and *The Nature and Destiny of Man*,
he located them more clearly in the nature of man as sinner,
offering a "gradual theological elaboration of what was at first
merely socio-ethical criticism." But even as he developed the
latter perspective, he still sharply distinguished between individual or personal and social ethics, contending that absolute
pacifism mistakenly tries to apply the personal ethic of self-
sacrifice and love to such social problems as war.[21]

If social life has such constraints and limits, how does one
respond to the argument that the Christian ought to surrender
the sphere of responsibility to others? Obviously the charges of
parasitic and ascetic relations to social life would be relevant,
but Niebuhr also held that withdrawal reflects a "very limited
concept of Christian citizenship." The pacifist recognizes his
responsibility to and for the state "up to a point." "But when
the state has to exercise its admitted central function as guar-
antor of order, then the state is abandoned on the ground that
the Christian has a higher loyalty and code of conduct. The
Christian is thus 'in the world' until coercion or violence enters the scene, when he becomes 'not of the world.'" The
Christian, from Niebuhr's standpoint, is obliged "to act responsibly in society at all times, and not merely when the state is at
peace."[22]

The basis of a more adequate conception of citizenship would
be the recognition that love has both vertical and horizontal

---

21 Reinhold Niebuhr, "Ten Years That Shook My World," *Christian Century,* LVI (April 26, 1939), 542; Reinhold Niebuhr and Angus Dun, "God Wills
Both Justice and Peace," *Christianity and Crisis,* XV (June 13, 1955), 76.
22 Niebuhr and Dun, "God Wills Both Justice and Peace," 76.

dimensions. In the former, it is self-sacrifice; in the latter, it is concern for all people, for justice, and for the mechanisms and instruments of justice. This horizontal dimension permits Niebuhr to show that his critics wrongly assume that "an ethic of responsibility is not part of a Christian way of life." When the pacifist looks only at the vertical dimension, he not only tries to apply personal ethics to social life, but he also ends up with ideological results: a preference for peace over justice and "a perverse preference for tyranny" over war. By stressing nonviolence, pacifists may "give an undue moral advantage" to those in power who use nonviolent coercion against the "disinherited." Such nonviolent coercion may even be "covert violence," Niebuhr suggested in a phrase that is now widely used. Unfortunately he did not develop this idea, which also appears in the Marxist conception of violence; the latter holds that "men are causally responsible for harm they could have prevented" and that "such harm may properly be regarded as a form of violence." After using the phrase *covert violence*, Niebuhr also referred to causal responsibility: "nonviolence may be covert violence. Children do starve and old people freeze to death in the poverty of our cities, a poverty for which everyone who has more than the bare necessities of life must feel some responsibility."[23] Niebuhr did not develop this thought, but recent theorists of violence have used such ideas to condemn covert and structural violence, while justifying the use of revolutionary violence. Acts of omission, specifically failures to effect institutional and structural changes, are condemned as violent as are the institutions and structures that result in harm. Numerous difficulties beset such attempts; for example, it is difficult to use the term *violence* to describe and

23 Niebuhr, "The Problem of a Protestant Political Ethic," 1086. Contrast Yoder, *Reinhold Niebuhr and Christian Pacifism*, 18; Niebuhr and Dun, "God Wills Both Justice and Peace," 75; Robertson (ed.), *Love and Justice*, 270, 257; Niebuhr, *Christianity and Power Politics*, Chap. 1; John Harris, "The Marxist Conception of Violence," *Philosophy and Public Affairs*, III (Winter, 1974), 192–93, and *Violence and Responsibility* (Boston: Routledge and Kegan Paul, 1980).

condemn some institutional arrangements while also using it to describe and praise some revolutionary acts.

It is important to deal with the concept of "responsibility" in relation to the concept of "necessity." John H. Yoder suggests that Niebuhr often used the concept of responsibility "to support that of necessity."[24] But I think that the relationship is somewhat different: necessity defines the parameters and some of the content of responsibility. This is an instance where the "real" becomes normative although it can never be accepted as finally or ultimately normative. At the very least, the "real" determines the application of the "ideal." Because coercion is necessary for order and justice, it becomes a matter of responsibility to use it in violent or nonviolent forms as the situation dictates. A person cannot be responsible if he forsakes what is necessary. Indeed, the idea of necessity is used to suggest a loss of choice. It indicates that some action is justified or excused because of that loss of choice. It functions in several legal and moral contexts, for example, in the right of necessity that has been alleged to exist under some extreme circumstances, such as among starving sailors in a lifeboat on the high seas. But as a judge held in one such famous case, "It is not correct . . . to say that there is any absolute or unqualified necessity to preserve one's life."[25] Niebuhr would certainly concur with that statement as applied to individuals, but he would qualify its application to societies. An individual can and should transcend his own interests to a much greater extent than can society; although he may well choose to sacrifice his life, such a sacrifice should not be expected of a society. There are some difficulties in this notion, for it is not clear whether Niebuhr *intended* to use it merely to set the boundary of the possible or also to determine the content of the responsible act. Does necessity apply to values (e.g., survival is a necessary value of society) as well as to means (e.g., war is sometimes necessary or is necessary in this context)? Is the claim about necessity general or specific?

24 Yoder, *Reinhold Niebuhr and Christian Pacifism*, 18.
25 *The Queen v. Dudley and Stevens*, 1884, 14 Q.B. 273.

Niebuhr clearly used both forms: coercion is necessary for order and justice, and specific forms of nonviolent and violent coercion are necessary in particular contexts. He insisted, for example, that one cannot disavow bombing cities without capitulating to the foe who refuses to disavow it. He also suggested that a nation cannot disavow the hydrogen bomb, but it can renounce its first use. "No man," he continued, "has the *moral freedom* to escape from these hard and cruel necessities of history," but he does have the freedom to do them without rancor or self-righteousness.[26] In terms of the diagram of Niebuhr's analysis of acts, "necessity" applies mainly to policies, objectives, and consequences, and their relationships. But moral freedom or transcendence is still possible, at least to a great extent, for motive. Agents cannot express pure goodwill, but they can avoid or reduce some attitudes such as hatred, rancor, and self-righteousness.

The language of necessity implies that the society has no choice and that some action, such as war, is thus justified or at least excused. But Niebuhr surely obfuscated matters by employing the language of necessity, which conceals specific value choices. A society can and perhaps in some contexts should choose to surrender its political autonomy or yield some of its territory without war. These choices can be made if political autonomy and territorial integrity are valued in certain ways. Thus, the term *necessity* appears to give weight and finality to a judgment that, after all, is based on a calculation that certain means are necessary to achieve certain ends; this calculation is susceptible to criticism and reevaluation. Niebuhr's language of necessity may only disguise human choices and thereby strengthen covert utilitarianism, for it says that a specific policy is necessary for objectives and consequences, but their weight is determined by the dialectic of norms and facts. Sometimes Niebuhr used the language of "necessary evil," which is open to the same difficulties. There are at least two versions of necessity, for example, in the military context. In the first version, a nation is on its knees with no other chance of sur-

26 Robertson (ed.), *Love and Justice*, 237, 223.

vival; in the second version, a nation is concerned to hasten victory and to end the war with less cost. The first version should be taken as the paradigm of necessity.[27] Niebuhr's language of "lesser evil," which implies that value judgments are involved in determining "lesser" and "greater," is more appropriate in most contexts.

Violence and Nonviolence

The general claim that coercion is essential for order and justice is the basis for establishing that some forms of violent as well as nonviolent coercion are essential at times and that the responsible agent cannot abjure them. But another step is also required. Niebuhr must show that the difference between violent coercion and nonviolent coercion is not very significant from a moral standpoint or, at least, that this difference is not absolute. Part of the rhetorical force of this denial of an absolute difference between violence and nonviolence depends on persuasive definitions of society and its forces; for example, for Niebuhr, society is a "perpetual state of war." This metaphorical use of *war* prepares us to accept the fact that *war* (now strictly defined) is not so unnatural, unnecessary, and unjustified. Because we are already and always engaged in "war," it is not so great a step to admit armed conflict between groups and nations. As Niebuhr said in 1928, "The world war was life, as it is lived on this little sphere." To underline the significance of such an approach, it is only necessary to consider other perspectives on politics for which martial metaphors would be inappropriate; for example, Jacques Maritain understands politics as "intrinsically moral" and refuses to emphasize its moral ambiguity. One issue is whether violence, or at least physical force and coercion, is one of the constitutive elements of politics. In the Weberian tradition, accepted by Niebuhr, one of the

27   See the discussion by Richard A. Falk, "The Shimoda Case: A Legal Appraisal of the Atomic Attacks upon Hiroshima and Nagasaki," *American Journal of International Law*, LIX (1965), 785.

essential elements of the state and hence politics is violence or physical force. By contrast, John H. Yoder argues for a different interpretation of *politics* in order to redefine Christian "political responsibility." For him, *political* refers to the "polis," that is, to "the structuring of relationships among men in groups." Therefore, nonresistance or nonviolence is not politically irrelevant or irresponsible.[28]

More than rhetoric is involved, and in getting at Niebuhr's view that the line between violent and nonviolent coercion is "important" but not absolute, I shall consider, first, his analysis of two factors that lead some pacifists to make nonviolence an absolute good and, second, his own positive argument for the important difference between violent and nonviolent coercion.

One factor that may account for the pacifist's interpretation of violence as intrinsically and absolutely wrong is "an uncritical identification of traditionalized instrumental values with intrinsic moral values," according to Niebuhr.

There are certain specific actions and attitudes which are generally not judged in terms of their adequacy in achieving an approved social end. Experience has established them; and their traditionalised instrumental value is regarded as an intrinsic one. Respect for the life, the opinions and the interests of another is regarded as intrinsically good and violence to the fellowman's life, opinions and interests is prohibited. It is not only assumed that they will have the right ultimate consequences but that they are the natural and inevitable expression of goodwill. In purely personal relations these assumptions are generally justified. The moral will expresses itself unconsciously in terms of consideration for the life, the interests and the rights of others; and the consequences of such consideration may be presumed to be good.[29]

What generally holds cannot be taken as absolute, and any reflective morality will have to reassess alleged intrinsic values in terms of instrumentality. Indeed, Niebuhr suggested that all

28 Niebuhr, *Christianity and Power Politics*, Chap. 1; Reinhold Niebuhr, "What the War Did to My Mind," *Christian Century*, XLV (September 27, 1928), 1163; Jacques Maritain, *Man and the State* (Chicago: University of Chicago Press, 1956), 58; John Howard Yoder, *The Politics of Jesus* (Grand Rapids, Mich.: Eerdmans, 1972), esp. 50 n.
29 Niebuhr, *Moral Man and Immoral Society*, 173.

morality really accepts the principle that ends justify means; this acceptance is sometimes concealed because of the assumption that the character of some immediate consequences (number 2 on the diagram) guarantees the character of the ultimate end and consequences (number 3 and number 4).

I have already mentioned a second factor that, according to Niebuhr, may account for the pacifist view that nonviolence is absolute. Pacifists assume that violence chosen as a policy, even on behalf of good ends and consequences, presupposes and derives from ill will, that is, intrinsic evil. They have transposed this condemnation of the supposed motive to the act of violence itself. Bernard Häring has said that violence is "always an undisciplined outburst, an expression of rancor." For Häring, the motive of "rancor" enters the definition of violence, which cannot then be justified. Niebuhr contended that, at least in society, one cannot move from the identification of an act as violent to its condemnation as an expression of ill will. (His definition of violence was, at this point, more neutral and definite than nonneutral and elastic.) I have already given examples from his writings to indicate that a person can love his enemy (in the sense of desiring his good) even while doing harm to him. Although such love (agape, not eros) is difficult to achieve, it reduces hatred, which has an egoistic root. Niebuhr's emphasis on motives and attitudes and his view that they can rarely be identified with specific acts and policies led him to insist that nonhatred is a more important symbol of the Christian faith than nonviolence.[30] Furthermore, the Christian has greater freedom in motives and attitudes than in acts, as the example about bombing cities and the discussion of responsibility and necessity suggested.

Niebuhr's argument against making nonviolence an absolute also involves the contention that violence and nonviolence are both forms of coercion and thus that the differences between

30   Bernard Häring, Theology of Protest (New York: Farrar, Straus, and Giroux, 1970); Donald Evans, "Paul Ramsey on Exceptionless Moral Rules," American Journal of Jurisprudence, XVI (1971), 193; Robertson (ed.), Love and Justice, 218–21, 258.

them are only extrinsic and not intrinsic. These are differences in degree, not in kind. Niebuhr and Robert Paul Wolff, among others, contend that because the differences between violence and nonviolence are extrinsic and only matters of degree, the selection of means of resistance is only a matter of pragmatic and teleological calculation. According to Niebuhr:

The religious radical is wrong in believing that there is an intrinsic difference between violence and nonviolence. The differences are pragmatic rather than intrinsic. The social consequences of the two methods are different, but the differences are in degree rather than in kind. Both place restraint upon liberty and both may destroy life and property. Once the principle of coercion and resistance has been accepted as necessary to the social struggle and to social cohesion, and pure pacifism has thus been abandoned, the differences between violence and non-violence lose their absolute significance, though they remain important.[31]

This is the heart of Niebuhr's argument, and despite its power, this argument is problematic. Ronald Stone contends that Niebuhr's "denial of an intrinsic difference between violence and nonviolence represents a polemic move against religiously based pacifism rather than careful analysis."[32] Closer attention to ordinary language would have improved Niebuhr's analysis at many points. For example, "murder" and "cruelty" may be examples of disrespect for others that are absolutely prohibited, whereas "violence" stands in need of justification that can sometimes be provided. But, in contrast to Stone, I suspect that Niebuhr's denial of an intrinsic difference between violence and nonviolence is more deeply rooted in his position and that even "careful analysis" would not have extirpated it. My contention is that Niebuhr's basic theses—that society requires coercion for order and justice as long as man is man, and yet coercion is always contrary to man's essential nature—require a *denial* of this intrinsic difference if he is to defend violence as a legitimate option and yet an *affirmation* of this difference if he is to refer to it as a "necessary evil."

31 Davis and Good (eds.), *Reinhold Niebuhr on Politics*, 141. *Cf.* Niebuhr, *Moral Man and Immoral Society*, 240, et passim.
32 Stone, *Reinhold Niebuhr*, 56.

A number of thinkers draw the important dividing line between nonresistance and resistance or between freedom and coercion in order to reduce the significance of the distinction between nonviolence and violence. For example, Robert Paul Wolff contends that coercion is intrinsically evil; otherwise we would not try to minimize and even eliminate it or use it only as a last resort. It is intrinsically although not absolutely evil not because it involves pain but because it is degrading. "To coerce a man rather than persuade him is to treat him as a thing governed by causes rather than as a person guided by reason."[33] Niebuhr did not explicitly develop such a Kantian understanding of coercion. Although he denied that the term is ethically neutral, he did not develop a clear statement of why coercion is intrinsically although not absolutely evil perhaps because he tended to view it less from the standpoint of the victim or patient and more from the standpoint of the agent and his motives and because he emphasized the tension between voluntary brotherhood and coercion. Because he emphasized the chasm between nonresistance and resistance, Niebuhr was not very interested in precise distinctions between degrees of resistance or types of resistance. The presence of coercion (forcing people against their wills to perform or refrain from some acts) marks the important transition in moral and political life. For a variety of reasons, it is possible to agree that it is prima facie wrong to limit anyone's freedom by sanctions or threats or that there is a moral rule against such conduct, without concluding that violence is wrong only because it is coercive or because it has bad consequences in some circumstances.

Even if we admit that much nonviolence involves some coercion (e.g., that it forces the other party to accede to demands against his will or reasoned judgment) and restriction of liberty, we have to ask whether all nonviolence involves coercion. Although this must be resolved empirically, it is

33 Robert Paul Wolff, "Is Coercion 'Ethically Neutral'?" in J. Roland Pennock and John Chapman (eds.), *Coercion*, Nomos XIV (New York: Atherton Press, 1972), 146.

plausible to hold that some forms of nonviolence rely more on persuasion or conversion than on coercion. Clearly we need a richer set of contrasts than violence and nonviolence. Such a set would help us see that not all acts of nonviolence are easily or equally justified, but it would not obliterate or reduce the significance of the contrast between violence and nonviolence. Now, Niebuhr's point may well be that when a person engages in nonviolent resistance and admits the importance of both resistance and coercion, he cannot or should not hold onto an absolute difference between violence and nonviolence. The core of both violence and nonviolence is coercion, and this contradicts love in the New Testament, which demands self-sacrifice and nonresistance. To engage in nonviolent coercion on pragmatic grounds is to base one's position on arguments that do not permit absolutism, for nonviolent coercion may be met by violence, or it may prove to be ineffective or extremely costly. Responsibility does not permit an agent to draw an absolute line in advance if he or she has made the commitment to use nonviolent coercion when it is necessary. But even if all these points hold, they do not constitute an argument against an intrinsic difference between violence and nonviolence: they are only an argument that we should not be absolutely committed to nonviolent persuasion or coercion.

In addition to stressing coercion, Niebuhr also emphasized that nonviolence may result in the destruction of life and property. No doubt nonviolent acts sometimes have such consequences, but such a concession does not demolish the distinction between violence and nonviolence or reduce it to ends and consequences. Recognition of these consequences may show a pacifist that nonviolent acts are not always justified merely because they are nonviolent. Justification does involve consequences as well as the form of acts. And nonviolence does not render an act or actor immune from criticism from a moral standpoint, for violence is not the only term for moral criticism. Thus, although Niebuhr's point is very important, it does not establish what he claims.

To admit that nonviolence may be coercive and may have

bad consequences and to grant that the differences between violence and nonviolence do not have absolute significance is not
to concede that the differences are only extrinsic, if *extrinsic*
means that the differences are found *only* in the ends and consequences. Nonviolence (or the rule "do no violence to anyone") has a moral priority over violence (the intentional infliction of harm on another person especially, but not exclusively,
through the use of physical force) that is not reducible to its
ends or consequences.

As can readily be seen, the distinction between acts and
consequences is very important. Niebuhr's point may be that it
is not always easy to distinguish between acts and their consequences, or that acts labeled violent or nonviolent can be redescribed in terms of their consequences. The issue here is not
merely that an act of violence can be justified by its ends and
consequences but that it can be redescribed in terms of them so
that the descriptive and evaluative labels of violence and nonviolence cease to be instructive.

Eric D'Arcy discusses genus terms (such as *honesty* and
dishonesty) and species terms (such as *murder, killing, theft,*
and *rape*), and argues that sometimes the latter cannot be redescribed or elided into their consequences. We cannot redes-
cribe the act of a man who killed four persons in order to save
ten persons as "saving lives"; from a moral standpoint it is
necessary to refer to the "killing." D'Arcy's point is not that such
terms refer to acts that are always wrong "but that they are so
significant for human existence and welfare and happiness that
they must always be taken into account before sound moral
judgment can be passed upon them; and if they are to be taken
into account, their presence must first be revealed."[34] Thus, they
cannot be elided into their consequences; they are always morally significant.

Perhaps *violence* and *nonviolence* are genus terms, rather
than species terms, for genus terms (in contrast to species

34 Eric D'Arcy, *Human Acts: An Essay in Their Moral Evaluation* (Oxford:
Clarendon Press, 1963), 38.

terms) often involve opposites, sometimes denote good as well as bad conduct, usually appear in the adjective form when we express an opinion about an act (e.g., "that was violent"), and are generally more evaluative and less descriptive.[35] There is usually more debate about what falls under genus terms. Even if *violence* is a genus term, acts that it encompasses (e.g., killing) may be nonelidable; that is, they may not be susceptible to redescription in terms of their consequences although, again, they may be justified by their consequences. Furthermore, much of what D'Arcy claims about species terms may apply to the genus term *violence*, which cannot be assimilated into its consequences. Its presence must be disclosed for moral evaluation. Insofar as Niebuhr claims that killing and violence are elidable, his position is weakened, but his language of "necessary evil," "lesser evil," and "*ultima ratio*" suggests that he does not finally or consistently allow this elision.

Like traditional just-war theorists, Niebuhr viewed violence as the *ultima ratio*, a matter of last resort. Such a notion may go beyond and even undermine his pragmatic approach. In order to determine whether it does, we must see how and why Niebuhr held the rule of nonviolence to be important. If this rule of nonviolence is taken as absolute, under no circumstances can it be overridden; the pacifist takes this stance toward at least one situation, usually war. If the rule is taken as relative, it functions as a rule of thumb or maxim with some illuminative but no prescriptive significance (as in Joseph Fletcher's "situation ethics"). In this form, it mainly represents the wisdom of the past, the "traditionalized instrumental values."[36] Finally, if it is taken as prima facie, it is viewed as binding, although it does not determine one's actual obligations in particular situations. Insofar as violence is a feature of an act, that act is wrong, although it may be actually right when all of its features and consequences are considered (e.g., it may be an

35   *Ibid.*, 25–26.
36   Robertson (ed.), *Love and Justice*, 296, 300. See Robert Paul Wolff, "On Violence," *Journal of Philosophy*, LXVI (October, 1969), 601–16, and Wolff (ed.), *The Rule of Law* (New York: Simon and Schuster, 1971), 243–52.

attempt to protect the innocent). From this third perspective, violence may be prima facie wrong, but actually right when all the prima facie claims are considered. At any rate, it can never be disregarded.

But suppose that an agent thinks that he should violate the prima facie duty not to injure or harm anyone in order to protect the innocent.[37] Even if his act is justified, the former prima facie duty is not cancelled or obliterated; it is overridden. And it should continue, thus, to influence the act as well as subsequent conduct; it should affect the way the act is performed and what the agent does later. For example, a violent resister against the state might warn government officials, publicly declare his intentions, exhaust other remedies, protect certain parties, and perhaps make reparations after the conflict. Certainly his prima facie duty not to harm others should affect his mental attitude as expressed in regret and perhaps remorse.

Accepting Niebuhr's explicit rejection of the absolute approach, we need to ask which view he took when he insisted that the difference between violence and nonviolence is "very important" and that violence is the *ultima ratio*. His argument points to the relative approach. It views the differences between violence and nonviolence as extrinsic and pragmatic; the violence of an act mainly involves some other evils to be weighed in the total calculation. From such an argument, one might conclude that in any situation of social conflict an agent should be genuinely pragmatic, inquiring at the outset whether violence or nonviolence would really be the most effective, least costly alternative. The distinction between violence and nonviolence would still have relative significance; it would suggest that we ought to examine the situation carefully because violence has *often* had greater costs or worse consequences than nonviolence. Niebuhr did not, to my knowledge, explicitly draw this

---

37   In developing this notion of prima facie duties I am indebted to various works by W. D. Ross and A. C. Ewing, among others. See also Robert L. Holmes, "Violence and Nonviolence," in Jerome A. Shaffer (ed.), *Violence* (New York: David McKay, 1971). I will develop this view of prima facie duties at greater length in Chapter 3.

conclusion, and his language of "necessary evil" and "*ultima ratio*" as well as his rhetoric pointed to the prima facie interpretation. There seems to be "something" wrong with violence beyond pragmatic matters, and this "something" led Niebuhr to continue to talk about even justified violence as "evil." His approach has been criticized on the grounds that he did not adequately distinguish between physical evil and moral evil, the latter occurring only when the agent intends to do something wrong. But "moral traces" (Robert Nozick's phrase), or residual effects of violated prima facie duties, are very important, and Niebuhr in particular extols the motive of love and nonhatred and feelings of guilt. But what Niebuhr's position only partially and inadequately expresses is that such attitudes presuppose something like a prima facie duty not to commit violence.

Another difficulty in Niebuhr's pragmatic approach to violence appeared in his view of means and ends. For example, Niebuhr insisted on construing responsibility in terms of ends and consequences in his debate with his brother, H. Richard Niebuhr, over the Sino-Japanese conflict in the 1930s. Reinhold Niebuhr restated his brother's position in his own terms of responsibility even though H. Richard Niebuhr was attempting to develop a position of *responding* to God within historical processes and without constant reference to ideals. Sometimes Reinhold Niebuhr related means to ends, while at other times he balanced immediate objectives and consequences against ultimate objectives and consequences. Whichever language he used, this pragmatic model must be reconsidered. As Antony Flew describes that model: "Talk of ends either justifying or not justifying means, of achieving good ends by evil means, and so forth, presupposes that we are dealing with something analogous to a field game in which the objective is unitary and given. The problem is to find some way to reach it, or to select one or another of various alternative routes, all of which lead to the same place." Flew calls this model into question, contending that different sorts of actions transform the ends, that people are affected by what they do, that morality is more a matter of meeting claims than of realizing ends and purposes, and that we are more often confronted with the difficulty of avoiding or removing evil than of realizing good.[38] Obviously not all of these points suggest difficulties in Niebuhr's position, for he avoided some of them and answered others. But they do suggest that any attempt to talk about violence and nonviolence merely as alternative means to ends cannot be successful. The issues are more than pragmatic, as Niebuhr's own language suggests.

Considerations of means and ends and of proportionality are not sufficient for either nonviolent or violent action. Other moral considerations are relevant and frequently decisive. First, even though nonviolence has moral priority over violence, it is not always justified even if it produces a net balance of good over bad consequences. It, too, is subject to other moral limits such as legitimate targets of action. Likewise, even if violent action and warfare appear to have a just cause, they may be subject to moral constraints such as the immunity of noncombatants from direct attack. In the next two chapters, I will explore just-war theories, which emphasize not only ends and consequences but also independent moral assessments of means. Niebuhr conceded that such theories, for example, in Roman Catholicism, rightly call "attention to the importance of means appropriate to the ends sought and to the danger of excessive violence." But he failed to pay serious attention to their moral constraints on means beyond proportionality, and he insisted that "efforts to construct a precise guide through detailed elaborations" of just-war criteria would "result in a rigid and highly artificial structure, more likely to confuse than illumine the conscience."[39]

38   See H. Richard Niebuhr, "The Grace of Doing Nothing," *Christian Century*, XLIX (March 23, 1932), 378–80; Reinhold Niebuhr, "Must We Do Nothing?" *Christian Century*, XLIX (March 30, 1932), 415–17; and H. Richard Niebuhr's communication, *Christian Century*, XLIX (April 6, 1932), 447. H. Richard Niebuhr's very different approach to responsibility in war can also be seen in his articles, "War as the Judgment of God," *Christian Century*, LIX (May 13, 1942), 630–33, and "War as Crucifixion," *Christian Century*, LX (April 28, 1943), 513–15. Antony Flew, "Ends and Means," *The Encyclopedia of Philosophy*, II, 509.
39   Niebuhr and Dun, "God Wills Both Justice and Peace," 77.

A good example of Niebuhr's reasoning can be seen in his discussion of just war in a nuclear age. He considered atomic warfare in relation to several ends and consequences, as assessed in relation to such values as justice, order, and peace. Caution is required because "the ultimate consequences of atomic warfare cannot be measured."

A war to "defend the victims of wanton aggression," where the demands of justice join the demands of order, is today the clearest case of a just war. But where the immediate claims of order and justice conflict, as in a war initiated "to secure freedom for the oppressed," the case is now much less clear. The claims of justice are no less. But because contemporary war places so many moral values in incalculable jeopardy, the immediate claims of order have become much greater. Although oppression was never more abhorrent to the Christian conscience or more dangerous to the longer-range prospects of peace than today, the concept of a just war does not provide moral justification for initiating a war of incalculable consequences to end such oppression.[40]

Conclusion

No doubt the power of Niebuhr's attack on pacifism results from the total vision of which it is a part. Indeed, if we examine each particular argument against pacifism, we discover that it lacks the power of the whole. Yet the whole is paradoxical and dialectical so that certain propositions are apparently both affirmed and denied. Specifically, Niebuhr's position seems to require both a denial and an affirmation of an intrinsic difference between nonviolence and violence. These and other assumptions of the "realist" approach to violence require more careful analysis; thus, the debate between the realist and the pacifist must go on.

Niebuhr's attack on pacifism was, unfortunately, limited to two main types, although there are other, perhaps more defensible, arguments for pacifism. Indeed, a pacifism developed on Niebuhr's own grounds would not be as vulnerable to his attacks largely because it would repudiate liberalism's assump-

40   Ibid., 78.

tion that persuasion is sufficient to effect social change. Such a
pacifism would start from the rule of nonviolence, as anyone
must if violence is prima facie wrong. As Howard Zinn has contended, "it is terribly important to understand that our starting
point should be pacifism, that the burden of proof should be
placed on the arguer for violence."[41] Then one could point to
(1) imperfect information and (2) ethical fallibility to show the
difficulty of predicting and assessing social consequences in
situations of multiple actors.[42] Such considerations would at
least increase the reluctance to depart from the rule of nonviolence. Because we cannot accurately predict the consequences
of our actions or adequately assess them, we should be very
hesitant to depart from nonviolence. For considerations of ends
and consequences to override the duty to refrain from harming
other persons, agents would need to be able to predict and assess consequences more fully and accurately than they can.

Versions of this argument have been offered by thinkers as
diverse as Hannah Arendt, Mohandas Gandhi, and Leo Tolstoy,
among others. Arendt, for example, argues in *On Violence*:
"Since the end of human action, as distinct from the end products of fabrication, can never be reliably predicted, the means
used to achieve political goals are more often than not of greater
relevance to the future world than the intended goals. . . . And
since when we act we never know with any certainty the even-
tual consequences of what we are doing, violence can remain
rational only if it pursues short-term goals." For Arendt, violence is rational only if it is directed toward short-term, concrete goals rather than long-term, abstract goals. Furthermore, it
is possible to claim that if an agent were forced to choose between committing bad acts for good ends and good acts for bad
ends, the world would be better if he chose the latter. Arendt's
view that the most probable result of violence is a more violent
world may appear to depend on a prediction of consequences,

41   Howard Zinn, "The Force of Nonviolence," in Thomas Rose (ed.), *Violence in America* (New York: Vintage Books, 1970), 20.
42   See the similar points in relation to political organization in J. R. Lucas,
The Principles of Politics (Oxford: Clarendon Press, 1967). Similar points are
often used to justify a democratic polity.

but central to her position is the unpredictability of consequences. "The reason why we are never able to foretell with
certainty the outcome and end of any action is simply that action has no end. The process of a single deed can quite literally
endure throughout time until mankind itself has come to an
end."[43] The unpredictability of consequences does not lead to
inaction, for we can and must make wagers and take risks. But
we have better odds in betting on the right act than on the good
consequences. For example, an act of nonviolence or truth-tell-
ing by its very performance is something good, but whether that
act will have good consequences depends on too many factors,
including the responses of others, to permit accurate prediction. Thus, the most probable result of violence is a more violent world because the act of violence itself adds to the violence. Arendt's view of violence is closely connected to her
understanding of human action and the inevitability of imperfect information.

For Gandhi, persistence in nonviolence is a necessary corollary of the fact that sincere striving after Truth leads to different conclusions. Absolute Truth and God are the same, but absolute Truth is a goal that cannot be realized in human relations
where we have only relative truths or many different interpretations of the Truth. *Satyagraha* means being firm and steadfast
in adhering to one's own conception of Truth until one is convinced that this conception is mistaken. Firm adherence should
not become stubbornness, and it should not become so certain
that the agent supposes that violence is justified. Gandhi expressed his point in many different ways. Truth "excludes the
use of violence because man is not capable of knowing the absolute truth and therefore is not competent to punish." There

43 Hannah Arendt, *On Violence* (New York: Harcourt, Brace, and World,
1970), 4, 79. See also J. M. Cameron, "On Violence," *New York Review of
Books* (July 2, 1970), 24ff. and the discussion in Yoder, *Nevertheless*, esp. 32–
45. Compare John Howard Yoder, *The Original Revolution: Essays on Christian Pacifism* (Scottdale, Pa.: Herald Press, 1971), 140. See, for example, Reinhold Niebuhr, *The Irony of American History* (New York: Charles Scribner's
Sons, 1952). Hannah Arendt, *The Human Condition* (Garden City, N.Y.:
Doubleday, 1959), 209.

can only be "experiments with truth." "*Ahimsa* is the farthest limit of humility." "We have always control over the means but not over the end." Gandhi also used the organic metaphor of the seed and the tree to express the interpenetration of means and ends.[44]

Obviously there are several differences between Arendt and Gandhi on violence; for example, Gandhi's notion of *karma*, or ethical retribution, undergirds his understanding of means and ends and his claim that evil means can never lead to good consequences. And there is a difference of emphasis, for Gandhi stressed ethical fallibility while Arendt stressed imperfect information.

Leo Tolstoy emphasized both ethical fallibility and imperfect information. His position on nonviolence, or nonresistance, has been misconstrued and consequently dismissed especially by those who identify him as a Christ-against-culture legalist. Yet he was not consistently and completely legalistic, particularly in his appeals to non-Christians. For example, he opposed those who wanted to depart from "God's law and reason's guidance" in this matter of nonresistance "because, according to their conception, the effects of actions performed in submission to God's law may be detrimental or inconvenient." One of his arguments against their position concerns man's mortality:

Astonishing delusion! A being who breathes one day and vanishes the next receives one definite, indubitable law to guide him through the brief term of his life; but instead of obeying that law he prefers to fancy that he knows what is necessary, advantageous, and well-timed for men, for all the world— this world which continually shifts and evolves and for the sake of some advantage (which each man pictures after his own fancy) he decides that he and other people should temporarily abandon the indubitable law given to

44   For a good discussion of Gandhi's views of ends and means, see H. J. N. Horsburgh, *Non-violence and Aggression: A Study of Gandhi's Moral Equivalent of War* (London: Oxford University Press, 1968), and Raghavan Iyer, "Means and Ends in Politics," in G. Ramachandran and T. K. Mahadevan (eds.), *Gandhi: His Relevance for Our Times* (Berkeley, Calif.: World Without War Council, 1971), 320–32. The most thorough study of Gandhi's moral and political thought is Raghavan Iyer, *The Moral and Political Thought of Mahatma Gandhi* (New York: Oxford University Press, 1973).

one and to all, and should act, not as they would that others should act toward them, bringing love into the world, but instead do violence, imprison, kill, and bring into the world enmity whenever it seems profitable to do so.

Both man's mortality and the shifting nature of the world undermine our capacity to predict and assess consequences. Tolstoy took the stock example of a criminal about to kill or molest a child and tried to show that for both the Christian and the non-Christian there is "no reasonable foundation" for the common conclusion that an act of violence against the criminal would be justified. First, Tolstoy stressed imperfect information. "By killing the former [the criminal] he kills for certain; whereas he cannot know positively whether the criminal would have killed the child or not." Then he emphasized ethical fallibility. "Who shall say whether the child's life was more needed, was better, than the other's life?"[45] While the Christian has special reasons within his faith for remaining nonviolent or nonresistant, every person, including the Christian, has sufficient reasons for such action (or insufficient reasons for violence) in imperfect information and ethical fallibility.

Despite their different philosophical and theological contexts, Arendt, Gandhi, and Tolstoy used very similar arguments for their reluctance to depart from nonviolence. Arendt's view is more relative, and it focuses on the question "when is violence rational?" Gandhi appeared to hold that violence is absolutely wrong, but he sometimes seemed to suggest that it is prima facie wrong (e.g., when he said that if there is only a choice between violence and cowardice, violence is morally preferable). Tolstoy's position, emphasizing nonresistance, is absolutist. Nevertheless, for all three thinkers, imperfect information and ethical fallibility provide strong reasons for varying degrees of reluctance to depart from nonviolence. Indeed, the appeal to imperfect information and ethical fallibility only deepens the reluctance we already have to use violence because of the moral priority of nonviolence.

45 Leo Tolstoy, Tolstoy's Writings on Civil Disobedience and Non-violence (New York: New American Library, 1968), 181–90.

Chapter Three

Just-War Criteria

If the distinction between nonviolence and violence is morally significant and if nonviolence has moral priority over violence, it is important to examine the criteria by which the transition from nonviolence to violence and from peace to war might be justified. In addition, it is important to examine the criteria for the right conduct of war. In this chapter I want to offer a general analysis and assessment of just-war criteria. Then in the following chapter I will offer a detailed study of one major theory of just war, emphasizing the laws of war.

There are at least two useful approaches to the criteria of just wars. One starts from basic ethical principles and asks what criteria of just wars can be derived from them. The other starts from the just-war criteria that we have inherited and criticizes them in terms of consistency, coherence, and fidelity to fundamental ethical principles and values. Within either approach, we move back and forth between our practices, including our ordinary judgments, and ethical principles and theories.

An example of the first approach is John Rawls's *A Theory of Justice*, which treats just-war criteria within the context of a systematic theory of justice as fairness. Unfortunately, his treatment is very sketchy and mainly reaffirms the traditional criteria without establishing the links between them and his theory of justice. Taking the second approach, several theologians and philosophers appropriate and apply traditional just-war criteria without adequately probing their bases, interrelations, and functions. In a recent article entitled "Just War Theory: What's

the Use?" James Johnson considers the implications and applications of this "broadly defined collection of practical principles" called just-war theory. He takes "classic just war theory"
(which is actually more a tradition than a single theory) as normative, viewing several developments in the last three centuries as dilutions and distortions. Indeed, he uses this classic
theory to expose contemporary misunderstandings of just-war
criteria. But he offers few arguments for taking particular "classic" formulations as normative and for viewing later developments as decline rather than progress.[1]

We should begin with the historical deposit of just-war criteria, now accessible in a number of fine historical studies.[2] But
we should not stop there, especially if just-war criteria are to be
defensible and usable for policy-makers and citizens. It is also
essential to offer a rational reconstruction of these criteria. I
will try to show how the traditional just-war criteria can be reconstructed, explicated, and defended in relation to the prima
facie duty of nonmaleficence—the duty not to harm or kill others. Then I will reconstruct their foundations and interrelations
before considering their order and strength. Finally, I will examine their function in a pluralistic society and ask what stake,
if any, pacifists might have in such criteria.

The Logic of Prima Facie Duties

The following criteria frequently appear in comprehensive just-
war theories: legitimate or competent authority, just cause, right

1 John Rawls, A Theory of Justice (Cambridge, Mass.: Harvard University
Press, 1971), #58; James T. Johnson, "Just War Theory: What's the Use?"
Worldview, XIX (July-August, 1976), 41–47. See Michael Walzer, Just and Un-
just Wars (New York: Basic Books, 1977), probably the best book on morality
of and in war in this century. See also my review of Just and Unjust Wars in
Bulletin of the Atomic Scientists, XXXIV (October, 1978), 44–48, and James
T. Johnson's review essay in Religious Studies Review, IV (October, 1978),
240–45.
2 See Frederick H. Russell, The Just War in the Middle Ages (New York:
Cambridge University Press, 1975); James T. Johnson, Ideology, Reason, and

intention, announcement of intention, last resort, reasonable hope of success, proportionality, and just conduct. All of these criteria taken together, with the exception of the last one, establish the *jus ad bellum*, the right to go to war, while the last criterion focuses on the *jus in bello*, right conduct within war, and includes both intention and proportionality, which are also part of the *jus ad bellum*.[3]

Many analogues to these criteria emerge when people reflect morally about several forms of conduct including the use of force and disobedience to the state. For example, Pauline Maier shows that many American colonists in the eighteenth century justified and limited their resistance to England by appealing to criteria in the Whig tradition that established several preconditions for justified violence: the ruler's violation of the ends of government, the failure of "all due means of redress," support by the people, right intentions and motives, reasonable chance of success, and proportionality. When the colonists acted, these criteria, as Maier notes, "proved to be as much a burden as a guide." Similar criteria are sometimes operative even when a person's ethical methodology appears to exclude them. For example, Dietrich Bonhoeffer, a theologian who was put to death for his involvement in the July 20, 1944, plot to assassinate Hitler, justified tyrannicide by some of the criteria of traditional just-war and just-revolution theories although his theological-ethical methodology appeared to exclude rules and principles. His "operative guidelines," for which his theological-ethical methodology made no provision, included clear evidence of serious misrule; respect for the scale of political responsibility and authority (those lower in or outside the political hierarchy

---

the *Limitation of War* (Princeton, N.J.: Princeton University Press, 1975); LeRoy Brandt Walters, Jr., "Five Classic Just-War Theories: A Study in the Thought of Thomas Aquinas, Vitoria, Suarez, Gentili, and Grotius" (Ph.D. dissertation, Yale University, 1971).

3   See Ralph B. Potter, Jr., *War and Moral Discourse* (Richmond, Va.: John Knox Press, 1969). One of the best systematic examinations of just-war criteria is Potter's article "The Moral Logic of War," *McCormick Quarterly*, XXIII (1970), 203–33.

should act only after others have failed); reasonable assurances
of successful execution; tyrannicide as a last resort; minimal
necessary force.[4] As in many justifications of revolution or tyrannicide, Bonhoeffer found a surrogate for the authority of the
government in the political hierarchy. Others have also appealed to the "lesser magistrates" and finally to the people.

Still others have dealt with civil disobedience and economic
boycotts by appealing to analogous criteria. For example, James
Luther Adams shows that "some of the most pertinent tests [for
determining justified civil disobedience] are similar to those
employed in the doctrine of the just war." And Paul Ramsey
insists that the use of various forms of economic pressure
"should conform to the ancient principles and limitations justifying a Christian in taking up any use of force." His discussion
parallels his examination of just-war criteria.[5] While Ramsey
and others account for these similarities by pointing to the presence of *force* in each of these modes of conduct, Adams thinks
that the similarities between the criteria for civil disobedience
and war stem from the fact that both actions deviate from normal procedures.

Actually we formulate and use criteria that are analogous to

4 Pauline Maier, *From Resistance to Revolution: Colonial Radicals and the
Development of American Opposition to Britain, 1765–1776* (New York:
Alfred A. Knopf, 1972), Chap. 2; Larry L. Rasmussen, *Dietrich Bonhoeffer:
Reality and Resistance* (Nashville: Abingdon Press, 1972), all of Pt. II, but
especially 145–46 and 154–55.

5 James Luther Adams, "Civil Disobedience: Its Occasions and Limits," in J.
Roland Pennock and John W. Chapman (eds.), *Political and Legal Obligations*, Nomos XII (New York: Atherton Press, 1970), 303. *Cf.* James F. Chil-
dress, *Civil Disobedience and Political Obligation: A Study in Christian Social Ethics*, Yale Publications in Religion, XVI (New Haven: Yale University
Press, 1971), Chap. IV; Paul Ramsey, *Christian Ethics and the Sit-In* (New
York: Association Press, 1961), 104. *Cf.* Ramsey, *War and the Christian Conscience: How Shall Modern War Be Conducted Justly?* (Durham, N.C.: Duke
University Press, 1961) and *The Just War: Force and Political Responsibility*
(New York: Charles Scribner's Sons, 1968). For an attempt to apply just-war
criteria to organ transplants on the grounds that both are instances of "the
controlled use of regrettable violence," see James B. Nelson, *Human Medicine*
(Minneapolis, Minn.: Augsburg, 1973), Chap. VII.

those that determine whether a war is just and justified whenever we face conflicting obligations or duties, whenever it is
impossible to fulfill all the claims upon us, to respect all the
rights involved, or to avoid doing evil to everyone. Sometimes
we confront two or more prima facie duties or obligations, one
of which we cannot fulfill without sacrificing the other(s). In
this sort of dilemma, we justify sacrificing one prima facie obligation to fulfill another only when we can answer certain
questions. We need to know whether we have a just cause,
proper intentions, a reasonable hope of achieving the end, a
reasonable balance between probable good and evil, and no
other courses of action that would enable us to avoid sacrificing
the obligation. Thus, the criteria for assessing wars and several
other actions are similar because war and these other actions
sacrifice some prima facie obligation(s)—a sacrifice that must
be justified along certain lines suggested by the criteria. Sometimes the use of force is important, but it is only one of numerous human actions that stand in need of justification because
they sacrifice prima facie obligations. Just-war criteria can be
illuminated by the language of prima facie obligations and the
content of the particular obligations not to injure or kill others
that the justification of war must override.

First, let us consider the notion of a prima facie obligation
or duty. (I am using *obligation* and *duty* interchangeably in this
context.) W. D. Ross introduced the distinction between prima
facie and actual obligations to account for conflicts of obligations, which, he maintained, proved to be "nonexistent" when
fully and carefully analyzed. When two or more prima facie
obligations appear to come into conflict, we have to assess the
total situation, including various possible courses of action
with all their features of prima facie rightness and wrongness,
to determine what we actually ought to do. The phrase *prima
facie* indicates that certain features of acts that have a tendency
to make an act right or wrong claim our attention; insofar as an
act has those features it is right or wrong. But our actual obligation depends on the act in its wholeness and entirety. For
"while an act may well be *prima facie* obligatory in respect of

one character and *prima facie* forbidden in virtue of another, it becomes obligatory or forbidden only in virtue of the totality of its ethically relevant characteristics."[6] *Prima facie* does not mean "apparent" in contrast to "real," for prima facie duties are real although they are distinguished from "actual" duties. Although some prima facie obligations are more stringent than others (e.g., nonmaleficence is more stringent than beneficence), it is not possible to provide a complete ranking or a scale of stringency of obligations.

To hold that an obligation or duty is prima facie is to claim that it always has a strong moral reason for its performance although this reason may not always be decisive or triumph over all other reasons. If an obligation is viewed as absolute, it cannot be overridden under any circumstances; it has priority over all other obligations with which it might come into conflict. If it is viewed as relative, the rule stating it is no more than a maxim or rule of thumb that illuminates but does not prescribe what we ought to do. If it is viewed as prima facie, it is intrinsically binding, but it does not necessarily determine one's actual obligation.

As individuals or members of institutions, we have a prima facie duty not to injure others. Injury may mean an unwarranted or unjustified harm or violation of rights, or it may mean inflicting actual harm (e.g., shooting someone) that may or may not be warranted or justified. In the first sense, it is, of course, always wrong by definition; an obligation not to injure others wrongfully would be absolute rather than prima facie. In the second sense, it is prima facie. Insofar as an act injures another, it is prima facie wrong and stands in need of justification. Although act-utilitarians imply that killing (which I am treating for the moment under injury) is morally neutral, William Frankena rightly insists that some kinds of action including killing are "intrinsically wrong." For they are "always prima facie wrong, and they are always actually wrong when they are

---

6   W. D. Ross, *Foundations of Ethics* (Oxford: Clarendon Press, 1939), 86. *Cf.* Ross, *The Right and the Good* (Oxford: Clarendon Press, 1930), Chap. II.

not justified on other moral grounds. They are not in themselves morally indifferent. They may conceivably be justified
in certain situations, but they always need to be justified; and
even when they are justified, there is still one moral point
against them." If the Fifth (or Sixth) Commandment reads "Thou
shalt not kill," it is prima facie rather than absolute, for the He-
brews admitted killing in self-defense, capital punishment, and
war. If it reads "Thou shalt not commit murder," it can then be
taken as absolute, but it leaves open the question which kill-
ings are to be counted as murder.[7]

It is not necessary to defend Ross's intuitionism in order to
hold that injury and killing are intrinsically prima facie wrong.
For Ross, both fall under the obligation of nonmaleficence. For
Rawls, there is a "natural duty," that is, a duty owed to persons
generally, not to injure or harm others and not to inflict unnecessary suffering; this natural duty can be derived from the original position.[8] Christian theologians might derive this obligation not to injure or kill others from the norm of *agape*. The
claim that injury and killing are prima facie wrong is compatible with a number of philosophical and religious frame-
works.

An overridden or outweighed prima facie obligation continues to function in the situation and the course of action one
adopts. It leaves what Robert Nozick calls "moral traces." It has
"residual effects" on the agent's attitudes and actions. As A. C.
Ewing suggests, "If I have a *prima facie* obligation which I cannot rightly fulfill because it is overruled by another, stronger
prima facie obligation, it does not by any means follow that my
conduct ought to be unaffected by the former obligation. Even
if I am morally bound to do something inconsistent with it, it

---

7 William K. Frankena, *Ethics* (2nd ed.; Englewood Cliffs, N.J.: Prentice-
Hall, 1973), 55–56. For some of the issues see J. J. Stamm with M. E. Andrew,
The Ten Commandments in Recent Research (London: SCM Press, 1967), 98–
99, which views what is prohibited as "illegal killing inimical to the community." See also Solomon Goldman, *The Ten Commandments* (Chicago:
University of Chicago Press, 1963).
8 Rawls, *A Theory of Justice*, 113–14.

should in many cases modify in some respect the way in which the act is performed and in almost all it should affect some subsequent action." For example, if I think that a stronger obligation requires me to break a promise, I should at least explain the situation to the promisee, ask him not to hold me to the promise, apologize for breaking it and even try to make it up to him later. At the very least, Ewing goes on to say, the prima facie obligation to keep the promise "should always affect our mental attitude toward the action" to the extent of evoking regret. According to W. D. Ross, "we do not for a moment cease to recognize a *prima facie* duty to keep our promise, and this leads us to feel, not indeed shame or repentance, but certainly compunction for behaving as we do."[9]

One important difference between many Protestant and Catholic interpretations of just war appears at this point. They differ on the appropriate attitude toward a just war that overrides the prima facie duty not to injure or kill others. In accord with their belief in the universality of sin, many Protestant theologians, such as Reinhold Niebuhr, insist that the decision to wage a just war is "the lesser of two evils," which they understand as "moral" as well as physical evils. Thus, remorse and repentance are proper responses. As Saint Augustine stressed, wars should be both just and mournful. Many Catholic theologians, joined by some Protestants, most notably Paul Ramsey, insist that "an act of self-defense or an act of vindictive justice, although imposed by circumstances which are regrettable, is morally good." For them, "war is not the lesser of two evils, but the lesser of two goods (one of which appears, at the moment of choice, unattainable)."[10]

---

9   Robert Nozick, "Moral Complications and Moral Structures," *Natural Law Forum*, XIII (1968), 1–50; A. C. Ewing, *Second Thoughts in Moral Philosophy* (London: Routledge and Kegan Paul, 1959), 110; Ross, *The Right and the Good*, 28. For a criticism of the view that prima facie obligations retain their tendency to be binding and thus occasion some measure of moral regret, see Maurice Mandelbaum, *The Phenomenology of Moral Experience* (Baltimore: Johns Hopkins University Press, 1969), 79–81.

10   See Henry Paolucci (ed.), *The Political Writings of St. Augustine* (Chicago: Henry Regnery, 1962), 162–83, and Roland H. Bainton, *Christian Atti-*

Whether a war that justly and justifiably overrides the prima facie duty not to injure or kill others should evoke regret or remorse may be debatable, but such a war engenders certain obligations as well as attitudes. The traces or residual effects of the overridden prima facie duty are extremely important, as will be clear in my discussion of such just-war criteria as right intention, proportionality, and just conduct.

Before I develop those criteria, I want to summarize and amplify some implications of the prima facie duty not to injure or kill others. They are actually presuppositions of many just-war theories that include both *jus ad bellum* and *jus in bello*. First, because it is prima facie wrong to injure or kill others, such acts demand justification. There is a presumption against their justification, and anyone who tries to justify them bears a heavy burden of proof. Second, because not all duties can be fulfilled in every situation without some sacrifices (this inability may be understood as natural or as the result of sin), it is necessary and legitimate to override some prima facie duties. Some other duties (for instance, the prima facie duty to uphold justice or to protect the innocent) may be more stringent and thus take priority over the duty not to injure others. War thus can be a moral undertaking in some circumstances. Third, the overridden prima facie duties should affect the actors' attitudes and what they do in waging the war. Some ways of waging war are more compatible than others with the overridden prima facie duties not to injure or kill others. War can be more or less humane and civilized. War and politics, or war and peace, are not two totally separate realms or periods.[11] Both are subject to moral principles and rules and, indeed, to many of the same

tudes *Toward War and Peace* (Nashville: Abingdon Press, 1960), 98; Joseph C. McKenna, S.J., "Ethics and War: A Catholic View," *American Political Science Review*, LIV (1960), 658, *cf.* 650. For Ramsey's theoretical statement, see *Deeds and Rules in Christian Ethics* (New York: Charles Scribner's Sons, 1967), 187–88. For some trends in recent Catholic moral theology that are similar to the language of prima facie duties proposed in this essay, see Richard McCormick, S.J., "Notes on Moral Theology, 1977: The Church in Dispute," *Theological Studies*, XXXVIII (1978), 103; Albert R. DiIanni, S.M., "The Direct/Indirect Distinction in Morals," *Thomist*, XLI (1977), 350–80.
11   Ramsey, *The Just War*, 55, 142, 143, 475, *et passim*.

principles and rules. War ought to fall within many of the boundaries that are also important to peace.

Theorists and practitioners are commonly tempted to make war merely an extension of politics so that it requires very little to justify waging war; or they are tempted to make politics and war so discontinuous that once one enters the state of war previously important moral, political, and legal considerations become irrelevant. Two points need to be affirmed. On the one hand, war must be justified because it violates some of our prima facie obligations, not because it is totally immoral or amoral or utterly discontinuous with politics. On the other hand, it can be more or less humane insofar as it is conducted in accordance with some standards that derive from the overridden prima facie obligations and other obligations that endure even in war. Furthermore, however much continuity there is between peace and war, peace remains the ultimate aim of a just war.

The model of war as a rule-governed activity stands in sharp contrast to the model of war as hell, which is accepted by most pacifists and by many "realists" who recognize no restraints other than proportionality. Both models are evident in the following passage from Rolf Hochhuth's play, *Soldiers*.

Bishop Bell of Chichester: We denigrate our men if we suggest that they require directives to tell them that the burning of defenseless persons is murder.

P.M. (savagely, not looking at Bell): War is murder. The murderer is the man who fires first. That man is Hitler.

According to one view, war is hell, murder, and there is thus only the crime of war, within which anything goes, for "all's fair . . . " According to another view, war is a gamelike (not in a frivolous sense) or a rule-governed conflict, within which one may legitimately injure, kill, and destroy, but not commit war crimes such as injuring or killing defenseless persons who are noncombatants or ex-combatants. For the view that war is "total" and without limits, the only critical moral factor is the decision to wage war, and moral blameworthiness may attach to the side starting the war, sometimes even to the side firing the first shot. For the view that war is a rule-governed activity, the *jus in bello* becomes very important. Any adequate theory, however, should *not* maintain that *jus ad bellum* is unimportant because the difference between war and peace is not all that great since some moral rules and principles persist in war. There is an important difference between them so that the *jus ad bellum* remains indispensable, but this difference is not to be described as that between morality and immorality or amorality. In Paul Ramsey's thought, for example, the emphasis is on the continuity between politics and war. Thus, he concentrates on the *jus in bello*, holding that the "*laws* of war are only an extension, where war is the only available means, of the rules governing any use of political power." Unfortunately, this emphasis on the continuity between politics and war may be excessive, since Ramsey does not pay enough attention to the moral issues in crossing the line between ordinary politics and war—the *jus ad bellum*.[12]

Grounds of Just-War Criteria

Most of the criteria traditionally associated with just-war theories emerge because war involves a conflict between prima facie obligations (when it is just and justified) and because the overridden prima facie obligations forbid us to injure and kill others. Many of these criteria apply in other areas, as I have suggested, because of similar conflicts between prima facie obligations, not because the prima facie obligations not to injure or kill others are involved at every point. Nevertheless, the

12 Rolf Hochhuth, *Soldiers: An Obituary for Geneva*, trans. Robert David MacDonald (New York: Grove Press, 1968), 208. The formulation of the ideas in this paragraph is indebted to some lectures on war by Michael Walzer at Harvard University, fall, 1972. The substance of these lectures appears in Walzer, *Just and Unjust Wars*. See Ramsey, *The Just War*, 144, *cf.* 475; James T. Johnson, "Toward Reconstructing the *jus ad bellum*," *Monist*, LVII (1973), 461–88.

content of the prima facie obligations that are overruled in just wars certainly shapes the criteria, particularly those having to do with *jus in bello*, since the conduct of the war should be as compatible as possible with the overridden prima facie obligations.

The first criterion of a just war is right or legitimate authority, which is really a presupposition for the rest of the criteria. In fact, it determines *who* is primarily responsible for judging whether the other criteria are met. As Quentin Quade indicates, "the principles of Just War become operative only *after* the classic political question is answered: who should do the judging?" Answering the authority question is a precondition for answering the others; it thus cannot be dismissed as a "secondary criterion." James Johnson appears to think that legitimate authority was a secondary criterion for Saint Augustine, but Augustine's writings indicate that the authority of the prince or state or God's direct authorization is indispensable for just war. In his attempt to reconstruct the *jus ad bellum*, Johnson does not address this criterion, except in passing, because he thinks that the current de facto definition of right authority (wherever there is sovereignty, there is right authority) is politically workable, although it has some moral difficulties. Nevertheless, any adequate just-war theory must seriously address this question "who decides?" Even in the use of these criteria for justifying and limiting revolution, surrogates for the established authority are often found in the revolutionary elite or the "people."[13]

After the proper authority has determined that a war is just and justified and thus overrides the prima facie obligation not to injure and kill others, citizens, including subject-soldiers, face a different presumption. Whereas the proper authority has to confront and rebut the presumption against war, the subject-

13 Quentin L. Quade, "Civil Disobedience and the State," *Worldview*, X (November, 1967), 4–9; Johnson, "Just War Theory," 42; Paolucci (ed.), *Political Writings of St. Augustine*, 163–66, *et passim*; Johnson, "Toward Reconstructing the *jus ad bellum*," 487 n. See also Richard Neuhaus' suggestions in Peter L. Berger and Richard J. Neuhaus, *Movement and Revolution* (Garden City, N.Y.: Doubleday, 1970), 164–78.

soldier now confronts the presumption that the war is just and justified because the legitimate authority has so decided in accord with established procedures.[14] In all political orders, the subject has a moral right and duty—although not a legal right—not to fight if the war is manifestly unjust. And in a democracy, the citizen is ruler as well as subject and thus has a greater responsibility to apply these criteria to war. As subject, however, his presumption is still that the authorities, if they are legitimate and have followed proper procedures, have decided correctly.

The requirement of a just cause is simply the requirement that the other competing prima facie duty or obligation be a serious and weighty one, e.g., to protect the innocent from unjust attack, to restore rights wrongfully denied, or to reestablish a just order. Because war involves overriding important prima facie obligations not to injure or kill others, it demands the most weighty and significant reasons. These obligations cannot be overridden if there are other ways of achieving the just aim short of war. War is the *ultima ratio*, the last resort, but the requirement that war be the last resort does not mean that all possible measures have to be attempted and exhausted if there is no reasonable expectation that they will be successful. James Johnson does not emphasize the criterion of "last resort" in part because he thinks that it tends to be understood as condemning the first use of force, but this requirement does not necessarily mean that the side that first resorts to armed force should be condemned.[15]

Insofar as a formal declaration is sometimes required, it stems not only from the nature of the political society, but also from the requirement that war be the last resort. Ultimata or formal declarations of war "are the last measures of persuasion short of force itself." Although a formal declaration of war may not be appropriate for various reasons, the significance of this cri-

14 See John A. Rohr, *Prophets Without Honor: Public Policy and the Selective Conscientious Objector* (Nashville: Abingdon Press, 1971), 98; Ramsey, *The Just War*, 98, 274–75, 360, et passim.
15 Johnson, "Just War Theory," 44, and "Toward Reconstructing the *jus ad bellum*," 487 (where this criterion is not included in the reconstruction).

terion, broadly understood, should not be underestimated. Conceding that the best publicists differed on the necessity of a declaration, Francis Lieber defended it because "decent regard for mankind" and "public good faith" require that a government explain and justify its departure from peace.[16] A failure to announce the intention of and the reasons for waging war is a failure to exercise the responsibility of explaining and justifying exceptional action to those involved. An announcement of intentions and explanation of reasons may be more appropriate than a formal declaration of war.

The requirements of reasonable hope of success and proportionality are closely related. If war has no reasonable chance of success, it is clearly imprudent. But more than a dictate of prudence is involved in the demand for a reasonable hope of success. If none of the just and serious ends, none of the other prima facie obligations, could be realized or fulfilled through the war, a nation should reconsider its policy, which, after all, involves overriding stringent prima facie obligations. Nevertheless, numerous qualifications are in order. This criterion applies more clearly to offensive than to defensive wars. In any war success may be broader than "victory." As Lieber wrote of John Brown's raid: it was irrational, but it will be historical! Success could include witnessing to values as well as achieving goals; for instance, a group might engage in resistance in order to retain self-respect even in its demise. Regarding the limited Jewish resistance in Nazi Germany, some Jewish thinkers have insisted that if the holocaust comes again Jews must not "die like sheep." Although Ralph Potter has derived the criterion of reasonable hope of success from the moral prohibition of suicide and from the fact that statesmen are stewards of a nation, heroic acts such as falling on a grenade to save one's comrades may be fitting for individuals and suicide itself may be justifiable in some cases, particularly if it can be a noble witness to some higher values in the face of certain and immi-

16 McKenna, "Ethics and War," 650. See my discussion of Lieber in the next chapter. This quotation comes from Francis Lieber, "Laws and Usages of War," lecture given at Columbia Law School, December 3, 1861.

nent death.[17] Even if a nation has good reason to think that it
will be defeated anyway, its vigorous resistance may preserve
significant values beyond number of lives and retention of territory or sovereignty. Furthermore, what is "reasonable" depends on the situations in which actors have to make responsible decisions; retrospective judgments by others should
include only what the actors could and should have foreseen.
Finally, this criterion appears only to exclude totally "useless"
or "pointless" or self-indulgent warfare, which reasonable people
cannot expect to achieve goals or to express values. Such warfare is excluded because it cannot override the prima facie duties not to injure or kill others, duties as binding on states as
on individuals.

Regarding proportionality, Ramsey writes: "It can never be
right to resort to war, no matter how just the cause, unless a
proportionality can be established between military/political
objectives and their price, or unless one has reason to believe
that in the end more good will be done than undone or a greater
measure of evil prevented. But, of all the tests for judging
whether to resort to or to participate in war, this one balancing
an evil or good effect against another is open to the greatest
uncertainty. This, therefore, establishes rather than removes the
possibility of conscientious disagreement among prudent
men."[18] Here, too, defensive measures are less restricted than
offensive ones, but this criterion includes the welfare of all
countries and peoples and not merely one's own country. Certainly the weight of the cause and the probability of success
enter the discussion of proportionality, but the probable negative consequences must also be considered—even beyond the
negative feature of injuring or killing others.

The last major criterion of the *jus ad bellum* is right or just
intention, which, along with proportionality, is very important
in particular battles, engagements, and acts within war and not
merely for the war as a whole. For the war as a whole, right

17 Potter, "The Moral Logic of War," 219.
18 Ramsey, *The Just War*, 195.

intention is shaped by the pursuit of a just cause, but it also encompasses motives. For example, as Augustine and others have insisted, hatred is ruled out. Some would hold that the dominance, if not the mere presence, of hatred vitiates the right to wage war even if there is a just cause. For example, Mc-Kenna holds that a "war which is otherwise just becomes immoral if it is waged out of hatred."[19] Such a contention, however, is difficult to establish, for if all the conditions of a just and justified war were met, the presence of vicious motives would not obliterate the *jus ad bellum*, although they would lead to negative judgments about the agents. Insofar as these vicious motives are expressed in such ways as the use of disproportionate force or the infliction of unnecessary suffering, one may condemn the belligerent for violating the *jus in bello*. Nevertheless, this criterion of right intention, understood not merely as pursuit of a just cause but also as proper motives, remains significant in part because war is conducted between public, not private, enemies. Furthermore, an attitude of regret, if not remorse, is appropriate when a prima facie obligation is overridden.

Another interpretation of right intention focuses on peace as the object or end of war. It too bridges the *jus ad bellum* and *jus in bello*, and I shall emphasize its impact on the conduct of war. Augustine and many others have affirmed that peace is the ultimate object, end, or intention of war. In short, war as injury, killing, and destruction is not an end in itself but a means to another end—a just or better peace. Even apart from the justice that is sought, peace retains its moral claim during war and thus constitutes an ultimate or final objective. There is a duty to restore the "normal" state of affairs as quickly and surely as possible.

It may be dangerous, however, to stress that it is urgent to restore peace, especially if peace is defined as the absence of conflict rather than a specific set of relationships that may include conflict. For such an emphasis may engender support for

19   McKenna, "Ethics and War," 652.

a quick, brutal, and total war that may undermine the limits set by the *jus in bello*. Paul Ramsey holds that, unless there is a morality that intrinsically limits the conduct of war, "then we must simply admit that war has no limits—since these can hardly be derived from 'peace' as the 'final cause' of just wars." But if one does not misconstrue peace as the total absence of conflict, one can see how the prima facie obligation not to injure or kill others persists even in the midst of war by mandating the ultimate object of peace. And through the object of peace (but not only this way), it imposes other restraints on the conduct of war. Since the aim of war is "a just peace," John Rawls contends, "the means employed must not destroy the possibility of peace or encourage a contempt for human life that puts the safety of ourselves and of mankind in jeopardy." General Orders No. 100 of 1863 insists that "military necessity does not include any act of hostility which makes the return to peace unnecessarily difficult."[20]

If peace does not require mutual goodwill, it at least requires some trust and confidence. Thus, perfidy, bad faith, and treachery are ruled out in part because they are destructive of the ultimate object of peace. If they are prevalent in war, to restore and maintain peace becomes very difficult short of the total subjugation of the enemy. Acceptable ruses of war, according to one commentator on the laws of war, are "those acts which the enemy would have had reason to expect, or in any event had no reason not to expect."[21] Perfidy or treachery involves the betrayal of a belligerent's confidence that is based on moral or legal expectations or both (such as the expected protection of prisoners of war). This requirement of good faith derives not only from the ultimate end of peace but also from the respect

---

20   Ramsey, *The Just War*, 152; Rawls, *A Theory of Justice*, 379. See the next chapter and Childress, "Francis Lieber's Interpretation of the Laws of War: General Orders No. 100 in the Context of His Life and Thought," *American Journal of Jurisprudence*, XXI (1976), 49, 63–65. On the dangers of an excessive emphasis on the end of peace, see Johnson, "Just War Theory," 43–44.

21   Frits Kalshoven, *The Law of Warfare: A Summary of Its Recent History and Trends in Development* (Leiden: A. W. Sijthoff, 1973), 102.

for the humanity of the enemy that is expressed in a number of prima facie obligations.

The prima facie obligation not to injure or kill others should also more directly affect the choice of weapons and methods to fight wars than should the ultimate object of peace. Since this prima facie obligation is not cancelled even when it is over-ruled, its impact can be seen in various restrictions of the *jus in bello*.

First, the immediate object is not to kill or even to injure any particular person, but to incapacitate or restrain him.[22] The enemy soldier is not reduced to his role as combatant, and when he surrenders or is wounded, he ceases to be a combatant be-cause he ceases to be a threat. He becomes an ex-combatant, and as a prisoner of war, he is entitled to certain protections. As a wounded person, he is entitled to medical treatment equal to that of one's own wounded comrades.

Second, to attack certain noncombatants directly is not le-gitimate. This principle is sound even if the distinction be-tween combatant and noncombatant is contextual and thus is partially determined by the society and the type of war. In the gray areas, noncombatants include those persons whose func-tions in factories and elsewhere serve the needs of the person *qua* person rather than his or her role as military personnel. Thus, while food is essential for the soldier to function, it is also indispensable for him as a human being. Similarly, chap-lains and medical personnel primarily serve the soldier as hu-man being even when their ministrations indirectly aid the war effort. Finally, indiscriminate methods of warfare are prohib-ited by this principle.

Third, the original prima facie obligation not to injure oth-ers also excludes inflicting unnecessary suffering. Thus, cru-elty (inflicting suffering for the sake of suffering) and wanton destruction (destruction without a compelling reason) are wrong. Such acts are not essential to the war effort. Acts that appear to fall under these vague categories of "cruelty" and "wanton de-

22   See Ramsey, *The Just War*, 397, 502, *et passim*.

struction" are not cruel or wanton if they are "necessary." The relation between military necessity and such categories is a serious problem area in the *jus in bello*, and I will return to it in the next chapter. At any rate, certain weapons (such as dumdum bullets and explosive or inflammable projectiles weighing less than four hundred grams) are prohibited because they are calculated to cause "unnecessary suffering" or "superfluous injury." The rationale is simple. An ordinary rifle bullet or projectile weighing less than four hundred grams is designed to incapacitate only one person. To make the bullet or projectile do more damage to that one person is to inflict suffering that is unnecessary or superfluous.[23] That suffering offers no military advantage. (Of course, not all suffering that offers military advantage is necessary and justified.)

Fourth, even the indirect, incidental, or obliquely intentional effects on civilians must be justified by the principle of proportionality.

I have not tried to offer an exhaustive list of the requirements of the *jus in bello*, but rather to show that some restrictions emerge from the continued pressure of the prima facie duty not to injure or kill others even when it is overridden by the *jus ad bellum*. That duty persists and imposes restrictions indirectly through the ultimate object of peace and directly as in the protection of certain classes, avoidance of unnecessary suffering, and care for combatants who are *hors de combat*.

Order and Strength of Criteria

How can these criteria be used to assess particular wars? How can we determine when a war is just and justified or unjust and unjustified? Various applications of just-war criteria have

---

23 *Weapons That May Cause Unnecessary Suffering or Have Indiscriminate Effects* (Geneva: International Committee of the Red Cross, 1973), 12–13. The quoted passage is from the St. Petersburg Declaration of 1868. See also Morris Greenspan, *Soldier's Guide to the Laws of War* (Washington, D.C.: Public Affairs Press, 1969).

been proposed and used. (1) Some just-war theorists contend
that the inability to meet any single criterion, such as last resort, renders a war unjust. Each criterion is necessary and all
are collectively sufficient.[24] (2) Under another theory the criteria establish prima facie duties, which follow the logic of such
duties, and the criteria should be met unless they are overridden by more stringent duties.[25] (3) Some theorists maintain that
no single criterion must be met, but at least several criteria must
be satisfied before a war can be justified. A war should approx-
imate the criteria, even though it cannot fully satisfy them. (4)
Other theorists contend that the criteria are "rules of thumb"
or "maxims" that identify some morally relevant considerations; they illuminate but do not prescribe what we ought to
do. (5) Still others arrange the criteria in a serial or lexical order so that some must be met before others can even be considered. For example, if there is no just cause, there is no reason
to consider proportionality, for the war cannot be justified.

There are other possible ways to apply just-war criteria, and
these five approaches can be combined in various ways. For
example, some of the criteria could establish necessary conditions for justified war, or at least prima facie duties, while others could serve as rules of thumb. The fifth approach is especially promising, and one possible serial or lexical order is
suggested in my arrangement of the criteria in the previous
section. Whether this fifth approach, perhaps in combination
with one or more of the others, could be developed is a subject
for further reflection. It is unfortunate that philosophers and
theologians have not devoted more attention to the order, mode
of application, and weight of the various criteria.

Proposals on these matters will depend, in part, on a particular theory's substantive view of justice and other moral principles. But they are not reducible to substantive interpretations
of justice, for my tentative order in the preceding section could
be justified in terms of the logic of overriding prima facie duties. For the most part, the conception of just-war criteria in

24 See Johnson, "Just War Theory," 42, 46.
25 D. Thomas O'Connor, "A Reappraisal of the Just-War Tradition," *Ethics,*
LXXXIV (1974), 167–73.

this essay is independent of substantive views of justice. It is not purely formal, however, for it hinges on material moral principles or prima facie duties (e.g., the duty not to injure or kill others). But it is intended to be accessible to many different theories of justice.

Paul Ramsey prefers to translate *justum bellum* as "justified war" rather than "just war," in part because he does not think that a substantive theory of justice in relation to ends can be developed or that one side can legitimately claim justice while denying it to the other.[26] Such an approach fits with a formal understanding of these criteria. When a policy-maker raises these formal questions of the *jus ad bellum* and gets affirmative answers, resort to war is "justified," although we cannot say that it is "just." A procedural justification is possible even when we lack a substantive theory of justice. Ramsey is more willing to provide content for *jus in bello* at least in terms of a principle of discrimination that rules out direct attacks on noncombatants. Indeed, he says very little about *jus ad bellum*, concentrating instead on *jus in bello*.

Many classic and contemporary theorists construe "just cause" to include last resort, reasonable chance of success, and proportionality. A nation does not have a just cause unless these other conditions are also met. Nonetheless, one way to use the distinction between just and justified war is to restrict the language of "justice" to war's cause or aim and then to determine whether the war is "justified" by reference to the other criteria, including last resort, reasonable chance of success, and proportionality. While a war may be "unjust," according to this approach, when its cause does not satisfy standards of justice, it is "unjustified" when it does not meet the other criteria. It is important to emphasize, as Joel Feinberg has pointed out, that one and the same act need not be both just and justified.[27] It may be just and unjustified, for example, if it renders various

26 Ramsey, *War and the Christian Conscience*, 15, 28, 31–32.
27 Walters, "Five Classic Just-War Theories," 316–20; William V. O'Brien, "Morality and War: The Contribution of Paul Ramsey," in James Johnson and David Smith (eds.), *Love and Society: Essays in the Ethics of Paul Ramsey* (Missoula, Mont.: Scholars Press, 1974), 181; Joel Feinberg, "On Being 'Mor-

parties their due but violates some other moral principles or results in terrible consequences, or it may be unjust and justified when, for example, an unfair act is required to prevent a disaster. Only when a war is both just and justified does a state have a *jus ad bellum*.

Does the *jus ad bellum* establish only a right or also a duty to go to war, at least under certain circumstances? Because the language of duty can lead to or support crusades and holy wars, it is somewhat suspect. There is no prima facie duty to go to war (*i.e.*, to injure and kill), but because some other prima facie duties, such as the duty to protect the innocent, may override the prima facie duty not to injure or kill, there may be an actual duty to fight, especially in a situation where the language of necessity seems appropriate. To say that war stands in need of justification because it violates certain prima facie duties is not to rule out the language of actual duty or obligation in a particular set of circumstances. To think of some wars as duties does not entail modifying or relaxing the *jus in bello*. Even a policeman who has a duty to try to stop an escaped criminal who has taken hostages still should respect certain moral and legal limits.

Another important distinction is between rights and right conduct or between rights and their exercise.[28] It is useful for construing the relation between *jus ad bellum* and *jus in bello*. For example, perhaps one side could meet most of the conditions of *jus ad bellum* but would have little chance of success without fighting the war unjustly and unfairly. We might say, "You have a right to go to war, but you ought not to exercise that right." Such an approach, however, favors the established military powers. Should a theory of just war make it impossible for one country or revolutionary movement to wage a "successful" war? Ideological bias and the tension between success and moral requirements must be confronted clearly and honestly.

In *Just and Unjust Wars*, Michael Walzer helpfully explores this tension between *jus ad bellum* and *jus in bello*, particularly

ally Speaking a Murderer,' " in Judith J. Thomson and Gerald Dworkin (eds.), *Ethics* (New York: Harper and Row, 1968), 295–97.
28   See A. I. Melden, *Rights and Right Conduct* (Oxford: Blackwell, 1959).

the tension between success or necessity and the protection of noncombatants. He wages a war, largely justified and justly conducted, against utilitarianism, but in the end he surrenders to one form of utilitarianism. In formulating and interpreting moral rules, he insists that utilitarian considerations such as proportionality are insignificant and that utilitarianism cannot generate other moral rules. It is not clear that rule-utilitarianism is as sterile as Walzer suggests, but his main point is well taken: even rules justified by their utility must be plausible on independent moral grounds. These grounds, according to Walzer, are moral rights, which constrain attempts to maximize the good. But utilitarianism may enter if we already know what the rules are and want to know when they may be broken. Part IV of *Just and Unjust Wars* is devoted to dilemmas that emerge when there is a conflict between *jus ad bellum* and *jus in bello* or when it does not appear to be possible to win the war without violating the limits on means set by moral rights.

Walzer considers four ways to deal with these conflicts.[29] First, he rejects the utilitarian attempt to set aside the rules of war because it reduces these rules to mere maxims or rules of thumb and misses their binding power. Second, another major position, which is widespread and can perhaps be found in John Rawls's *A Theory of Justice*, advocates a "sliding scale": "the more justice, the more right." The side with more justice can violate more of the rules because its violations will ultimately serve justice. The rules of war can be gradually eroded. Against such an approach it is important to argue that the rules of war have an independent moral foundation; the *jus in bello* cannot be reduced to the *jus ad bellum*. From the standpoint of the *jus in bello* the justice of the cause is irrelevant. A third position is absolutism, which insists on adherence to moral rules and principles regardless of the circumstances and consequences; its motto is "do justice even if the heavens fall." This hard-line approach, according to Walzer, is not morally plausible in the face of terrible aggression.

Finally, Walzer discusses and defends an "utilitarianism of

29 Walzer, *Just and Unjust Wars*, Chap. 14.

extremity." Its motto is "do justice unless the heavens are (really) about to fall." Its key words are *emergency* and *necessity*. It is possible to argue that certain violations of the rules of war are justified in extreme situations where the only requirements are usefulness and proportionality between probable good and evil consequences. Walzer does not lightly appeal to necessity or emergency, for he insists that the nature and the imminence of the danger are of primary importance. His utilitarianism of extremity is not reducible to ordinary utilitarian calculation, such as the number of lives that will probably be saved or lost by a particular strategy. It requires extraordinary circumstances. For example, British terror bombing of German cities was possibly justified early in the war when the outcome was in doubt because there was a danger "of an unusual and horrifying kind." Nazism was "an ultimate threat to everything decent in our lives" and the consequences of its final victory "were literally beyond calculation, immeasurably awful."[30]

What is gained by Walzer's approach to breaking moral rules of war? Ordinary utilitarianism denies the strength of rules of war; the sliding scale allows gradual erosion; and absolutism is unrealistic; but extraordinary utilitarianism, "utilitarianism of extremity," allows a sudden break after long and deep resistance to it. From Walzer's moral perspective, it is sometimes necessary to violate moral rules of war when the conditions are extreme and there are no alternatives. But the rights that are violated are not set aside or diminished; they are acknowledged to continue to have force and to endure even when they are violated. As a consequence, the agents who violate these rights for collective security, even when they have no other choice, are guilty because, after all, their hands are dirty. Any "moral theory that made their life easier, or that concealed their dilemma from the rest of us, might achieve greater coherence, but it would miss or it would repress the reality of war." In supreme emergencies, Walzer contends, we are compelled to say both

30   *Ibid.*, Chap. 16. See also Michael Walzer, "World War II: Why Was This War Different?" *Philosophy and Public Affairs*, I (Fall, 1971), 3–21.

"right" and "wrong" about the same act and perhaps to refuse to honor those who have dirty hands even for sufficient reasons (e.g., the British refusal to honor Arthur Harris who directed the strategic bombing of Germany). Even necessary breaches of the rules of war are "a kind of blasphemy against our deepest moral commitments."[31]

This moral perspective on dilemmas is one of Walzer's most distinctive contributions, but it raises many questions. First, the appeal to necessity may lack adequate controls, for "utility" can easily become "necessity" in the face of real and imaginary dangers in war. Second, "necessity" can easily be a matter of "bad faith," if agents claim that they have no choice when in fact they do. Their choices may hinge on values that are subject to criticism, correction, and choice. Does necessity apply to values (e.g., survival is a necessary value of society) as well as to means (e.g., violations of the rules of war are sometimes necessary for survival)? Necessitarian language often obscures specific value choices. A society can, and perhaps in some cases should, surrender its independence and its territory rather than violate some rules of war. When the plea to necessity is acceptable, does it justify the act or excuse the agent? If it does neither, as Walzer seems to suggest when he insists on the agent's guilt, its function is unclear. As these comments suggest, a more systematic treatment of necessity, guilt, and value choices would have been useful.

Third, Walzer may not recognize his affinities with some of the "realists" whom he sharply criticizes while overlooking some subtle but important differences in the realist camp.[32] For instance, Reinhold Niebuhr's perspective on moral tragedy and necessity is, in general terms, strikingly similar to Walzer's. For Niebuhr, the moral agent who acts responsibly must be ready to incur guilt by choosing the lesser of two evils. His religious doctrine of justification by faith could ease the fear to act that

31   Walzer, *Just and Unjust Wars*, 323–27. See also Michael Walzer, "Political Action: The Problem of Dirty Hands," *Philosophy and Public Affairs*, II (Winter, 1973), 160–80.
32   Walzer, *Just and Unjust Wars*, 110, 342 n, 117, *et passim*.

might result from such a heavy sense of moral ambiguity, tragedy, and guilt.

Fourth, many theorists of just war, including most Roman Catholics and some Protestants such as Paul Ramsey, have held that once we have formulated certain rules, it is never right to violate them, for it is never right to do (moral) evil that good might result. But many of these theorists allow more room than Walzer does for military necessity and utility in the formulation and interpretation of the rules. And they might seek to justify a particular policy that apparently contravenes a moral rule by probing the meaning of the rule or by stressing that the apparent violation is only an indirect effect. Walzer, however, takes relatively definite moral-legal categories such as "murder" and holds that acts that fall under these categories can be justified in situations of necessity although the agents who perform them are nevertheless guilty.

The difference in perspective between Ramsey and Walzer can be seen in their discussions of nuclear weapons and deterrence. They agree that nuclear weapons *per se* cannot be condemned as immoral; their morality or immorality depends on their use, that is, on their targets. Both contend that using nuclear weapons against population centers is immoral; Walzer, of course, would have to recognize the possibility of a situation of necessity, which did not exist when the United States used the atomic bomb against Hiroshima. Ramsey does not appear to allow necessity such leeway.

But what about the system of nuclear deterrence? In several earlier writings, Ramsey attempted to stretch the meaning of the rule of double effect to cover a policy of nuclear deterrence that targeted enemy population centers. He insisted that "the question is whether 'possession' of massive nuclear weapons is reducible to the crime of planning to use them over civilian targets. The question is whether 'having' or 'possession' implies a criminal intention to use them murderously, or a conditional willingness to do so." Such weapons have dual uses; they may be used against strategic forces or against population centers. And, Ramsey contended, the deterrent effect flows from a "studied ambiguity" rather than from an intention to use the weapons immorally, such as, for example, directly against population centers. The intention to deceive should be distinguished from the intention or even the conditional willingness to commit murder.[33]

Walzer contends that the system of nuclear deterrence is immoral because it rests ultimately on an immoral threat, the threat that we will act immorally by killing people who are not direct threats to us. This is the threat of murder. Walzer thinks that Ramsey wants to "clear our intentions without prohibiting those policies that he believes necessary." Walzer wants us to face the truth about our immoral threats. Attempts to show that nuclear deterrence can be accommodated within the *jus in bello* (for example, by expanding the categories of double effect or collateral damage) are risky, he argues, for they ultimately "corrupt the argument for justice as a whole and . . . render it suspect even in those areas of military life to which it properly pertains." His main concern is to show us how to think morally about nuclear deterrence. But, although we should seek alternatives, nuclear deterrence may actually be justified at this time. "Deterrence itself, for all its criminality, falls or may fall for the moment under the standard of necessity."[34] Thus, even when Walzer and Ramsey agree about policies, they sharply disagree about the relation of moral rules to necessity.

The Function of Just-War Criteria

It is important to examine the possible function of just-war criteria in a society that has several competing theories of justice

33 Ramsey, *The Just War*, 252–58. He later retracted this position. "I now think that an input of deliberate ambiguity about the counter-people use of nuclear weapons is not possible unless it is (immorally) meant, and not a very good idea in the first place." Ramsey, "A Political Ethics Context for Strategic Thinking," in Morton A. Kaplan (ed.), *Strategic Thinking and Its Moral Implications* (Chicago: University of Chicago Center for Policy Study, 1973), 142.
34 Walzer, *Just and Unjust Wars*, Chap. 17.

and to determine the pacifist's stake, if any, in such a function. Many recent attempts to restate just-war criteria apparently treat them as questions that policy-makers and others ought to consider. These criteria constitute a formal framework and structure for moral debates about the use of force. They are important and even essential because of the prima facie duty not to injure or kill others, and they identify the kinds of questions that should be answered affirmatively before war and other acts that override prima facie duties can be justified. Perhaps because they are empty, they can serve to organize and orchestrate disputes in the public arena; even pacifists could and did appeal to these criteria to condemn the war in Vietnam. In democratic theory and practice, formal procedures can accommodate conflicts about moral convictions and interests; they do not dictate the material outcome. Similarly, just-war criteria constitute a formal framework within which different substantive interpretations of justice and morality as applied to war can be debated. For example, the formal interpretation holds that it is morally mandatory to determine that one has a "just" cause, but exactly what constitutes a "just" cause will depend on substantive convictions about justice and morality. This formal function of the criteria is hardly what traditional just-war theorists expected, for they developed their criteria within substantive theories of justice and the common good.

Some critics of a formalist interpretation of just-war criteria contend that such an interpretation cannot be accepted or supported because it does not serve, in fact, to restrain and limit war. Nevertheless, one of its manifest functions can be viewed as restraining and limiting war because it holds that only some wars, and only some acts within war, justifiably override the prima facie duty not to injure or kill others. The formalist interpretation fulfills this function, however, in the context of the legitimation of war as an exceptional practice. Its function is both positive (legitimation) and negative (limitation). It justifies but also restrains.[35]

35   For a discussion of legitimating and restraining functions of just-war theories, see Walters, "Five Classic Just-War Theories," 414–18, *et passim*.

Some critics are not satisfied with this explanation of the dual function of just-war theories.[36] They insist that this formalist interpretation fails to give clear and precise determinations regarding the justification of actual wars. In particular, they contend, it fails to give clear and precise *negative* answers. It fails to specify when particular wars or acts within wars are unjust or unjustified. In short, these critics wonder whether a formalist interpretation of just-war criteria can overcome the emptiness and vacuity that are deficiencies of most formalist theories in ethics. Agreement is possible precisely because they do not involve material content.

What these critics expect of just-war criteria is available only within *substantive* theories. There is no single substantive theory of just war. But these critics ask that the just-war criteria serve the same function now as they served in a different era when (presumably) there were strong shared convictions about justice and accepted arbiters of justice of and in war. This is impossible in a pluralistic society. But even in a pluralistic society, just-war criteria as defined in this chapter have the important function of serving as a framework for debates about which wars, if any, are justified.

Just-war criteria within a substantive theory should indicate when war is unjust and when it is conducted unjustly. They should define not only just cause, but also such terms as *innocence* and *discrimination*. I have not tried to develop a substantive theory of just war in this chapter, but I have tried to show that just-war criteria are important and even indispensable moral standards apart from any particular theory of justice. They are explicable, I have argued, by reference to the no-

---

36 Similar criticisms were offered by John Howard Yoder in an exchange in "Can Contemporary Armed Conflicts Be Just?" (Evening Dialogue at the Woodrow Wilson Center of the Smithsonian Institution, Washington, D.C., October 5, 1978). Yoder, James T. Johnson, and I presented papers, to which Bryan Hehir and Seymour Siegel responded. Since that time and subsequently John Howard Yoder's similar criticisms emerged in the context of an oral debate, I do not wish to suggest that he holds them in the form they take in this essay.

tion of prima facie duties and, specifically, to the prima facie duty not to injure or kill.

If we accept this prima facie duty of nonmaleficence and if we accept the responsibility to think morally about the use of force in a sinful world, we should be committed to a framework and procedure of reasoning that is at least analogous to just-war criteria. Furthermore, it is important to secure support for this formal framework in order to avoid the amoral approaches to power that only appreciate "national interest" (as defined in nonmoral terms) or Machiavellian maneuvers. If the pacifist admits that there will always be "wars and rumors of wars"—an admission that will depend on his theology and anthropology— then he too has an important stake in the moral assessment of wars and acts within wars. He too should provisionally accept something analogous to just-war criteria.

There may be some misunderstanding of the nature and function of just-war criteria. They are not designed to answer the question of the justification of war in general but the question of the justification of particular wars. That is, they do not determine *whether* war as an institution or practice can ever, or in principle, be justified; they rather indicate *when* particular wars can be justified. They presuppose an affirmative answer to the question whether war can ever be justified and then pinpoint the conditions required for the justification of any particular war. Just-war criteria, thus, are not involved in the debate between the pacifist and the just-war theorist over *whether* war can ever be justified. This debate hinges on such general theological, anthropological, and moral convictions as sin, the place and function of the state, and political responsibility. It focuses on whether any moral principles and values, such as justice, can ever outweigh or override the prima facie duty of nonmaleficence.

But if just-war criteria presuppose an affirmative answer to the question whether war can ever be justified, how can the pacifist appeal to these criteria in discourse about a particular war? Sometimes in the moral assessment of particular wars, pacifists are ignored or excluded on the grounds that "we already know their conclusions."[37] Because the pacifist does not accept the premise of just-war theories that war can, in principle, be justified as an exceptional practice, so the argument goes, he cannot participate openly and impartially in the debate. But this argument is not cogent. The pacifist can apply the criteria of just war, as accepted by other groups, to a particular war. He can be sensitive to the implications of the criteria and whether they are satisfied by the factual circumstances, for example. He need not accept the premise of just-war theorists; his premise may be only that "of all possible wars, one that meets these criteria is less evil than one that does not."

In conclusion, pacifists and just-war theorists are actually closer to and more dependent on each other than they often suppose. Just-war theorists sometimes overlook the fact that they and the pacifists reason from a common starting point. Both begin with the contention that nonviolence has moral priority over violence, that violent acts always stand in need of justification because they violate the prima facie duty not to injure or kill others, whereas only some nonviolent acts need justification (e.g., when they violate laws). While pacifists can remind just-war theorists of this presumption against violence, pacifists also need just-war theorists. In a world in which war appears to be a permanent institution, debates about particular wars require a framework and a structure that can be provided by the criteria of the just-war tradition properly reconstructed. In addition, there are degrees of justice and humanity within violence and warfare, and the just-war theorist can emphasize these moral constraints, which the pacifist view of war as hell or murder (shared by some realists) tends to obscure. Even the pacifist has a stake in the integrity of just-war criteria as the coin of the political realm. The pacifist finally cannot be satisfied with that coin, just as the just-war theorist finally cannot be satisfied with the weight pacifism gives to the duty not to injure or kill others. The pacifist may charge that concentration on just-war criteria assumes the inevitability of war and makes

37   See Ramsey, *The Just War*, Chap. 12: "Can a Pacifist Tell a Just War?"

war more likely by making it appear acceptable as long as it respects some limits and boundaries. But the just-war theorist may respond that concentration on the avoidance of war may weaken the sense of limits that should prevail even in war. Despite their differences, what the pacifist and the just warrior share—the moral presumption against war—can be neglected only at great peril to all of us.

Chapter Four

Francis Lieber's Interpretation of the Laws of War

One of the most important monuments of the American Civil War is General Orders No. 100, which was approved by President Lincoln and issued by the Adjutant General's Office April 24, 1863. Published under the title, *Instructions for the Government of Armies of the United States in the Field*, this code was prepared by Francis Lieber and revised by a board of officers. Although there is some debate about its immediate impact on the Civil War, its long-term significance cannot be denied. Lieber was aware of its imperfections, but he rightly predicted that "Old Hundred," as he fondly called it, would "do honor to our country" and would "be adopted as a basis for similar works by the English, French, and Germans. It is a contribution by the U.S. to the stock of common civilization." Others also shared his judgment. General Ethan A. Hitchcock suggested that "the *Code* must gradually become the law of the civilized world in war." August W. Heffter, a German jurist, insisted that the "precious" *Instructions* "is calculated to form the foundation of a general code of international law of war, or . . . , rather, is already such a basis." Heffter's response was particularly gratifying to Lieber, for, he admitted, he had hoped that his code would become just such a foundation. He wrote: "It was one of my objects in drawing up this code; but, of course [I] did not speak to any one about it. It gave me joy therefore to see that this great jurist found it to be such."[1]

1 General Orders No. 100 was published under the title *Instructions for the Government of Armies of the United States in the Field* (New York: D. Van Nostrand, 1863). It is reprinted in Leon Friedman (ed.), *The Law of War: A Documentary History* (2 vols.; New York: Random House, 1972), I, 158–86,

These prophecies were soon fulfilled, for in 1866 Johann K. Bluntschli of the University of Heidelberg published *Das moderne Kriegsrecht der civilisirten Staaten als Rechtsbuch dargestellt*, which was inspired by and modeled after Lieber's code. Indeed, Bluntschli acknowledged: "The articles of war, drawn up by Professor Lieber in New York and issued in 1863 by President Lincoln for the army of the United States, have served as a model for this work. To my knowledge, a similar code of war does not yet exist in European literature. These articles of war have been greatly and often literally used." Other countries developed similar codes, and the work of the conferences of Brussels in 1874 and The Hague in 1899 and 1907 clearly reflects the *Instructions'* influence, which was also important although less clear and direct in the Geneva Conventions of 1949.[2]

---

and elsewhere. Francis Lieber to Henry W. Halleck, May 20, 1863, Ethan A. Hitchcock to Lieber, October 22, 1863, August W. Heffter to Lieber, August 26, 1863 (and Lieber's translation from the German), Lieber to Samuel A. Allibone, November 9, 1863, all in Lieber Papers, Henry E. Huntington Library, San Marino, Cal. Unless otherwise indicated, all references to Lieber's correspondence, manuscripts, notes, and other papers are to materials in the Lieber Papers, Huntington Library. Some of Lieber's letters also appear in Thomas Sergeant Perry (ed.), *The Life and Letters of Francis Lieber* (Boston: James R. Osgood, 1882). Unfortunately, this collection, hereinafter cited as Perry (ed.), *Lieber*, is extremely unreliable because of editorial inaccuracies, including numerous changes in the letters, the omission of passages without indication of the omissions, and conflation of letters.

2 Johann K. Bluntschli, *Das moderne Kriegsrecht der civilisirten Staaten als Rechtsbuch dargestellt* (Nördlingen: C. H. Beck, 1866), Foreword. For Lieber's inspiration and encouragement, see Bluntschli, "Lieber's Service to Political Science and International Law," in Daniel Gilman (ed.), *The Miscellaneous Writings of Francis Lieber* (2 vols.; Philadelphia: J. B. Lippincott, 1881), II, 13, hereinafter cited as *Miscellaneous Writings*. Also see Lieber's discussion of Bluntschli's volume in the New York *Tribune*, May 25, 1866 (clipping in the Lieber Papers). See Elihu Root, "Francis Lieber," *American Journal of International Law*, VII (July, 1913), 456–58, and George B. Davis, "Memorandum Showing the Relation Between General Orders No. 100 and The Hague Convention with Respect to the Laws and Customs of War on Land," *ibid.*, 466–69; Richard Sallet, "On Francis Lieber and His Contribution to the Law of Nations of Today," in Gottlinger Arbeitskreis, *Recht im Dienste der Menschenwürde: Festschrift für Herbert Kraus* (Würzburg, 1964), 279–306.

Although some recent scholars have almost fully and completely traced the growth of the *Instructions*, no one, to my knowledge, has yet subjected it to careful scrutiny in the context of Lieber's political ethics and jurisprudence, as expressed not only in his books and articles but also in his voluminous correspondence, notes, and lectures. The fine studies by Frank Freidel deal with the growth of the code and some of its ideas, especially on military government, but they do not attempt a systematic treatment of its rules in the context of Lieber's thought. Richard Baxter studied the code particularly in relation to Lieber's lectures on the "Law and Usages of War" and his manuscript notebook and concluded that Lieber's was "a mature and logically consistent system, developed and systematized over many years of thinking and teaching." But Baxter's excellent discussion neglects some of the inconsistencies and tensions in Lieber's thought, which are revealed by a more comprehensive examination of his unpublished materials. No one has as yet fully analyzed the continuities and changes in his interpretation of the laws of war over time.[3]

While the code described the laws and practices of nations in war—indeed, "the common law of war"—it could not be merely descriptive given Lieber's understanding of the union of law and morality and of the methods of the historical and phil-

3 Frank Freidel, *Francis Lieber: Nineteenth-Century Liberal* (Baton Rouge: Louisiana State University Press, 1947), and "General Orders 100 and Military Government," *Mississippi Valley Historical Review*, XXXII (March, 1946), 541–56; Richard R. Baxter, "The First Modern Codification of the Law of War: Francis Lieber and General Orders No. 100," *International Review of the Red Cross* (April, 1963), 170–89, and (May, 1963), 234–50; Francis Lieber, "Law and Usages of War" (8 lectures given at Columbia Law School, October 21, 1861–February 6, 1862, in Lieber notebooks, Eisenhower Library, Johns Hopkins University). Also valuable are Charles B. Robson, "Material in the Papers of Francis Lieber in the Huntington Library Relating to General Orders No. 100: *Instructions for the Government of Armies of the United States in the Field*" (typescript in Lieber Papers), and James G. Garner, "General Order 100 Revisited," *Military Law Review*, XXVII (January, 1965), 1–48. See also Brainerd Dyer, "Francis Lieber and the American Civil War," *Huntington Library Quarterly*, II (July, 1939), 449–65, esp. 452–57, and William S. Shepard, "One Hundredth Anniversary of the Lieber Code," *Military Law Review*, XXI (July, 1963), 157–62.

osophical schools of jurisprudence. Neither positivism nor mere philosophical speculation would suffice. As Bluntschli rightly observed about the *Instructions*, "Throughout this work . . . we see the stamp of Lieber's peculiar genius. His legal injunctions rest upon the foundation of moral precepts. The former are not always sharply distinguished from moral injunctions."[4] Thus this first modern codification of the laws of war to be adopted by a state has its foundation in its author's distinctive perspective on international law, war, and political ethics. Because the code omits the reasons for many rules and provisions, its presuppositions must be sought in Lieber's general thought.

Equally interesting and significant is Lieber's understanding of the application of these principles and rules to actual cases on which his opinion was requested (and often expressed when not requested!) by General Henry W. Halleck, Attorney General Edward Bates, Senator Charles Sumner, and many others. Since General Orders No. 100 simply embodies "the principles of the laws of war, or the general rules," as General Halleck suggested, it is important to see how Lieber thought they should be applied in actual and hypothetical cases.[5] Not only the presuppositions but also the implications of the *Instructions* merit attention mainly, though not exclusively, through an analysis of Lieber's unpublished papers.

At a time when the laws of war are undergoing reexamination not only for possible revisions but also in terms of their general consistency, coherence, and utility, such a study of General Orders No. 100, a source of much of our thinking in this area, may illuminate some contemporary issues. Because current debates cover somewhat different ground as a result of technological and other developments since the Civil War, this study will seek only indirect illumination of contemporary issues through an analysis of the rules and principles in their philosophical setting.

4 Bluntschli, "Lieber's Service," II, 12. Contrast Root, "Francis Lieber," 456.
5 Halleck to S. A. Hurlbut, June 22, 1863, *cf.* Halleck to Hitchcock, August 12, 1863, both in Eldridge Papers, Huntington Library.

After briefly sketching the evolution and structure of the *Instructions*, I shall place Lieber's approach to the laws of war in the context of his experiences of war; his arguments against pacifism, which was defended by several of his friends and associates; and his defense and explication of a theory of just war that does not allow the justice of a belligerent's aims to cancel its obligations to the enemy. Then I shall examine the reasons and principles at work in and the implications of particular rules in the *Instructions*, especially those having to do with classes of the enemy, means and weapons, faith and confidence, necessity and retaliation.

The Evolution and Structure of General Orders No. 100

Through Lieber's manuscripts and correspondence, as well as official documents, it is possible to trace the evolution of General Orders No. 100. Although Lieber had previously expressed an interest in codifying the laws of war, his opportunity finally came through his contact with General Henry Halleck. "Old Brains," as Halleck was called, was extremely interested in practical questions of the laws of war for his command in the western theater and, after July 11, 1862, as general-in-chief of the Union army. Already in 1861 he had published a book entitled *International Law*, approximately two-thirds of which was devoted to the laws of war. From the outset Lieber and Halleck's correspondence and personal contact often touched on the laws of war. Lieber's first letter mentioned his lectures on this subject in the Columbia Law School and his disappointment that Halleck's *International Law* had only just arrived since he was interested in considering "so important a work written by a jurist and a soldier." Halleck in turn requested copies of Lieber's lectures, which were not sent because they were not printed. When Lieber later mentioned that he was examining the subject of guerrilla warfare with reference to the laws and usages of war, Halleck asked to see the results, issued an official request that Lieber present his views to the public—as

Lieber had proposed—and ordered five thousand copies for army distribution.[6]

In November, 1862, Lieber suggested to Halleck that "the President ought to issue a set of rules and definitions providing for the most urgent cases, occurring under the Law and Usages of War, and on which our Articles of War are silent." The rationale for such a code was obvious to Lieber, and he emphasized the current confusion about such critical matters as parole, the treatment of fugitive slaves, the use or confiscation of the enemy's property, and the question of which people should be treated as prisoners of war. The confusion was exacerbated by certain features of the Civil War. It was being fought over a large area by large numbers of men unfamiliar with the laws of war and deprived of the tight military organization that prevailed in Europe.[7] While Lieber's concern to codify the "common law of war" had affinities with the general movement to codify the common law, it was motivated and shaped by the peculiar problems of international law, war in general, and the Civil War in particular. Not only would such a code indicate what the Union army could do, but it would also indicate to the enemy what it could expect. For example, the South would be notified to expect retaliation for mistreating or killing Negro prisoners of war.

6   Henry W. Halleck, *International Law* (San Francisco: D. Van Nostrand, 1861); Lieber to Halleck, January 30, February 7, July 23, August 1, 9, 1862, Halleck to Lieber, February 3, 11, July 30, August 6, 19, 20, 1862; Francis Lieber, *Guerrilla Parties Considered with Reference to the Laws and Usages of War* (New York: D. Van Nostrand, 1862). Excerpts and summaries of Lieber's lectures ("Law and Usages of War") did appear in the New York *Times*, January 13, February 4, 10, March 4, 17, 1862, but there is no evidence that Lieber sent clippings to Halleck. For Lieber's interest in writing a code, see Lieber to Allibone, August 18, 1861, and Lieber to Charles Sumner, August 19, 1861. Lieber used Halleck's *International Law* (which frequently refers to Lieber's *Manual of Political Ethics* [Boston: Charles C. Little and James Brown, 1839]) and spoke favorably of it to Halleck, but he considered it to be distinguished mainly "by careful and ample collection of authorities and citation and complete use of his predecessors in the literatures of the various nations." Lieber to Allibone, December 12, 1862, and see December 14, 1863.
7   Lieber to Halleck, November 13, 1862, and see also November 20, 25, 1862.

Although Halleck protested that he was too busy to pursue the matter immediately, he was successful within a few weeks. The Adjutant General's Office called Lieber to Washington in December and appointed him with four military men to a board under the chairmanship of General Ethan A. Hitchcock. The board was instructed "to propose amendments or changes in the Rules and Articles of War and a code of Regulations for the government of Armies in the field as authorized by the laws and usages of war."[8]

After discussions in Washington over several days in December, Lieber began to prepare a code, relying on his *Political Ethics*; his lectures, particularly on the laws and usages of war, at the Columbia Law School; other writers on international law; notes; and newspaper clippings. On February 20, 1863, he sent members of the board and several other persons printed copies of *A Code for the Government of Armies in the Field as Authorized by the Laws and Usages of War on Land*.[9] In an accompanying letter, Lieber claimed, with some exaggeration, that "nothing of the kind exists in any language. I had no guide, no groundwork, no textbook. I can assure you . . . that no counsellor of Justinian, sat down to his task of the Digest with a deeper feeling of the gravity of his labour, than filled my breast in the laying down for the first time such a code, where nearly everything was floating. Usage, history, reason, and conscientiousness, a sincere love of truth, justice, and of civilization, have been my guides; but of course the whole must be very imperfect." Lieber earnestly solicited suggestions from the board and others. He continued to rework the code, especially by adding sections, and within two weeks he had a "new manuscript" that "added much," some of it in response to suggestions that he had received from Halleck and others.[10] Following Halleck's insistence that "the civil war articles should by all means be

8   Adjutant General's Office, Special Order No. 399, December 17, 1862.
9   Hereinafter cited as *A Code*. For a list of the classic and contemporary interpretations of the laws of war with which Lieber was familiar, see Freidel, *Francis Lieber*, 333 n.
10   Lieber to Halleck, February 20, 1863 (accompanying copies of the code) (*cf.* Lieber to Sumner, February 21, 1863), Lieber to Halleck, March 2, 1863,

inserted," Lieber wrote a section entitled "Insurrection-Rebel-lion-Civil War-Foreign Invasion of the United States," which he described as "ticklish work" (and which the board later reduced drastically). Some of this section was indebted to Halleck, especially to his letter to General William Rosecrans. Indeed, Lieber felt that Halleck's name should have been clearly linked with the code because of his influence on it.[11]

The board examined the revised code in April, and made some changes (mainly changes in wording), additions, and deletions, after which the secretary of war approved it. Lieber thought that the generals of the board had added "some valuable parts," but he very much regretted some of the omissions, many of which had to do with the reasons—both philosophical and historical—for particular rules. For example, Lieber commented to Halleck on the drastic cuts in the section on insurrection: "I was aware when I wrote Rebellion & c., that I wrote something betwixt a code and a book—it was all new ground; and I thought it might be necessary to lay and show the foundation for the new structure—*giving the reasons*. But if you and competent authorities say it is not necessary, I have no objections."[12] Despite Lieber's arguments for retaining the word *code* in the title, or for having some "citable name," General Orders No. 100 was issued as *Instructions for the Government of Armies of the United States in the Field.*

Lieber's interest in the laws of war did not diminish with the publication of "Old Hundred." Indeed, he ventured several proposals, some stemming from his desire to have the code approved by Congress, others resulting from his concern for

---

Hitchcock to Lieber, March 6, 1863, Halleck to Lieber, February 23, 28, March 4, 13, 18, April 8, 1863, Alexander D. Bache to Lieber, February 25, 1863, Hamilton Fish to Lieber, March 10, 17, 1863, Lieber to Fish, March 12, 19, 1863, John P. Usher to Lieber, February 26, 1863, C. E. Detmold to Lieber, February 25, 1863. A photostatic copy of *A Code* with Halleck's notations and question marks is in the Lieber Papers, Huntington Library, and the original is in the Eisenhower Library, Johns Hopkins University.

11   Halleck to Lieber, February 28, April 8, 1863, Lieber to Halleck, March 4, 23, April 10, May 20, 1863.

12   Lieber to Halleck, May 20, April 10, 1863.

promulgating the reasons for particular rules and delineating their significance for particular cases. His interest in the justification of particular rules flowed in part from his view, shared with Bluntschli among others, that international law ultimately derives its force from public opinion. He was never enthusiastic about proposals for a permanent international congress to settle questions of justice in conflicts between nations; nor did he consider an "International Judicial Institution for the Prevention and Repression of Infractions of the Convention of Geneva" to be desirable or feasible because of the necessary autonomy of nations and the lack of means of enforcement. "Hugo Grotius," he wrote, "was quoted as authority at the Congress of the European nations at Vienna; but he was thus quoted above monarchs, ministers, and nations, *because* he was an unofficial man, absent from the strife, and who had written his work on Peace and War at the dictation of reason and justice, without any special connexion with the cases in question, appealing to reason, justice, and equity alone." More effective and beneficial for intercourse between nations in war and peace would be a "meeting of the most prominent jurists of the law of nations" in their private capacities, one from each country, to settle unresolved questions such as neutrality. Lieber explained, "I mean *settle* as Grotius *settled* . . . by the strength of the great argument of justice. A code or proclamation, as it were, of such a body would soon acquire far greater authority than the book of the greatest single jurist."[13] He had no illusions about the adequacy of reason to settle conflicts and avoid war, but he considered public opinion, informed about the moral reasons for certain rules and policies, to be the foundation and force of international law.

His interest in the justification of particular rules also resulted in part from his conviction that legal positivism in inter-

13 Lieber to G. H. Dufour, April 10, 1872, Lieber to Judge Thayer, May 7, 1869. See also Lieber to Bluntschli, April 16, 1866, Lieber to Sumner, December 27, 1861. For his support of international conferences, including the Geneva Conference of 1864, see Lieber to Halleck, June 18, 25, 1864, and Halleck to Lieber, June 30, July 7, 1864. Lieber was also influential in the founding of the Institut de Droit International. See Root, "Francis Lieber," 464.

national law is inadequate. For instance, he did not expect very much from a new book which was "represented as exclusively 'positive' " since it would merely try to determine "what the positive, settled and acknowledged law is, not ascertaining the principles and applying them to new cases and widening regions." In his effort to codify the "common law of war," Lieber did not merely attend to the practices of nations, although these were important. His procedure is evident in his letter to General Montgomery C. Meigs regarding the use of prisoners of war for work: "If then it is the universal usage of war to make prisoners work and thus to re-imburse in part the expenditure they cause, the only remaining question for me in drawing up the little Code was: Is there any reason of honor or humanity, why this usage should be stopped? There is none whatever." As he remarked elsewhere, the law of war "consists like all international law of precedents, that is things done, gravely and thoroughly discussed and recommending themselves, not indeed by the mere fact of having been done, but *by the reasons of justice found in the case*, by judges, by writers, by governments and by the common sense of assenting mankind."[14]

Because of his fundamental convictions, Lieber pursued every opportunity to explicate the code and perfect it. He wanted to publish General Orders No. 100 with notes, and apparently the secretary of war approved the plan and even ordered that the document be published. However, it does not seem to have appeared.[15] Lieber lobbied for the opportunity to give a course of ten to fifteen lectures on the laws of war at the United States Military Academy at West Point. He wrote Senator Charles Sumner: "I wish I could have accompanied this *projêt* [A Code] with the '*Motives*', but they would have required a volume. I would gladly give the latter in a course of

14   Lieber to Halleck, January 6, 1864, Lieber to Montgomery C. Meigs, January 24, 1864 (contemporary copy enclosed in Meigs to Lieber, February 1, 1864); "Law and Usages of War," December 3, 1861, my italics.
15   Lieber to Halleck, May 20, 30, June 18, 22, July 25, 1863, Halleck to Lieber, May 25, 28, June 19, 1863, all in Lieber Papers; Lieber to Daniel Gilman, June and August 2, 1863, both in Eisenhower Library.

lectures at Westpoint."[16] Lieber also had a strong desire to perfect the *Instructions* before the Civil War ended. As he expressed to General Halleck: "If ever it becomes necessary to re-
print No. 100, would it not be advisable that the Secretary of
War first have it revised? I should like much to make a few
changes and a few additions. A war like ours is a furnace, not
only for the nation at large, but also for the minds of single
thinkers and those that feel and love right. Considering 'One
Hundred' one of the products of this war, I naturally desire to
see it perfected before this war ends." Holding that law and literature are the major monuments of a country, he thought that
a new redaction of the code, passed by Congress with "very few
additions indeed and still fewer corrections might make it a
nice little thing and quite a little monument erected in honour
of this war."[17]

Experiences of War

Because a legal code cannot elaborate all the reasons that the
philosopher desires, it is necessary to look elsewhere for the
author's reasons. A good starting point is the author's own experiences of war. One common criticism of the *Instructions* is
that its author was not a military man and, hence, was not
aware of many important features of war and battle.[18] Although
Lieber never had the responsibility of making decisions as a
commander in battle, his own numerous and profound experi-

16   Lieber to Sumner, February 21, 1863; *cf.* Lieber to Halleck, March 10, 16,
April 26, December 21, 1864. His "Proposal to Offer a Course of Lectures to
West Point Students on the Subject of the Law and Usages of War on Land,"
May, 1862, has been preserved in the Lieber Papers. He gave a lecture on
"Military Ethics" at West Point June 6, 1838, and his notes for it have been
preserved.
17   Lieber to Halleck, December 21, 1864, Lieber to Allibone, October 4,
1865, Lieber to Halleck, February 11, 1865.
18   See Percy Bordwell, *The Law of War Between Belligerents: A History and
Commentary* (Chicago: Callaghan, 1908), 74. Theodore Woolsey attributed
the harshness of some of Lieber's comments about war to the fact that lawyers, in contrast to military officers, "see war only in its abstract features."

ences of war certainly influenced his interpretation of the laws of war.

Lieber's life and thought—to use an image that Paul Tillich applied to himself—was "on the boundaries." Not only was he a citizen of two worlds because of his birth in Prussia in 1798 (he claimed 1800) and his emigration to the United States in 1827, but Lieber also lived and taught in both the South and the North, at South Carolina College from 1835 to 1856 and at Columbia College and then the Law School from 1857 until his death in 1872. Even his teaching and research defied the boundaries of particular disciplines. On the boundary of reflection and action, he regretted throughout the Civil War that he was denied the "happiness of acting," and yet he traversed the boundary between private and public citizen to make significant contributions to the Union through his work as a publicist and his advice to civil and military officials. He is recognized, according to Brainerd Dyer, "as one of the most active and helpful of private citizens during the Civil War." Finally, on the boundary between war and peace much of his life, he insisted that morality and law are present in the former as well as in the latter.[19]

Lieber's autobiographical account stresses the intense humiliation and shame that he felt when the French soldiers marched through conquered Berlin in October, 1806. He stood at the window crying so loudly and uncontrollably that his father had to remove him forcibly so that the passing soldiers would not hear him. He had prayed that one of his heroes, Ferdinand Baptista von Schill, would be successful in his courageous defense of a garrison in Colberg. When Schill returned to Berlin, young Lieber was almost trampled by the enthusiastic

See Lieber, *Manual of Political Ethics*, ed. Theodore Woolsey (2nd ed., 2 vols.; Philadelphia: J. B. Lippincott, 1881), II, 453.

19   See Hugo Preuss, *Franz Lieber: ein Bürger zweier Welten* (Berlin: 1866). On action, see Lieber to Halleck, February 8, November 20, 1862, April 15, 1865. Brainerd Dyer, "Francis Lieber and the American Civil War," *Huntington Library Quarterly*, II (July, 1939), 449. Freidel's biography, *Francis Lieber*, is indispensable and illuminating on these matters.

crowd when he and his father tried unsuccessfully to get a glimpse of their hero. Later the boy visited Schill and received his seal.[20]

Lieber developed a strong sense of nationalism and extreme hostility toward the French. In 1813 when his brothers answered the king's call to resist the French, he took an oath to try to assassinate Napoleon, for as he wrote many years later, "the idea of sacrificing two armies while the sacrifice of one life might stop all misery, seemed to me preposterous." Then in March, 1815, "'Boys, clean your rifles,' said my old and venerable father, entering my room, where I was just studying Loder's Anatomical Tables. 'He is loose again.' —'Napoleon?' —'He has returned from Elba.' My heart beat high; it was glorious news for a boy of sixteen, who had often heard with silent envy the account of the campaigns of 1813 and '14 from the lips of his two brothers." Lieber and one of his brothers joined the Colberg regiment on the assumption that it would soon be in the thick of the fighting. At Ligny, Lieber reported, "we saw innumerable troops ascending the plain with flying colors, and music playing. It was a sight a soldier loves to look at." His first shot in battle having killed a Frenchman, he was delighted to learn that it was "really a good sound battle" since he had feared that he would "not have the honor of assisting in a thorough battle." His company decimated by battle and its survivors weakened by hunger and fatigue, the Colberg regiment stood in reserve and watched the battle of Waterloo. Marching another night and day, his regiment engaged the enemy in battle at Namur, where Lieber was shot through the neck and then in the chest and left to die. Later he graphically described his feelings and emotions, his attempt to get a comrade to shoot him, the way some peasants searched for his watch and money as booty, and the kindness of comrades, even wounded ones.[21]

20 Lieber, "A Reminiscence," Southern Literary Messenger, II (June 28, 1836), 535–38.
21 Ibid.; Lieber to George S. Hillard, April 1, 9, 1858; Lieber, "Personal Reminiscences of the Battle of Waterloo," Miscellaneous Writings, I, 151–71. See also Lieber to James A. Garfield, December 10, 1870. Many years later

Such experiences, including the "indelible horror" of the agony at Ligny, did not dampen his enthusiastic romanticism and idealism. In 1821 he and other Philhellenes sailed for Greece to aid the Greeks in their resistance to the Turks, "led by the youthful ardor to assist the oppressed and struggling descendants of that people whom all civilized nations love and admire." His venture was abortive and frustrating because he was unable to get to the fighting, barely able to survive, and increasingly contemptuous of the Greeks.[22]

After he came to the United States, Lieber opposed the War with Mexico on moral grounds (which I shall discuss later), but he enthusiastically supported many of the policies of the Radical Republicans in the Civil War and lamented his inability to "act" as a political or military figure. But the fact that two of his sons were in the Union army and another in the Confederate army again put him on the boundaries and led him to exclaim, "Behold in me the symbol of civil war." After the death of his son Oscar, who had joined the Confederate army, Lieber wrote, "Civil war has thus knocked very loudly at our door." His son Hamilton was wounded at Fort Donelson, and the anxious father went west to look for him. "I knew war as [a] soldier, as a wounded man in the hospital, as an observing citizen, but I had yet to learn it in the phase of a father searching for his wounded son, walking through the hospitals, peering in the ambulances." Truly, Lieber participated in the Civil War, as he later wrote, "with my whole soul, my whole mind, and my whole family."[23]

Lieber sensitively interpreted the motives of his friend Karl Sand, who killed August von Kotzebue, a reactionary playwright, in 1819, but he emphatically denounced assasination as a means, even in war. Lieber to Hillard, April 19, 1858, and Lieber to James H. Hammond, April 18, 1860. On Lieber's nationalism, see Merle Curti, "Francis Lieber and Nationalism," *Huntington Library Quarterly*, IV (1941), 263–92.

22 Lieber, "Reminiscences of Barthold George Niebuhr," *Miscellaneous Writings*, II, 56–57. See also Perry (ed.), *Lieber*, 34–41.

23 Lieber to Hillard, May 11, 1861, Lieber to Halleck, August 9, 1862, *cf.* Lieber to Dr. S. Tyler, January 14, 1867 [reprinted in Perry (ed.), *Lieber*, 367–68], Lieber to Sumner, March 23, 1862, Lieber to Karl Josef Anton Mittermaier, March 1, 1866.

Such experiences gave Lieber a realistic appreciation of the suffering of war (the reason that war always stands in need of justification) and a humanitarian concern to limit and restrain the conduct of war. But they also led him to stress the positive moral elements and effects of war. In a spirit of moderation he wrote, "though an economist, who knows that war can never increase wealth; though a publicist who knows that peace is the normal state of man; though a Christian that knows the message of the energizing love of the gospel, I am no vilifier of war under all circumstances." Perhaps because of his polemical context, including a strong peace movement until it was muted by the Civil War, Lieber constantly reiterated the "great advantages" of just wars. Several pages of his *Political Ethics* extol the qualities and effects of (just) wars in order to educate those "who have an inadequate idea of what war actually is, what a general has to do, and into what parts war resolves itself." His rhapsodic descriptions include the intellectual strength and "moral vigor" of generals, the arousal of a "public spirit" because war requires unselfishness, the formation of lasting friendships, and the elevation of the "tone of morality." According to Lieber, "no one who is acquainted with all the details can deny that the whole moral tone of the German nation has been eminently raised by their late struggle for national independence against the French—a moral elevation which shows itself in all spheres and all branches; and it was universally observed at the time, that the soldiers had returned from those wars with high and elevated tone of moral feeling." He attributed his love of war not to an "ursine nature" that qualified him to be a pirate, but to his feeling that "danger is alluring" and that it "is vivifying to be in the midst of 'working' things," and he resisted the temptation to volunteer for a commission in the war with Mexico only by reminding himself that it was a bad war. Lieber's perspective was so shaped by the glories of war that he frequently dated his letters by the famous battles that had occurred on that day.[24]

24 Lieber to Hillard, April 18, 1854, reprinted in Perry (ed.), *Lieber*, 270–71; Lieber, *Political Ethics*, Pt. 2, pp. 645, 633, 545–46; Lieber to Hillard, April, 1847. See also his description of war in Lieber, "Battle," *Encyclopedia*

Nevertheless, although he consistently praised war and gave less attention to its follies and futilities, Lieber could not agree with the slogan "La guerre est divine." He was aware that prostitution, roasting children, and slavery had all been viewed as divine, but he could not think of anyone, even "old Hobbes," who had held that war is divine. And yet Lieber did identify certain wars with the divine will and affirmed that war is one of God's ways of leading man to new stages of development so that its absolute condemnation is an act of impiety. Although war is not divine, particular wars are not always unjustified, and their conduct cannot always be described by the image of "hell." When a person crosses the boundary from peace to war, he does not leave a moral state of affairs for an amoral or immoral one. The phrase *laws of war* is not a contradiction in terms; war has its laws. "War is the exceptional—if not the abnormal state of society. The exception has its rule as the regular state."[25] Against the pacifists, Lieber, influenced by his own experiences of war, contended that war can be justified, that it can be fought in accord with its own laws, and that its laws are morally significant.

Against Pacifism

Although Lieber's own experiences in war led him to stress its positive features and effects, his sociopolitical context in the United States was profoundly affected by numerous individuals and societies who opposed war until their pacifism collided

Americana (Philadelphia: Desilver, Thomas, 1838), I, 614–16. (Lieber was general editor of this encyclopedia.) J. Glenn Gray, in *The Warriors: Reflections on Men in Battle* (New York: Harper and Row, 1970), includes delight in destruction among the attractions of war, a point of view that Lieber concurred in, at least implicitly, by his insistence that "destruction and obstruction" characterize war. Lieber to Hillard, April, 1847. For examples of letters dated by battles, see Lieber to Sumner, October 18, 1865 (Battle of Leipzig), June 16, 1864 (Day of the Battle of Ligny).

25 Lieber to Halleck, July 19, 1864, marginal note in *La Charité sur les champs de bataille*, Lieber to Sumner and Hillard, March 16, 1844, note attached to a clipping from *National Gazette* reporting a sermon by William

with their abolitionism in the wake of the Civil War.[26] Thus Lieber was more or less compelled to deal with pacifist arguments against physical force generally and war specifically despite his personal predilections. Although he conceded that it would be better to discuss war in a work on the law of nations and international ethics and that it was beyond the scope of political ethics as he defined it, he defended his decision to examine this topic in the last chapter of his *Political Ethics.* "So much has been advanced of late regarding war as affecting the morality of the individual, and so many cases, to be decided on ethic ground by the individual, necessarily happen in every war, that I feel obliged to add this chapter to the present work although international ethics in general have been excluded from it."[27] However, he limited his discussion to two major issues: "the admissibility of war among rational and moral beings" and the individual's conduct in war.

In response to nineteenth-century pacifism, Lieber analyzed and criticized the putative grounds for the inadmissibility of war in Christianity, morality, and utility. First, in his arguments relating to Christianity, he reveals familiarity with only a small portion of the pacifist literature, although the two works that he cites are among the best and most influential pacifist literature of his time. The pamphlet *An Inquiry into the Accordancy of War with the Principles of Christianity*, by a British Quaker,

---

Ellery Channing in Boston, January 25, 1835, in "File on War, c. 1835," all in Lieber Papers. It is necessary to use Lieber's notes with caution and mainly to amplify views clearly expressed elsewhere, for Lieber warned: "Do not think, however, should the paper [Notes for *Political Ethics*] become your property, that all I have written down, was intended for use, or was my view. I often represent a subject clearly to myself, by treating it as my adversary would do." Lieber to Sumner, June 18, 1836.

26 Although the term *pacifism* is a twentieth-century development (see *OED*, supplement), it is the most useful general term, since *nonresistance* and some other labels are more confusing. For the conflict between pacifism and abolitionism, see Peter Brock, *Pacifism in the United States* (Princeton, N.J.: Princeton University Press, 1968), Merle Curti, *Peace or War: The American Struggle, 1636–1936* (New York: W. W. Norton, 1936), and Merle Curti, *The American Peace Crusade, 1815–1860* (Durham, N.C.: Duke University Press, 1929).

27 *Political Ethics*, Pt. 2, p. 629. *Cf.* Pt. 1 (1838), 71–73.

Jonathan Dymond, was a standard and significant work in the American peace movement among Christians and non-Christians alike. Much of the pamphlet is directed against the arguments offered by William Paley in *The Principles of Moral and Political Philosophy*. Against Paley's distinction between individual and community conduct, with expediency the norm for the latter, Dymond tries to show that Christ's commands relating to nonresistance are literal, universal, and absolute: "that the pacific injunctions of the Christian Scriptures do apply to us, under every circumstance of life, whether private or public, appears to be made necessary by the universality of Christian obligation." Dymond, like most Quakers, insists that what is right is also efficacious. "What then is the principle for which we contend? *An unreasoning reliance upon Providence for defence, in all those cases in which we should violate His laws by defending ourselves*." He appeals to several historical examples such as the response of the Indians to Quakers in Pennsylvania.[28]

Although Lieber does not treat Dymond's views systematically, he suggests that Dymond expresses "all [the] objections which have been raised on the ground of the Christian religion against war," and he adresses several of Dymond's main theses. First, insisting that Christian scriptures and tradition do not repudiate war, Lieber interprets biblical passages that seem to condemn war "in conjunction with the whole bible," particularly Romans 13. Christ's statements, such as his injunction to turn the other cheek, must not be taken literally. "Christ taught principles, not absolute mathematical formulas; he addressed them to rational beings, who with reason therefore must apply them."[29]

28   See William Paley, *The Principles of Moral and Political Philosophy* (6th American ed.; Boston: John West, 1810), 477–92; Jonathan Dymond, *An Inquiry into the Accordancy of War with the Principles of Christianity* (3rd ed., corrected and enlarged; Philadelphia: William Brown, 1834), 107, 136.
29   Lieber, *Political Ethics*, Pt. 2, p. 639. On the interpretation of texts, see Lieber, *Legal and Political Hermeneutics* (Boston: Charles C. Little and James Brown, 1839).

Lieber invokes several related distinctions between individual and society, person and role, attitude and action, and he develops them under the rubrics of love and justice. For a proper understanding of Christianity, he contends, one must carefully and precisely distinguish and relate love and justice.

Christ came to infuse the spirit of kindness, not to abrogate the principles of God's creation. A stone is attracted by the centre of the earth, now, as before Christ; a conclusion, drawn according to the logic laws of reasoning, is now as binding as before Christ; and the eternal principles of justice are now as strong, as imperative and as sacred as before Christ. Let the law do justice and full justice alone, and leave love to the individual; for sacred as it is, it becomes only so if added to justice, but not if it abolishes it.

Although the language suggests Thomistic views that grace completes but does not abolish nature, the idea is more Lutheran, particularly in the *way* love is added to justice through the individual's spirit of kindness in his role as government official or soldier. A soldier fighting in a just war under the call of his government does not shoot "from hatred or revenge" and excludes "all personal cruelty," even caring equally for wounded enemy and friend after the battle. Like so many of Lieber's comments on war and battle, this one is idealized, but his point is critical to his argument. Dymond had argued that soldiers do not die for their country (since they would not be willing to be quietly executed for their country in a foreign land) and that their motive must be "glory alone." Not only did Lieber reject this argument by trying to show that genuine patriotism is often present, but he also contended that war can be fought without motives of personal hostility and animosity, especially by the operation of "necessity," which forces one to act and in no way depends on one's motives of hatred or revenge. In short, the Christian must uphold the order of justice by fighting if necessary, and he must respect love by expressing certain attitudes, which are also expected of all participants. Lieber did not sufficiently relate these issues to other elements in his description of modern wars (e.g., to masses fighting for other men). But because many pacifists oppose the *spirit* of war as much as killing, Lieber's attempt to deal with this issue is significant even if unsuccessful.[30]

Because he had read Dymond and perhaps because he had contacts with Quakers in his work for prison reform, Lieber tended to think of Christian pacifism as Quaker pacifism.[31] He exhibited little interest in or understanding of other Christian pacifist positions as can be seen in his dismissal of the Anabaptists as those who had used force "in order to compel others into their belief of non-resistance," or in his statement: "I do not know that the entire denial of our right to use arms, or in other words, of the legality of war has ever been adopted into any system, except by Quakers, before Mr. [Francis] Wayland's Elements of Moral Science." This very popular textbook by the president of Brown University argued not only that "all wars are contrary to the revealed will of God" but also that a nonresistant nation probably would not be harmed. "There is not a nation in Europe that could be led on to war against a harmless, just, forgiving and defenceless people." If such an approach failed, the nation should simply suffer the injury. Against Wayland, Lieber used many of the points that I have already mentioned, emphasizing that "government cannot act in many cases by way of benevolence, but must go by the principles of justice." But Lieber's reading of the historical evidence regarding the effectiveness of pacifism was also quite different from Wayland's or Dymond's. Whereas Dymond stressed the pacific responses to the Quakers by the Indians and others, Lieber took the attacks on the Quakers in New England as paradigmatic. "The fact is, an undefended state known to suffer everything, would become the prey of all the others."[32] Behind such inter-

30   Lieber, *Political Ethics*, Pt. 2, 637–638; 634–35, 666, *et passim; cf.* Lieber to S. B. Ruggles, September 9, 1860, Library of Congress.

31   Lieber's personal copy of Dymond, *An Inquiry*, in the Huntington Library, is inscribed, "Received from Roberts Vaux Esq. [a Quaker prison reformer] June, 1835. F. Lieber."

32   Lieber, *Political Ethics*, Pt. 2, pp. 637, 664, 665–66; Francis Wayland, *Elements of Moral Science* (New York: Cooke, 1835). In his lecture on the "Law and Usages of War," October 21, 1861, Lieber again singled out Dymond and Wayland when he mentioned the "voluminous literature" during the "anti-war period" from 1815 to 1855. Indeed, he only identified these two.

pretations of the past and predictions of the future are divergent views of the nature of man and of the universe, including divine providence.

Turning from Christianity to "the score of ethics alone," Lieber considers six main objections to war: (1) that rational beings should use reason, not force, since the latter reduces them to the level of animals; (2) that a victory does not prove right; (3) that many who had nothing to do with bringing about the war suffer in it; (4) that "war is immoral, because it is a cessation of morality, and, in addition, it breeds immorality"; (5) that its evil effects outweigh its benefits; and (6) that national disputes ought to be settled by a congress of nations. Although Lieber treats these arguments point by point, his main theses, already evident in the discussion of Christianity, are that "the ancient *vim vi repellere licet*, is not only justifiable, but is one of the principles of God's whole creation, and extinguished from it would create universal moral and physical disorder," and that the effects of wars are often good and noble. For objections 4 and 5, Lieber's own experiences in war play a significant part in the argument.[33]

Although Lieber devotes considerable attention to pacifism, he not only fails to appreciate the variety of Christian pacifism, but he also misses some of the pacifists' central claims. For example, he makes the following point against pacifism: "As *life* is not the greatest good, so is *dying* not the greatest evil."[34] But few, if any, pacifists have claimed that *dying* is the greatest evil; instead they have claimed that *killing*, at least in war, is the greatest moral or religious evil! Or they have said that the *system* of killing called war is the greatest evil.

One of the foremost defenders of this last proposition in the nineteenth century was Charles Sumner, a Boston lawyer and later United States senator. Lieber's friendship and voluminous correspondence with Sumner indicate his continued exposure to and rejection of pacifism. A participant in the American Peace Society, Sumner in the late 1830s declared war to be "un-

33   Lieber, *Political Ethics*, Pt. 2, pp. 640–53, 639. *Cf.* Halleck, *International Law*, 312ff.
34   Lieber, *Political Ethics*, Pt. 2, p. 667.

just and un-Christian." Later, answering the charge that he entered the peace movement and supported other reforms very late and only in order to attract public attention, Sumner insisted that "my ripened convictions were known to my friends, and were often the subject of conversation." He pointed to his participation in the American Peace Society and his service on its executive committee. Nevertheless, his views did not become a significant part of the public debate until he was invited to deliver Boston's 1845 Fourth of July oration. He gave a speech entitled *The True Grandeur of Nations* with the central thesis: "In our age there can be no peace that is not honorable: there can be no war that is not dishonorable." Although the speech contained few original ideas, it had an "epoch-making significance in the history of the peace movement," largely because of its setting, its historical and classical learning, and the author's position in Boston society. The Boston *Post* rebuked him for offering "a discourse appropriate perhaps for an insane Quaker in his dotage."[35]

Sumner only repudiated war for his age, while refusing to judge or condemn past wars such as the American Revolution. Some twentieth-century pacifists, relying on standards of discrimination between combatants and noncombatants and proportionality, have also repudiated only modern wars. But their technological pacifism, based on the logic or effects of modern warfare, has little in common with Sumner's position, which concentrated on the motives for war and war as a process. He

35 Sumner to Lord Morpeth, March 22, 1839, Sumner to George Putnam, April, 1848, both in Edward L. Pierce, *Memoir and Letters of Charles Sumner* (Boston: Roberts Brothers, Vols. I & II, 1877, Vols. III & IV, 1893), II, 820, III, 68, hereinafter cited as Pierce, *Sumner*. See also David Donald, *Charles Sumner and the Coming of the Civil War* (New York: Alfred A. Knopf, 1960), 107, *et passim*. Charles Sumner, *The True Grandeur of Nations* (Boston: William D. Ticknor, 1845), 4; Curti, *The American Peace Crusade*, 120; Boston *Post* quoted in Donald, *Charles Sumner and the Coming of the Civil War*, 112. For the controversy surrounding the oration, see Pierce, *Sumner*, II, 337–84, and Worthington Chauncey Ford (ed.), "Sumner's Oration on the 'True Grandeur of Nations,'" *Proceedings of the Massachusetts Historical Society*, L (1971), 249–307.

admitted that defensive wars could be justified. He had, for example, believed that the defense of English subjects and representatives justified England's war with China. But Sumner held that no wars in his time could be defensive and pointed particularly to the feud with Mexico. Modern nations (or at least Christian nations) can only wage war at this time in order to determine justice. Given this essential premise, which he nowhere clearly and solidly established, he employed an analogy between contemporary wars and medieval trials by battle. Because both try to determine justice by force and chance, they must be denounced as "monstrous and impious."[36] Force and chance cannot determine justice for individuals or for nations, and to claim God's presence in such processes is impious.

In short, Sumner defended a version of the second ethical objection to war in Lieber's list: war does not determine right. In contrast to many in the peace movement, Sumner tried to make his argument "entirely independent of the texts of the Gospels," though he appealed to Christianity and acknowledged his indebtedness to Channing, Dymond, Wayland, and others. In *The True Grandeur of Nations*, he examined Christian principles only in order to show how Christian support for war has no foundation.

Not only was Sumner's argument temporally limited ("our age") and in some statements geographically limited ("our country"), it was also limited to the use of physical force in one context: war between nations. He claimed that his position did "not in any way interfere with the right of self-defence or the stability of government or the sword of the magistrate." His alternative to war was some form of negotiation, arbitration, mediation, or congress of nations: only through such proceedings can nations establish justice. For example, since the conflict with Mexico concerned the title to a piece of land, it "should be tried, as other titles are tried, by arbitration, or by some tri-

36 Sumner to Richard H. Dana, Jr., August, 1845, Sumner to Lieber, January 5, 1842, both in Pierce, *Sumner*, II, 377, 198. See also Sumner, *The True Grandeur of Nations*, esp. 19–27. Lieber believed that England was justified in compelling China to enter into communication with other nations.

bunal having in it the elements of justice." Thus, he combined ethical objections 2 and 6, occasionally incorporating elements of the others that Lieber rejected in *Political Ethics*. Taken as a whole, Sumner's ambiguous position was "near pacifism," as Peter Brock has suggested.[37]

The nature, extent, and basis of Sumner's pacifism should be noted, for Lieber was in constant contact with him, especially through correspondence. Indeed, between 1835 and 1872 (with a break in correspondence from 1853 to 1861), Lieber wrote approximately a thousand letters and notes to Sumner.[38] Furthermore, Lieber was in Boston July 4, 1845, and heard Sumner's famous oration, as he noted in his diary:

July 4 Sumner's Anti-War oration, which seemed to me the worst advised, and one of the worst reasoned speeches I have ever heard.
July 7 Dined at Longfellow's with Sumner, Hillard, Felton, and Doctor Frothingham. Long, animated, but very pleasant conversation on War.[39]

Lieber ridiculed Sumner's optimistic hopes for the elimination of war by teasing him about assuming the posture of "a new Archangel Michael with a flybrush instead of a sword." Even before Sumner's oration, Lieber suggested that "indiscriminate railing against war" involves "a degree of impiety" because God uses war, among a thousand other means, to take man through different stages of civilization. "Blood is occasionally the rich dew of History."[40]

37   Sumner to Putnam, April, 1848, Sumner to his brother George, August 26, 1844, Sumner to Lieber, June 27, 1843, Sumner to Dana, August, 1845, all in Pierce, *Sumner*, III, 68 (*cf.* II, 379), II, 313–14, 212, 377; Brock, *Pacifism in the United States*, 633. Sumner was clearer about the limits of his claims in "The War System of the Commonwealth of Nations," an address before the American Peace Society in Boston, May 28, 1849, in *The Works of Charles Sumner* (15 vols.; Boston: Lee and Shepard, 1894), II, 171–277.
38   See Freidel, *Francis Lieber*, 110, and Charles B. Robson, "Papers of Francis Lieber," *Huntington Library Bulletin*, No. 3 (February, 1933), 135–55.
39   Perry (ed.), *Lieber*, 198; see also Frothingham to Sumner, Aug. 25, 1845, in Ford (ed.), "Sumner's Oration," 281–82.
40   Lieber to Sumner, June [25?], 1846. Lieber to Sumner and Hillard, March 18, 1844, in a section addressed to Hillard, but obviously intended for Sumner too, especially in the light of Sumner's contention that war is impiety.

Lieber's friendship with Sumner suffered a rupture from 1853 to 1861 that had its beginning, according to Lieber, in their disagreement over war. "When he first came out with his Antiwar, 4th of July oration," wrote Lieber in 1858, "he did not take my dissent well." Five years earlier he had written Hillard, "The tree of our friendship has begun to show yellow leaves ever since Sumner's speech on War." As for Sumner, he had written to his brother George, shortly after the speech, "All my friends here except Lieber agree with me." In a footnote to the printed speech, he castigated Lieber, "He advocates war with the ardor of one inspired by the history of the past, and looking no higher than to history for rules of conduct, while his own experience of suffering on the fields of slaughter has failed to make him discern the folly and wickedness of such a mode of determining questions between nations." Ironically, in 1835 Sumner had wanted Lieber's account of the battle of Waterloo reprinted as a peace tract or as an article in a peace journal because it "gives the most vivid sketch I ever read of the horrors of war, because it embodies them in the experience of one individual, without resorting to any of the declamatory generalities which are generally used with that view." At the time, Lieber supported the project.[41]

Anticipating Sumner's argument, Lieber contended in his *Political Ethics* that wars "are not like the ancient ordeals, a supposed trial of justice," or an appeal to arms. In the late 1840s he thought that Sumner "unreasonably" maintained the analogy between wars and duels or ordeals. In effect, Sumner confused end and process or activity as Lieber suggested in different language. One may fight for a just end or cause without supposing that the war will settle the issue of justice. As Lieber argued, "We undertake wars in order to obtain right, and if victory is doubtful, and we still undertake it, we do it, because we

41   Lieber to Dorothea Dix, April 18, 1858, Lieber to Hillard, May 29, 1853; Sumner to his brother George, August 16, 1845, in Pierce, *Sumner*, II, 378; Sumner, *The True Grandeur of Nations*, 7; Sumner to Lieber, April 7, 1835, *cf.* Sumner to Lieber, August 25, 1835, both in Pierce, *Sumner*, I, 167, 170; Lieber to Sumner, August 24, September 31, 1835.

believe the loss by submission would be so great that we must at least try to protect ourselves, and hope that God will grant victory to the just cause." A nation does not fight in order to convince the other side that its cause is just, and "although war is not of an ethical nature, so far as the physical force goes, it is not immoral on that account. A dinner is not an ethical procedure, but it is not immoral." Lieber also refused to accept Sumner's sharp distinction between war and other uses of force, holding instead that "the question of war is only a subdivision of the larger question may we or may we not morally use means of physical defence or coercion under certain circumstances." Nor could he concede a fundamental distinction between previous wars and current wars, with a condemnation of the latter implying nothing about the former. The pacifists, including Sumner, could not give cogent reasons for this distinction.[42]

Even in Sumner's stage of "near pacifism," the differences between Lieber and Sumner were partly matters of emphasis, and the issues at stake included the proper description of war and its effects as well as the causes that can justify war. Sumner clearly did not rule out all force or even all wars. But for him war is horrible and wicked, and it can only be justified if it is defensive. For Lieber war is less than divine, although divine providence uses it, and it can be justified on a number of different grounds in addition to self-defense. During the Civil War, their differences were negligible, for Sumner was a spokesman for radical republicanism and Lieber defended many of its programs. After the war, when Sumner revised his writings for his collected works, he made several important alterations in the text of *The True Grandeur of Nations*. For example, he changed his thesis into a question: "Can there be in our age any peace

42   On the analogy between ordeals and wars, see *Political Ethics*, Pt. 2, p. 643, Lieber's note on his copy of Sumner's *The War System*, and "Notes on the case of Alexander MacLeod in Connection with International Law," June 11, 1842, which maintains that "War is not resorted to, to settle any question" (Lieber Papers). For the other criticisms of Sumner's distinctions, see "Law and Usages of War," October 29, 1861, and *Political Ethics*, Pt. 2, interleaved copy, 664 (both in Eisenhower Library, Johns Hopkins University).

that is not honorable, any war that is not dishonorable?" The statement that "Christianity forbids war in all cases" was weakened to "the whole custom of war is contrary to Christianity." Sumner also deleted his criticism of Lieber's views on war.[43]

Just War

Despite Lieber's disagreements with the pacifists, he shared a few very important themes with them, particularly the conviction that war stands in need of justification because of the suffering it involves. Not only his personal experiences but also his debates with the pacifists probably helped to make this theme central. "A just war implies that we have a just cause, and that it is necessary: for war implies sufferance in some parties, and it is a principle of all human actions that, in order to be justified in inflicting sufferance of any kind, we must not only be justified, but the evil must be necessary."[44] With the pacifists, Lieber held that there is a presumption against war, but against the pacifists, he held that the presumption is rebuttable when certain conditions are met. Despite the fervent hopes of some pacifists, he did not believe that war could be abolished. Like many in the just-war tradition, he sketched both *jus ad bellum* and *jus in bello*, although he did not use those terms. He kept the two concepts distinct and even separate, as many in the tradition did not. When he discussed the laws of war, including both legal and moral rules and principles, he was clearly talking of *jus in bello*. The *jus ad bellum* is the right to wage war when the conditions that can rebut the presumption against war are met. When Lieber used the phrase *just war*, he meant a war that is just and justified, but such a war may be fought fairly or unfairly, according to or in violation of the laws of war. *Just war* indicates the right to make war.

How does one determine that a war is just and justified, and

43 Charles Sumner, *Charles Sumner: His Complete Works* (15 vols.; Boston: Lee and Shepard, Statesman Edition, 1899), I, 9, 34, 58.
44 *Political Ethics*, Pt. 2, p. 635, *cf.* 649–50.

that a nation thus has the right to wage it? Lieber's criteria fall within the broad just-war tradition. "A war, to be justifiable, must be undertaken on *just grounds*, that is, to repel or avert wrongful force, or to establish a right; must be the *last resort*, that is, after all other means of reparation are unavailable or have miscarried; it must be *necessary*, that is, the evil to be averted or redressed should be a great one; and it must be *wise*, that is, there must be reasonable prospect of obtaining reparation, or the averting of the evil, and the acquiescence in the evil must be greater than the evils of the contest." Underlining these criteria of just cause, last resort, necessity (or substantial cause), reasonable prospect of success, and proportionality, he omits, or rather simply assumes, other criteria that often fall under *jus ad bellum*: right intention, peace as the ultimate object of war, public declaration of war, and public authority. Elsewhere he claims that the ultimate object of a (just) war is peace. Although this claim is fundamental in his discussion of the laws of war, it plays no explicit role in his discussion of the *jus ad bellum*. Likewise, right intention is important in the right conduct of war, and Lieber apparently assumes that wrong intention (e.g., cruelty and revenge) in the war as a whole is excluded by the other criteria such as just cause and necessity.[45]

The other two omitted or assumed criteria are also related. While Lieber in *Political Ethics* does not require that a war be publicly declared in order to be just, he contends that such a

---

45   Lieber, *Political Ethics*, Pt. 2, pp. 653–54, 638. When Lieber discussed just war, he emphasized "just cause" and "necessity." See *Political Ethics*, Pt. 2, pp. 635, 653. Perhaps his position could be construed as taking these two characteristics as the "justice" in the just war and the other criteria as determining the fuller justification of the war. For example, a nation might have a *just* and *necessary* cause in his sense of serious or great evil to be averted, but its resort to war would not be *justified* unless it had exhausted other remedies. Or a Nation might have a *right* to wage war because of, say, the justice of its cause, but it might not be *right* for it to undertake a war because of the suffering that would result for all parties. Although the distinction between justice and justification appears in Lieber's thought, he tended in his discussion of war to use these terms interchangeably. Furthermore, although he thought of some wars as *duties*, this conception had no effect on the operation of *jus in bello*.

declaration implies an acknowledgment of certain obligations. His lecture on the "Laws and Usages of War," December 3, 1861, admits that the best writers differ on the necessity of a declaration, but he appears to defend it because "decent regard for mankind" and "public good faith" require that a government explain and justify its departure from peace. A declaration permits other countries and people to prepare their maritime commerce and determine their responses (e.g., whether they will remain neutral). Indeed, other countries would severely rebuke any sudden rupture of peace. His argument, of course, assumes that peace is the normal state of affairs and that the exception called war requires justification. He also notes that in the United States, a declaration of war can only be made by the full Congress, both House and Senate, while the president, with the consent of the Senate, can make peace.

Only the public authority can declare war. While the criterion of public authority appears to exclude rebellions and some other conflicts, Lieber takes a somewhat broader definition of war than those who limit it to a contest between states, stressing instead "protracted and active enmity" in which both parties are willing to use other means than intellectual ones to achieve their ends. Such a definition includes insurrections and civil wars as well as international conflicts. Thus, the authority of the state would not be a prerequisite for a just war. Yet Lieber generally assumes this criterion and therefore exempts the individual soldier from "all obligation" to "decide upon the justness of war." Lieber favored conscription of armies, and he clearly emphasized the duty of obedience, but he by no means denied the moral right of selective conscientious objection—objection to a particular war because of its injustice. For example, in a revolution, a soldier may have to determine whether "it is a case of utmost extremity, and whether the most sacred duties do conflict."[46] But there is no general rule for deciding such cases, and there is a presumption against disobedience.

46 Lieber, "[Memorandum on] Conscription," July 23, 1864; Lieber, *Political Ethics*, Pt. 2, p. 667. Furthermore, Lieber insisted during the Civil War that treatment of the enemy according to the laws of war does not imply an

Lieber drew a sharp distinction between the freedom of a person already in the army (or drafted) and a volunteer. In the late 1830s, commenting on one of William Ellery Channing's lectures on war, which, he insisted, was "not much," he wrote, "I like something more than seeing ministers of the gospel preach peace and keep it; when parsons tell the people quite as a general rule that they must in each war judge for themselves and not fight when their government calls upon them, they transcend . . . their proper limit." Nevertheless, Lieber also affirmed another version of selective conscientious objection when he considered "whether a man whose government has gone to war has a *right to volunteer*, if he considers the war unjust." Far from being merely theoretical, this was a practical issue for Lieber in the war between the United States and Mexico in 1846, and he would have solicited a commission in that conflict "had it not been for this ethical consideration." His love of war, the lure of danger, and the fulfillment of acting and making history could not overcome his belief that the war with Mexico began "in wanton injustice on the part of the U.S." and that it was a "cabinet war" brought about by President Polk with Congress out of session.[47] In short, while there is a clear presumption against disobedience, the soldier may face a *Grenzfall* in which he disobeys orders because they conflict with other duties and the ordinary citizen may apply just-war criteria in deciding not to volunteer despite his government's entreaties.

Unfortunately Lieber generally did not indicate the bases of the criteria for determining the *jus ad bellum* or their status, function, and interrelationship. Thus, it is not clear whether each criterion must be met for a war to be just and justified, or whether the determination of the justice of a war is a matter of

acknowledgment of the enemy's authority to wage war or its sovereignty. See General Orders No. 100, #152.

47   Lieber to Hillard, April, 1847, and May 19, 1839; interleaved copy of *Political Ethics*, Pt. 2, opposite p. 667 (Eisenhower Library, Johns Hopkins University), partially incorporated in the revised second edition of *Political Ethics*, ed. Woolsey, Pt. 2, p. 457; "Notes and Extracts for *Political Ethics*," Huntington Library; "Laws and Usages of War," December 3, 1861. For Lieber's praise of obedience, see "Obedience" (MS in Lieber Papers).

approximation, a matter of more or less. But certainly there is no right to wage war without a just cause. In contrast to Sumner in his stage of "near pacifism," Lieber did not restrict just causes to self-defense but also included insurrections for liberty, wars to unite states, wars of chastisement, and "cases of war, where the possession of some place or province becomes absolutely necessary for the safety or existence of a state or nation." For example, he wrote, "If Louisiana had not peaceably joined America, and the United States, recognizing her high mission, had not obtained possession of the mouth of the Mississippi by offers of compromise, would it not have been her *duty* to have acquired it by force?" Lieber admitted that this category of "national necessity" is risky and dangerous, but his inclusion of it in the list of just causes also led him to emphasize that "there are wars where the right is on both sides."[48] This statement grants *objective* right to both sides, in contrast to a view that in every war one side undertakes a just war while the other side wages an unjust one and that, at best, the unjust side can be *subjectively* right through sincere belief and invincible ignorance.

It is easy to see how a recognition that both parties in a conflict may have objective right on their sides could lead to an emphasis on the restraints of the *jus in bello*. But fundamental to Lieber's formulation of the laws of war is the conviction that the justice of a cause does not free its defenders from obligations to the other side: "War . . . by no means absolves us from all obligation toward the enemy." He also used familial imagery to express this idea. "The fundamental idea of all international law is the idea that the civilized nations of our race form a family of nations. If members of this family go to war with one another, they do not thereby divest themselves of the membership—neither toward the other members, nor wholly toward the enemy."[49] These obligations set limits on what the belliger-

48 Lieber, *Political Ethics*, Pt. 2, pp. 654–57; Lieber to Franz von Holtzendorff, May 26, 1872, in Perry (ed.), *Lieber*, 424–25.
49 Lieber, *Political Ethics*, Pt. 2, p. 657; Lieber, "Twenty-Seven Definitions and Elementary Positions Concerning the Laws and Usages of War" (MS in Eisenhower Library), #20.

ents may do in prosecuting the war; even if only one side objectively has *jus ad bellum*—or is convinced that its cause is just and necessary—these obligations endure. Certitude about the *jus ad bellum* does not cancel or weaken the restraints of the *jus in bello*.

The importance of Lieber's defense of this thesis can be illustrated by contrasting it with some other widespread views during the Civil War. General William Tecumseh Sherman decided to secure Atlanta by evacuating its population and eliminating the need for a garrison to control it. In answer to protests from the mayor and council of Atlanta, Sherman wrote, "You cannot qualify war in harsher terms than I will. War is cruelty and you cannot refine it; and those who brought war into our country deserve all the curses and maledictions a people can pour out. I know I had no hand in making this war, and I know I will make more sacrifice to-day than any of you to secure peace."[50] Although Sherman did not put into writing the famous words attributed to him—"War is hell"—his other expressions such as "War is cruelty" and "War is barbarism" attest to this motif in his thought and give credence to the testimony of his hearers that he also used the more famous words. At any rate, the idea is clearly present, and it could be used to justify not only such evacuations but other conduct less consistent with the laws of war. If war itself is the moral problem— also one of the main pacifist objections to war—only those who are responsible for starting it, for releasing its fury, are to be condemned, not those who fight the war. Indeed, no important moral judgments can be made about the latter's conduct. If war is hell, the conduct of generals and soldiers cannot be subjected to moral scrutiny and censure, which must be reserved for those who started the war. Although there is a crime of war, there are no war crimes. While Sherman probably did not fully accept the logic of this position, others came close to it, often emphasizing more strongly the justice of their cause than the intrinsic characteristics of war itself.

50   B. H. Liddell Hart, *Sherman: Soldier—Realist—American* (New York: Dodd, Mead, 1929), 310.

One of Lieutenant General Thomas J. "Stonewall" Jackson's biographers wrote that when Jackson and others were unable to prevent the Civil War, they felt the Confederate army should "take no prisoners" since "the war was an offence against humanity so monstrous that it outlawed those who shared its guilt beyond the pale of forbearance." In effect the restraints of the laws of war cease to operate when the enemy's cause is so unjust (although the requisite degree of injustice is rarely specified). Some unjust causes render their defenders "outlaws," and their opponents "crusaders."

In a communication to the New York *Times*, Lieber repudiated Jackson's position. "An individual of fervent, and even grim devotion, undertaking to decide for himself whether a war (mark, it is the war he speaks of, and not any acts done by the enemy) so outrages all humanity that it outlaws those who share in it, as if civilization had not established the law of war for the very purpose of preventing people from acting on this idea, which, as a matter of course, has always been maintained by many in every war."[51] In a note, probably written a few years later, he developed this theme, which undergirds General Orders No. 100. Confederates told "suffering Union prisoners that they had no business to come and attack innocent people who wanted to be left alone. This is the reason why I put in Genl. Order No. 100, year 1863 (what I fear some people at a distance have thought strange, because unnecessary) that the motives or presumed motives of a belligerent for going to war do not in the least affect the laws of war regarding the treatment of prisoners or concerning the treatment of the enemy in general." From the standpoint of the laws of war, the belligerents are equal. There is not one body of law for a just war, and another for an unjust war. "The law of nations allows every sovereign government to make war upon another sovereign state, and, therefore, admits of no rules or laws different from those of regular warfare, regarding the treatment of prisoners of war, although they may

51   Lieber to New York *Times*, January 7, 1865. His communication concerned R. L. Dabney, *The Life of Lieut.-General Thomas J. Jackson* (London: 1865). He also enclosed this clipping from the New York *Times* in a letter to Halleck, January 9, 1865.

belong to the army of a government which the captor may consider as a wanton and unjust assailant." Regardless of the justice of their cause, when nations resort to force, they invoke
two principles that are important in all law of nations: "what is
right for one, is right for the other (or perfect equality of the
belligerents) and the principle of retaliation." The law and
usages of war provide rules of action, developed as a common
law in "our family of nations," for the "peculiar and abnormal
relations" that characterize the state of war.[52]

Lieber's conception of the relation between the right to wage
war (just war) and the obligations that persist in war (laws of
war) has its philosophical foundation in his conviction that the
notions of right and obligation are "inter-completing." According to Lieber, "right and obligation are twins. . . . [They are]
each other's complements, and cannot be severed without undermining the ethical ground on which we stand—that ground
on which alone civilization, justice, virtue, and real progress
can build enduring monuments. Right and obligation are the
warp and the woof of the tissue of man's moral, and therefore,
likewise, of man's civil life. Take out the one, and the other is
in worthless confusion." This highly metaphorical statement is
not merely a repetition of the view, held by Paley and others,
that obligation is the corollary of right and that *my right thus
entails another's duty.* Lieber's point is rather that *my right* is
connected with and completed by *my duty:* "right alone, des-
potism,—duty alone, slavery. I consider *right* completing the
idea of *duty as vice versa*; and I speak of duty in the *possessor*
of the right, not in the one on whom the claim is made—all
right consisting in a claim upon another."[53] A nation does not

52   Lieber, "[Notes on] Retaliation," *ca.* 1867 (MS in Lieber Papers); *Instructions,* #67; Lieber, "Law and Usages of War," December 13, 17, 1861.
53   *Miscellaneous Writings,* I, 264; Lieber to Thayer, November 5, 1869, in
Perry (ed.), *Lieber,* 391–92. He frequently used the slogan "No Right without
its Duty; No Duty without its Right," even on his stationary, and he thought
of it as "perhaps the only thing I shall have contributed to jurisprudence
when I die." Lieber to Allibone, February 15, 1870. Lieber reacted vehemently
to the Marxist use of this slogan because he viewed it as his creation and the

have the right to wage war without simultaneously being subject to the obligations that constitute the laws of war. But to determine exactly how the right to wage war, established by just-war criteria, and the obligations of laws of war are "inter-completing," it is necessary to examine the different grounds of these obligations.

Grounds of Obligations

Lieber's *Political Ethics* does not give "an outline of the law of war," but rather deals with "some points of importance in public ethics." Among these important points—some of which are only suggested in the *Instructions*—are four grounds of obligations toward the enemy: (1) the object of war; (2) the humanity of the belligerents; (3) the declaration of war, which implies a "tacit acknowledgment of certain usages and obligations"; and (4) the involvement in wars of masses "who fight for others, or not for themselves only."[54] Although his discussion, unfortunately, is not systematic and comprehensive, it does indicate the direction of his thought and what is back of General Orders No. 100.

It appears that the fourth ground (in conjunction with the second) establishes that a soldier is a public and not a private enemy. One of the ethical objections to war is that many who

---

expression of man's individual and social dimensions. Lieber to von Holzendorff, The Day of Sedan, 1871. When Lieber studied in Berlin, he heard sermons and lectures by Friedrich E. D. Schleiermacher whom he greatly admired. This theologian's influence can probably be seen in Lieber's thesis which was the basis of the relation of right and duty: "Man's individuality and sociality form the two poles round which his whole life revolves." Lieber, *Political Ethics*, Pt. 1, pp. 20–33, 57–63; Freidel, *Francis Lieber*, 21–22, 151–54. Although Lieber also was indebted to Kant for several themes (e.g., on universalizability), he found Kant less helpful in social and political philosophy. Contrast Wilson Smith's interpretation in *Professors and Public Ethics: Studies of Northern Moral Philosophers Before the Civil War* (Ithaca, N.Y.: Cornell University Press, 1956).

54 Lieber, *Political Ethics*, Pt. 2, pp. 657, 629.

have nothing to do with starting a war suffer in it. Lieber's answer, in part, is that "it is the plan of the creator that government and people should be closely united in weal and woe."
And he uses the analogy of a criminal whose just punishment
also affects his innocent wife and children. But here Lieber's
point is that because the soldier fights under the authority of
the government for public causes, he is not to be treated as a
private criminal, nor is he to be held responsible for the war
itself. He is to be treated according to the laws of war. "So soon
as a man is armed by a sovereign government, and takes the
soldier's oath of fidelity, he is a belligerent; his killing, wounding, or other warlike acts, are no individual crimes or offences.
No belligerent has a right to declare that enemies of a certain
class, color, or condition, when properly organized as soldiers,
will not be treated by him as public enemies."[55]

On the third ground, when a nation declares war or enters
into a state of war, it tacitly or silently acknowledges certain
usages and obligations, such as honoring flags of truce and protecting heralds and envoys. The interdependence of these
grounds of obligation (any obligation may rest on more than
one ground), as well as their scale of importance, can be seen in
Lieber's appeal to reasons other than tacit acknowledgment for
respecting these customs. They must be kept not only because
of the honor involved but also because they are necessary
"either for mitigating the evils of war and bringing it within the
sphere of civilisation, or for . . . obtaining . . . the end of
peace."[56]

Clearly the object of war and the humanity of the belligerents are the most important sources of obligations toward the
enemy. Although Lieber's statements about the object of war appear to be contradictory because they both include and exclude
destruction, his apparent confusion is easily explained by an
analysis of several levels of objects of war. The immediate objects or means of war are deception, injury, and destruction.

55   Ibid., Pt. 2, p. 644; Instructions, #57.
56   Lieber, Political Ethics, Pt. 2, p. 664. See also Instructions, #114.

While he uses the language of both object and means in discussing these actions, the language of means better fits his considered position in the *Instructions*. "Modern wars are not internecine wars, in which the killing of the enemy is the object. The destruction of the enemy in modern war, and, indeed, modern war itself, are means to obtain that object of the belligerent which lies beyond the war."[57] Although Lieber refers to our duty to injure our enemy and describes the destruction of the enemy as an object, the logic of his position requires that injury and killing be considered merely as means to render the enemy harmless. The "next object" of the war encompasses both the aims of particular campaigns and battles and also the ends for which the war is fought. Whatever the end or cause of the war, the "ultimate object" is peace, "on whatever conditions that may be." For nations, "peace is their normal condition; war is the exception. The ultimate object of all modern war is a renewed state of peace."[58]

"Old Hundred" does not explicitly derive particular obligations from this "ultimate object" of peace, although it states that "military necessity does not include any act of hostility which makes the return to peace unnecessarily difficult." In *Political Ethics*, however, Lieber appeals to this ultimate object in order to establish some obligations and general policies. For example, although removing works of arts from a conquered country cannot be absolutely denied on any "jural ground," it should generally be avoided because the hostility it engenders makes peace more difficult, for peace "requires mutual good will." Nevertheless, he permits such conduct when it is necessary, perhaps to chastise a nation for waging an unjust war, although he rules out destruction of art. Furthermore, we should not in-

---

57 *Instructions*, #68.
58 Lieber, *Political Ethics*, Pt. 2, pp. 658–60; *Instructions*, #29, #30. But destruction is frequently if not generally the object in naval engagements. See Lieber's article, "Battle," *Encyclopedia Americana* (1836), I, 615, and "Twenty-seven Definitions and Elementary Positions Concerning the Law and Usages of War," #13. The latter was delivered as part of his lectures on the "Law and Usages of War."

flict an injury upon an individual which "will cruelly inflict him after he has ceased to be an enemy" if we can avoid it. Nor is assassination permitted since "it would lead to deplorable evils which would greatly impede the ultimate end of war—*quod est Pax*."[59]

Even when "mutual good will" is weak, *confidence* may be sufficient for a limited peace. Certainly it is indispensable, and thus perfidy, bad faith, and the breaking of faith are prohibited. These categories do not include deception in war, for military necessity "admits of deception, but disclaims acts of perfidy."[60] Within war, a capitulation or an agreement, such as an armistice or a permitted convoy, is "above the declaration of war." Such acts depend on confidence, and violations would destroy the confidence that is the basis of the peace that is ultimately sought. Lieber appeals to both logic and expediency. First, in a Kantian argument of universalizability, he contends that it "would be illogical" to adopt treachery as a principle of war. "We could not carry on anything in war, but destruction itself, if treachery were adopted as principle (which besides would be *illogical*, for we require first the *trust*, in order to break it, hence we could not make treachery general)." Second, "on the ground of expediency, it would be better to abstain from treachery." If treachery and perfidy became widespread in war, numerous limits would fall and "all possibility of ultimately concluding peace would vanish."[61] Similarly, some provisions of treaties concluded in times of peace deal with conduct during hostilities and should be observed for the same reasons.

59   *Instructions*, #16; Lieber, *Political Ethics*, Pt. 2, p. 661; Note, Columbia, S.C., January, 1841, Lieber Papers, *cf. Instructions*, #148. A Code prohibits destruction of works of art "in the name of common humanity and civilization," but this phrase was omitted from *Instructions*. See *Instructions*, #35, #36, and *Political Ethics*, Pt. 2, p. 663.
60   *Instructions*, #16. This phrase was added at Halleck's suggestion; see Lieber's revised, interleaved copy of *A Code. Cf.* Lieber, *Political Ethics*, Pt. 2, pp. 658, 661.
61   Lieber, *Political Ethics*, Pt. 2, p. 662; *Instructions*, #11, #15; "Law and Usages of War," December 17, 1861, and a summary in the New York *Times*, January 13, 1862, p. 8.

Lieber emphasizes the importance of confidence for achieving peace. "Indeed, if no degree of confidence remains between the belligerents, every war would become an internecine war; and so it is the case between all savage tribes, who have lost all confidence in one another." But he also recognizes other "moral points remaining in a state of force." Beyond explicit agreements, there are requirements of good faith "supposed by the modern law of war to exist."[62]

But within war what is the distinction between deception and perfidy? It can be unpacked by examining relevant passages in *Instructions*:

#63. Troops who fight in the uniform of their enemies, without any plain, striking, and uniform mark of distinction of their own, can expect no quarter. . . .

#65. The use of the enemy's national standard, flag, or other emblem of nationality, for the purpose of deceiving the enemy in battle, is an act of perfidy by which they lose all claim to the protection of the war. . . .

#117. It is justly considered an act of bad faith, of infamy or fiendishness, to deceive the enemy by flags of protection. Such an act of bad faith may be good cause for refusing to respect such flags.[63]

Perfidy emerges in two main situations. In the first, a belligerent believes that he will receive protection and acts on this belief, perhaps surrendering under certain conditions. In the second, more common situation, a belligerent believes that he must grant protection to certain persons, or at least that he does not have to take serious precautions in relation to them. For example, the use of the enemy's national flags, or civilian disguise, or hospital flags on military factories may lead the enemy to suppose that certain persons are harmless and merit protection or that certain property is not a legitimate military target.

The *Instructions* indicate that these deceptions are instances of perfidy, probably because such "moral points . . . in a state of force" as the protection of civilians could not endure without

---

62 Lieber, *Political Ethics*, Pt. 2, pp. 662–63; *Instructions*, #15.

63 Halleck suggested the last sentence; see Lieber's revised, interleaved copy of *A Code*, where this is marked in blue. See also Lieber to Halleck, February 20, 1863.

confidence that the enemy will not take advantage of them. It is difficult to ensure the protection of civilians when belligerents have reason to believe that soldiers on the other side will frequently appear as civilians. On the other hand, a contemporary interpreter of the laws of war describes acceptable ruses of war as "those acts which the enemy would have had reason to expect, or in any event had no reason not to expect."[64] Perfidy appears when one belligerent's confidence, based on moral or legal reasons or both (such as the expected protection of prisoners of war), is betrayed. Perfidy thus combines a betrayal of trust with unfairness, for one belligerent takes advantage of the other's adherence to the laws of war in order to advance his own cause. A belligerent may use camouflage and other modes of deception, but he is guilty of perfidy and treachery if he puts legitimate targets of attack under legally protected categories, relying on the opponent's adherence to the laws of war. Because of the gravity of perfidy, each of the passages from the *Instructions* provides a serious sanction.

The requirements of good faith and fairness rest not only on the ultimate object of war but also on the humanity of the belligerents. This final ground of obligation figures prominently in the *Instructions*. "Men who take up arms against one another in public war do not cease on this account to be moral beings, responsible to one another, and to God." The humanity of the belligerents serves as the most general and comprehensive reason for the rules of war. It rules out cruelty, which is "the infliction of suffering for the sake of suffering or for revenge." It thus excludes unnecessary suffering, for the direct and avoidable infliction of suffering that is not related to the general object of the battle or the war is directed against private individuals (or soldiers as private individuals) who "do not impede my way." "So soon as an enemy is rendered harmless by wounds or capitivity, he is no longer my enemy, for he is no enemy of mine individually." When a soldier is *hors de combat*, perhaps

64 Frits Kalshoven, *The Law of Warfare: A Summary of Its Recent History and Trends in Development* (Leiden: A. W. Sijthoff, 1973), 102.

because of wounds, he ceases to be a legitimate target of attack precisely because his humanity is not wholly and exhaustively expressed in his role as soldier. Thus, "the wounded on the battlefield is protected in his misfortune; the wounded enemy is a sacred person; he is of course a prisoner, but must be provided for by him into whose hands he falls. . . . The wounded of both parties should be treated the same."[65]

Who is the Enemy?

The last ground of obligations to our enemy—their humanity— is also evident in Lieber's treatment of what he takes to be the fundamental question in the laws of war: *who is the enemy?* "Properly speaking, the enemy is the hostile state, next represented for the belligerent in the hostile army, but also in all its citizens, from whom the means of carrying on the war are drawn, or who furnish them." In effect Lieber begins by making the state and everyone in it the enemy. Although the preceding quotation might seem to exclude citizens who are not able to work (e.g., elderly people), *Instructions* closes that loophole by declaring that the citizen or native of a hostile country is "an enemy, as one of the constituents of the hostile state or nation, and as such is subjected to the hardships of the war." But then Lieber makes some distinctions that effectively restrict the legitimate targets of direct attack among the enemy and that identify the different categories of the enemy toward whom the belligerent has different obligations. Although it is impossible finally to separate the grounds of obligations from the groups toward whom obligations are directed, I have done so for ana-

---

65 *Instructions*, #15, #16; Lieber, *Political Ethics*, Pt. 2, p. 659, *cf.* 658; "The Usages of War," New York *Times*, February 4, 1862, p. 3. It is also cruel to torture for information. See New York *Times*, January 13, 1863. In discussing slavery, Lieber contends that Negro slaves coming into Union lines must be treated as free men, for the only question in determining humanity is whether an individual belongs to "a class of beings who, in their normal state, speak." Lieber to Sumner, December 19, 1861.

lytic purposes. Of the two main strands of the laws of war, one
concentrating on war casualties and noncombatants and the
other concentrating on military operations and methods of warfare, including weapons, Lieber in principle emphasized the
former.[66]

After making everyone in the hostile country subject to the
hardships of war, *Instructions* distinguishes "the private individual belonging to a hostile country and the hostile country
itself, with its men in arms."[67] The private, unarmed, inoffensive, harmless citizen, the noncombatant, is spared "in person,
property and honor as much as the exigencies of war will admit." Lieber's distinction between combatant and noncombatant has nothing to do with a person's subjective guilt or innocence, but with his objective position, impeding or obstruct-
ing the opposing belligerent in his war aims. Thus, Lieber
frequently uses the adjectives *harmless* or *inoffensive* to describe such persons.

Despite his emphasis on categories of persons who receive
various degrees of protection from the laws of war, Lieber did
not elaborate the category of the noncombatant, which, instead,
is residual in his interpretation. Furthermore, although he insisted upon the protection of noncombatants, he added very
little to the extension of their protection over against the exigencies of war and failed to indicate how much risk combatants

66 *Political Ethics*, Pt. 2, p. 658; *Instructions*, #21; "War. Who is the *enemy*?
Fundamental Question treated philosoph. by myself Pol Ethics last Chapter
vol II" (Note in "Notes and Clippings Assembled by Lieber as Working Material on the Law of War, 1840–1869," Lieber Papers). See Sydney D. Bailey,
Prohibitions and Restraints in War (London: Oxford University Press, 1972),
esp. Chap. 3. A clear example of the tension in Lieber's thought about the
"enemy" can be seen in the first printed draft of the section "Insurrection-
Civil War-Rebellion," which was written after *A Code* and then drastically
reduced for the final version of *Instructions*. First, Lieber wrote that the word
enemy in the law of nations means "the sovereign government, at war with
another sovereign, and those armed persons in the service of a sovereign, who
fight against others." But then he divided "all enemies in regular war" into
two general classes, combatants and noncombatants or unarmed citizens.
Only the latter was retained in *Instructions* #155, and it is consistent with
#21.
67 *Instructions*, #22.

should take in order to protect enemy noncombatants. For example, General Orders No. 100 allows the starvation of unarmed belligerents, permits a besieger to send expelled noncombatants back into a besieged place to hasten surrender (although this is an extreme measure), and holds that the common law of war does not require that a bombardment be announced so that the noncombatants may be removed although such an announcement is recommended "whenever admissible." Lieber's analysis also suggests but does not develop important distinctions between direct and indirect, and avoidable and unavoidable destruction. "Military necessity admits of all direct destruction of life or limb of *armed* enemies, and of other persons whose destruction is incidentally *unavoidable* in the armed contests of the war."[68] Much of his discussion of cases concerns the treatment of different types of belligerents and especially the protection that they should receive when they are captured. Not everyone who is a legitimate target for direct attack is also qualified for the privileges of prisoners of war. Some belligerents do not benefit from the protection of the laws of war upon capture; often they are left unprotected in part because they concealed the fact that they were legitimate targets by assuming the appearance of civilians.

The question of belligerents "wholly unprotected by the Law of War" ("unprivileged belligerents" in Richard Baxter's phrase) emerged with special urgency when the Confederates claimed that their men who went within Union lines in civilian clothing to attack troops and destroy property were entitled to be treated as prisoners of war instead of being executed as spies or marauders. They even threatened to retaliate by executing Union prisoners of war. Emphasizing that this was "substantially a new topic in the law of war," Lieber tried to draw several distinctions between the enemy combatants, offering protection to regular soldiers, partisans, and participants in risings *en masse* and denying it to guerrillas generally, war-rebels, con-

---

68   *Ibid.*, #17–19, #15. Lieber's second draft of the code did not stress these distinctions: "Martial Necessity allows of all destruction and obstruction, requisite for the speedy obtaining of the end of the war, short of cruelty" (p. 2).

spirators, spies, brigands, armed prowlers, freebooters, and those, including regular soldiers, who violate the laws of war.[69]

As these lists suggest, among the variables that determine whether particular individuals and groups should be treated as prisoners of war are their acts (whether they violate the laws of war that prohibit the infliction of unnecessary suffering, the use of poison, the use of an enemy's emblem of nationality or uniform in battle, the refusal to give quarter, and other such acts); their authorization (whether they are self-constituted and unorganized); their location (whether they are in occupied territory); and their dress (whether they are in civilian clothing). Certain acts in violation of the laws of war will cancel their protection, and because conducting an unauthorized, purely private war for personal gain is criminal, the perpetrators will not be treated as public enemies. Since the size of the group in question relates to its power and is usually correlated with organization, discipline, and the ability to fight openly and take prisoners, it may decisively affect the protection that its members will receive. When the group is large, it is more likely to receive protection. Regarding the paper on *Guerrilla Parties*, Lieber wrote to Halleck, "As jurist, you will not expect much; for you know that such persons . . . have always been treated as *brigands* whenever the captor felt he had the power and did not fear a greater evil to result from retaliation." According to the laws of war, guerrillas are not "public enemies" and may be treated as brigands, although "prudential mercy" may lead to different results in particular cases. A government cannot extend important privileges, such as acceptance as prisoners of war, to guerrillas because they cannot reciprocate. In most cases, they cannot take prisoners of war. But reciprocity is "the first basis on which all mitigations of modern war are based."[70]

69   See Halleck to Lieber, August 6, 1862, official request, reprinted in Lieber, *Guerrilla Parties*, 5; Richard Baxter, "So-Called 'Unprivileged Belligerency': Spies, Guerrillas, and Saboteurs," *British Year Book of International Law*, XXVIII (1951), 323–45.
70   Lieber to Halleck, August 9, 1862; Lieber, *Guerrilla Parties*, 20, and *Instructions*, #82, *et passim*; Lieber, notebook with manuscript of *Guerrilla Parties*, Lieber Papers.

At stake is not merely size, power, the concomitant threat of retaliatory measures, and the impossibility of reciprocation, but also the fact that guerrilla parties, war-rebels, and many of the other unprivileged combatants interfere "with the mitigation of the severity of war, which it is one of the noblest objects of the modern law of war to obtain." War-rebels rise against the army of the occupied country and, like spies, are especially dangerous because they make "hostile use of the protection which, by the modern law of war, the victor extends to the persons and property of the conquered." War-rebels are to be distinguished from risings *en masse* in unoccupied territories, and guerrilla parties are to be distinguished from partisans who are "armed and wearing the uniform of their army" though detached from the main body to make inroads into the enemy's territory. Participants in such risings *en masse* and partisans are accepted as prisoners of war. Both the necessities of fighting a war and the principle of protecting noncombatants require severe measures against certain belligerents such as "armed prowlers."[71]

Among the "unprivileged belligerents" are spies, and many of the most urgent cases on which Lieber's opinion was requested involved the treatment of captured spies. According to the laws of war, what may be done with a spy and who is to be counted as a spy? Discussing authorities on spies in international law, Lieber insisted that General Orders No. 100 was the most significant. "Upon my word I know nothing so full as Old Hundred, or rather, I know that no where the *spy* is treated of so plainly." According to Old Hundred, a spy may be put to death. In *A Code*, Lieber had written that "the spy *is punished* with death," but the revision in the *Instructions* altered this statement to "The spy *is punishable* with death."[72] In the evolution of the code, there are numerous similar changes, indicating different emphases in the understanding of the relation be-

71   Lieber, *Guerrilla Parties*, 13–14; *Instructions*, #81, #84, #85.
72   Lieber to Halleck, February 4, 1865; *Instructions*, #88. Lieber had received a request from Major John A. Bolles, judge advocate, for information about the law of war on spies; see Lieber to Bolles, February 28, 1865, which contains a long discussion of disguise and spying related to the case of John Beall.

tween what is required and what is permitted and between practice and prescription.

But why does the law of war permit belligerents to execute spies? Many writers on international law, including Emmerich de Vattel and General Halleck, had argued that capital punishment is permitted because spying is a crime, a violation of the laws of war. From this standpoint, the spy may be executed even if he is captured after having completed his mission and resumed his normal military role. But this position cannot easily deal with the realities of war in which both sides use spies even as they execute enemy spies. Thus, Vattel stressed the inconsistency of putting a man to death for spying and yet simultaneously and avowedly employing spies.[73] Holding that there is no more inconsistency in the treatment of spies than in war generally, Lieber contended that spying is not a crime against the laws of war, which, at least in this instance, are not a criminal or penal code. Death for the spy is not a punishment but a penalty. This point is critical, for it relates to the spy's susceptibility to later retribution. Number 104 of the *Instructions* indicates that a spy who has completed his mission and rejoined his own army must be treated as a prisoner of war if he is later captured, unless he is guilty of other crimes. Of course, a spy against his own country is a criminal and remains a spy subject to punishment under his country's laws, but while a murderer remains a murderer, a "military spy, serving against a hostile government, ceases to be a spy the moment he has done with his work and he has plainly escaped."[74] But if the spy is caught in the act or before his return, he may justifiably be put to death in self-defense (although it is not clear why imprisonment would not be sufficient) and for deterrence. According to Lie-

73 Emmerich de Vattel, *Law of Nations*, trans. from the French (Philadelphia: T. & J. W. Johnson, 1855); Halleck, *International Law*, 400–410.

74 In his revision of *A Code*, Lieber prefaced the section that became #104 in *Instructions* with an explanation that was deleted by the board: "Yet the law of war is not a penal law." Without this explanation, Lieber's use of the language of punishment, for which he could find no substitute, could be misconstrued. See Lieber to Halleck, October 3, 1863, in which he offered what he calls "my reasons" for this rule.

ber, "the avoiding of *danger* is one of the chief elements in met-
ing out preventive measures, in the Law of War." As he wrote
on another occasion, "the Law of War is not a Penal or Criminal
Law. You do not *punish* a spy; you kill him to repress his
trade."[75] The spy's activity within and behind enemy lines in
civilian dress clearly makes "hostile use" of the protection ac-
corded civilians, and upon capture the spy cannot claim protection as a civilian or as a prisoner of war. The difficulty of
guarding against spies and the danger that they pose are the
fundamental reasons for the penalty of death, as Number 101 of
the *Instructions* indicates. "While deception in war is admitted
as a just and necessary means of hostility, and is consistent with
honorable warfare, the common law of war allows even capital
punishment for clandestine or treacherous attempts to injure
an enemy, because they are so dangerous, and it is so difficult
to guard against them."[76] Spying is not perfidy in part because
it does not violate the laws of war, but the realities of war permit severe penalties to deter such activity.

In 1863 when the Confederates executed Spencer Kellogg on
the charge that he had been a spy prior to his capture as a member of the Union forces, General Halleck asked for Lieber's and
Horace Binney's opinions about the adequacy of *Instructions*
Number 104 as a statement of international law so that the government could consider retaliation for this unjustified execution. Lieber offered his "reasons" for the rule that a person cannot be executed for his past spying if he has returned to his own

---

75   Lieber to Halleck, December 17, 1864, October 3, 1863. Even some "unprivileged belligerents" such as spies may have the privilege of trials in some
circumstances, however. Lieber to Halleck, March 18, 1865. Indeed, the common practice in the Civil War was to grant trials to spies, and sometimes spies
were not hanged but imprisoned. According to Lieber, the Union army's "de-
viations from the common usages of war" were "toward a milder course"
even when they were not wise. Lieber to B. J. Lossing, August 21, 1862, Library of Congress.

76   Lieber did not like this language; he wrote Halleck (May 20, 1863): " 'So
dangerous' and 'so difficult' are not dignified expressions in a code. I avoid
them even in letters. Whose are they? I have no doubt they merely slipt in."
His own words were "on account of their great danger and the difficulty to
guard against them." See Lieber's addition to *A Code*, Lieber Papers.

forces, and Binney supported Number 104, but retaliation was
not offered because Kellogg had also been convicted of being a
deserter from the Confederate army, in which he had enlisted
during his espionage.[77]

Another difficult case involved Captain John B. Castleman
of the Confederate army, who had escaped to Canada and was
attempting to return to his command in citizen's clothing and
under an assumed name when he was captured in Indiana. According to *Instructions* Number 83, he could be treated as a spy,
although Confederate officials insisted that there was no difference between his case and that of Union prisoners of war in
Confederate camps who had used disguises to facilitate their
escape. If the latter were still entitled to prisoner-of-war protections, the former should also be treated as a prisoner of war.
Holding that it was natural for an escaped soldier to use civilian
clothing, General Grant concurred that Castleman should not
be treated as a spy. Halleck vehemently disagreed with Grant.
He did not contest the principle that a prisoner of war may use
civilian disguise to try to escape, but he insisted that it did not
apply to this case, for Castleman "*came* within our lines from a
foreign country *in the disguise of a citizen*." Halleck tried to
strengthen his hand by soliciting Lieber's opinion, which
agreed "fully" with Halleck's although it also acknowledged
that expediency should determine whether death should be the
penalty in this case; the secretary of war adopted their opinion.
In 1865 Castleman was released on the condition that he leave
the country and never return.[78]

---

77   See Halleck to Lieber, September 30, 1863, and Halleck to Binney, October 1, 1863; both letters are printed in *The War of the Rebellion: A Compila-
tion of the Official Records of the Union and Confederate Armies* (130 vols.;
Washington, D.C.: Government Printing Office, 1894–1927), Ser. I, Vol. VI, pp.
327–28, 332 (hereinafter cited as *Official Records*), which also has information about this case. See also Lieber to Halleck, October 3 (two letters), 6, 7,
12, 15, 1863, Halleck to Lieber, October 1, 4, 7, 13, 24, 1863, and *Instructions*,
#48.

78   Halleck to Lieber, December 14, 1864 (with copies of Robert Ould's letter
and Grant's and Halleck's endorsements), Lieber to Halleck, December 17,
1864, Halleck to Lieber, December 19, 25, 1864; Lieber to Bolles, February 28,
1865. See *Official Records*, Ser. II, Vol. VIII, pp. 704–705.

For spies, as for so many other groups of the enemy, their treatment in part hinges upon their clothing although some interpreters have thought it strange that rights in war should hinge upon such matters. One reason for the emphasis on clothing, however, is connected with trust and confidence that are so important in Lieber's interpretation of the laws of war. Generally the combatant and noncombatant can be distinguished by clothing, but the spy and guerrilla depend on their disguise as protected civilians. For treatment of soldiers or a rising *en masse*, the presence or absence of a uniform is not critical; treatment depends on "whether the absence of the uniform is used for the purpose of concealment or disguise." But an individual soldier found within or behind the lines of the enemy in civilian dress or in the uniform of the enemy is presumed to be a spy "unless very positive and direct proof to the contrary can be adduced."[79]

Surgeons and other medical personnel may be treated as prisoners of war although in a sense they are not *hors de combat* but *hors de guerre*. They and chaplains "are not prisoners of war, unless the commander has reasons to retain them."[80] Even if they may be made prisoners of war, they should not be aimed at directly, whatever unavoidable harm may befall them. Instead of spelling out the reasons for exempting medical personnel and chaplains, Lieber used rhetorical questions: medical personnel "are ministering angels bringing comfort to the wounded, and should not be shot any more than a chaplain, and who would fire upon a chaplain?"[81] But it is easy to reconstruct his reasons. Just as the soldier's humanity is not exhausted in his role, so activities that serve that humanity do not directly aid the war effort as their primary purpose. What is necessary for life is necessary for fighting, but Lieber seeks a more direct connection between the service and the war than

79   Lieber, *Guerrilla Parties*, 16; See Lieber to Bolles, February 28, 1865; *Instructions*, #83.
80   Lieber to Halleck, June 18, 1864; *Instructions*, #53. Contrast note "Military," August, 1861: "Surgeons not to be subject to *capture*. Even most laws against duelling make a difference, at least on continent of Europe."
81   "The Usages of War," New York *Times*, February 4, 1862, p. 3.

medical and religious assistance. Surgeons "do not impede my way." Nor do sutlers, editors, reporters, or contractors as citizens accompanying an army who may also be made prisoners of war.[82]

But which persons in the supporting services can be considered both as legitimate targets of attack and as entitled to prisoner-of-war status? To the categories soldiers and risings *en masse*, *Instructions* adds "all those who are attached to the army for its efficiency and promote directly the object of the war, except such as are hereinafter provided for." In *A Code*, Lieber had included "such as officers of the commissariat or teamsters" after the "object of the war." The revision appears to include them in the sense that they are not later "provided for" under some separate heading.[83]

---

82   Lieber, *Political Ethics*, Pt. 2, p. 659; *Instructions* #50. *A Code* appeared to hold that sutlers "are" prisoners of war, whereas *Instructions* #50 indicates that they "may be made prisoners of war." Similar important changes are evident elsewhere in the different versions of the code. I have generally omitted Lieber's rules and principles relating to property. He was influenced greatly by Locke. See Lieber, *Essays on Labour and Property* (New York: Harper's, 1854), and Lieber to Sumner, September 15, 1841. But his discussion of contraband of war illuminates his discussions of different classes of the enemy: "*contraband of war* is everything, animate or inanimate, deemed at the time necessary for commission of acts of hostility between belligerents on sea or land, or for the direct pursuit of the war in general . . . [but] does not consist in material of universal sustenance or of common comfort and necessity, although they are especially used, and in exceptionally large quantities in war,—nor in those materials which are used for the alleviation of bodily harm and suffering inflicted by war." He excludes flour, beef, leather, boots and shoes, shirts, cotton, drugs, hospital furniture, surgical instruments, ambulances for use in battle, and disinfecting materials from contraband. Lieber to Fish, October 8, 1870, in Perry (ed.), *Lieber*, 399–400. He also drew a distinction between materials that are "exclusively or almost exclusively used for that purpose." Gunpowder and arms fall under the first category, and saltpeter under the second. Both may be considered contraband of war. Lieber, "On the Sale of Arms," *Miscellaneous Writings*, II, 318.

83   *Instructions*, #49. Lieber thought that teamsters are "actively helping the war which is not the case with surgeons." Comment in a notebook listing several headings for the laws of war, "Notes . . . on the Law of War, 1840–1869," Lieber Papers. He had considerable difficulty in determining where to

An interesting special case is that of the sentinel. According to *Instructions* Number 69, "Outposts, sentinels, or pickets are not to be fired upon, except to drive them in, or when a positive order, special or general, has been issued to that effect." Richard Baxter has noted that it is "difficult to follow Lieber's reasoning for this provision." However, its rationale is implicit in its context (clearer in *A Code* than in the *Instructions*), which stresses the avoidance of all unnecessary destruction of life since killing the enemy is not the object of modern wars. Lieber insists elsewhere that "firing upon a single man for no other purpose than killing him is murder." An army may warn the other side to keep sentinels away from a certain place and then fire if the warning is not heeded. "This is right, chivalrous and Christian."[84]

Lieber's treatment of the detached soldier has some affinities with discussions of the sleeping soldier. Is the soldier who is asleep or engaged in some other nonmilitary activity really an obstacle to be removed? If one draws a distinction between being "engaged in an attempt" to obstruct rather than "attempting" to obstruct, then even when the soldier is asleep he is "engaged in the attempt" to obstruct although he is not "attempting" anything, for the former is not full-time work.[85] Nevertheless, Lieber generally viewed the sentinel as detached from other men, with no specific military mission that requires his being rendered "harmless" by being killed. Although he may try to kill one's comrades the next day, or in the next battle, he is not now a threat. Given the distinction between "engaged in the attempt" and "attempting," no requirement of justice, rooted in

---

place sutlers, private citizens who follow an army to sell provisions to the soldiers. In the first two drafts of the code (one consisting of notes and the other of the first manuscript), he put *sutlers* after *teamsters*; the word was followed by a question mark in the first draft and enclosed in parentheses in the second draft.

84 Baxter, "The First Modern Codification of the Law of War" (May, 1963), 242. Lieber, "Law and Usages of War," and summary in the New York *Times*, February 4, 1862.

85 See Jeffrie G. Murphy, "The Killing of the Innocent," *Monist*, LVII (October, 1973), 532.

the temporary noncombatant status of the sentinel, dictates restraint. But where killing is not related to military ends and is
not necessary, it is murder.

Weapons and Methods of Warfare

By what means and weapons may one belligerent attack the
combatants of another belligerent? Most of Lieber's attention in
the *Instructions* and elsewhere was devoted to the different
classes of enemy and their privileges and obligations, and what
he had to say about means and weapons was quite limited, un-
developed, and inconsistent. Predisposed to permit all means
and weapons of direct attack, he did recognize some limits.

His starting point, chronologically and logically, was the
conviction that since short wars are better for humanity, wars
should be fought intensely, vigorously and with all arms, advantages, and means of destruction—a position defended by
Bynkershoek on whom Lieber drew, but rejected by Vattel
whom Lieber criticized as "Father namby pamby." Lieber's dependence on Bynkershoek can be seen in his early contention
that the poisoning of wells does not violate the laws of war. But
between the writing of *Political Ethics* in the late 1830s and
Instructions, Lieber decided that "the use of poison in any way"
is a violation of the laws of war, not warranted even by military
necessity. "The use of poison in any manner, be it to poison
wells, or food, or arms, is wholly excluded from modern warfare. He that uses it puts himself out of the pale of the law and
usages of war." An historical allusion that offered both an example and a motivating reason appeared in *A Code* but was
omitted from the final *Instructions*, possibly by the board.
"Thousands of years ago it was held that no one who fears a
supreme avenger of wrong, will poison his arrow."[86]

86 Cornelius van Bynkershoek, *A Treatise on the Law of War*, trans. Peter
Stephen du Ponceau (Philadelphia: Farrand and Nicholas, 1810), 2. Lieber to
Halleck, October 3, 1863; *A Code*, #37. Lieber followed Bynkershoek more

This prohibition may have been a concession to the dominant opinion among international lawyers, for Lieber did not seem to recognize the principle back of it when he faced similar cases. Having read about the Confederate army's use of explosive traps in abandoned redoubts, he inquired of Halleck: "Suppose it true—what does the *jurist* think of the lawfulness of the thing? The soldier within me revolts at the thing. It seems so cowardly. The jurist within me cannot find arguments to declare it unlawful. National battles are no Quixotic tournaments. Nothing more common in sieges than undermining and blowing up the enemy, or pitfalls, as you, the engineer, know full well. I should like to know what you think about it, not what you feel. I know you feel as I do." Halleck replied that explosive traps in abandoned redoubts "are of the same class as poisoning springs, provisions, & c." In his *International Law* he had stressed the universal condemnation of the use of poisoned weapons and the practice of poisoning wells, springs, waters, and any kind of food, arguing that "by poisoning waters and food, we may destroy innocent persons, and non-combatants."[87] The discrimination of such modes of warfare cannot be ensured; the agents lose control over them, creating the possibility that "harmless" persons will be killed. Lieber, on the other hand, clearly thought of them as independent means or weapons without grasping their relation to the distinction between classes of the enemy. He later appeared to condemn the "land infernal machines" used at Yorktown, but without giving his reasons, and he condemned the Confederate proposal to engage in germ warfare by spreading yellow fever, smallpox, and pestilence in the United States.[88]

---

closely on weapons and means of direct attack than on the repudiation of the distinctions between classes of the enemy, for Bynkershoek "defended . . . the killing of common prisoners of war." Lieber, *Guerrilla Parties*, 16; Lieber, *Political Ethics*, Pt. 2, p. 66.

87   Lieber to Halleck, August 24, 1863, Halleck to Lieber, August 26, 1863; Halleck, *International Law*, 399–400.

88   Lieber, "On the Sale of Arms," *Miscellaneous Writings*, II, 320. Bluntschli connected the prohibition of germ warfare to the rule against the use of poi-

The main reason for prohibiting the practice of poisoning water and food is not, of course, operative in the prohibition of poisoned weapons, which rests instead on the principle that a belligerent should not act cruelly or inflict unnecessary suffering. Although Lieber discussed this principle in *Political Ethics*, he did not use it to condemn poisoned weapons. In *Instructions*, however, the paragraph that prohibits the use of poison in any manner is followed by a paragraph that implicitly invokes this principle: "Whoever intentionally inflicts additional wounds on an enemy already wholly disabled, or kills such an enemy, or who orders or encourages soldiers to do so, shall suffer death, if duly convicted, whether he belongs to the army of the United States, or is an enemy captured after having committed his misdeed."[89] Since weapons or arms without poison will presumably "disable" the enemy combatant and render him harmless, the use of poison inflicts additional or unnecessary suffering. The object is to remove the enemy as an impediment and opponent, in short, to place him *hors de combat*, not to kill him. Lieber did not, however, connect these points (which he affirmed throughout his writings) to the use of poison.

In notes and correspondence, Lieber mentioned some weapons of war that others had rejected because of unnecessary suffering, but he did not condemn such weapons as incendiary balls, "Greek Fire," and explosive bullets that scatter lead in the body. He clearly and emphatically stated his general

---

son, and although Lieber did not indicate its rationale, he probably used the same one. See Bluntschli, *Das moderne Kriegsrecht*, 11, #47. Lieber asked Halleck (letter, November 17, 1865) to treat in his abridged *International Law* what the law of war allows and to examine in some detail what "the rebels have thought they had liberty of perpetrating against us, such as land infernal machines, setting clandestinely cities on fire, depriving un-besieged places of water, assassination. Not only are persons guilty of such crimes, or attempts, treated as outlaws, but no honourable soldier will resort to such things." Brig. Gen. William F. Barry, Inspector of Artillery, U.S. Army, discussed these "infernal machines" in a letter to Brig. Gen. G. W. Cullum who wanted the information for Lieber. *Official Records*, Ser. I, vol. XI, part 1, pp. 349–50.
89 *Instructions*, #70, #71; *wholly* was probably added to this paragraph by the board; it does not appear in any of Lieber's drafts or revisions.

principle in a note: "The modern law of war allows of all weapons and other means of direct destruction and obstruction. It excludes no projectile on account of the certainty of its aim, the comprehensive destruction it causes, the character of the wounds it produces, or the mode by which it produces instant death without preceding wounds [stink pots]; but it discards the use of poison in any manner."[90] He thus excluded poisoned weapons, probably on grounds of unnecessary suffering, but he did not apply this principle to any other weapons. Furthermore, it is possible that some weapons cannot be employed in such a way as to discriminate between combatants and noncombatants, for example, because of uncertainty of aim. Starting with the distinction between classes of persons, theorists might find it necessary to reject some weapons. Lieber's inclination to start with and to emphasize the distinction between classes of persons was sound, even though he failed to draw out all its implications. Bluntschli, who followed Lieber's code, and various laws of The Hague attempted to prohibit certain weapons, but this strand of the laws of war has been less efficacious than the protection of certain classes of persons.[91]

Lieber also included some other restrictions on the means and methods of conducting war; torture even to gain informa-

90 "Remarks on 'Incendiary Balls' and 'Rifle Bombs' used by Confederate Army," with several newspaper clippings, note in "Addenda and Notes to Be Included in Lieber's Code . . . ," 1863, both in Lieber Papers. General McClellan had remarked in 1861 that "such means of destruction [as Greek Fire] are hardly within the category of those recognized in civilized warfare." *Official Records*, Ser. III, vol. I, p. 606. On Greek Fire, see "Greek Fire, and Other Inflammables," *United States Service Magazine*, I (January, 1864), 50–55.
91 Under the heading of "Prohibited Means," Bluntschli's code has ten paragraphs, including a few matters, such as assassination and the use of poison, that Lieber's code also covers but adding prohibitions of weapons that cause unnecessary suffering, such as arrows or darts with barbs, chopped lead, and glass fragments. There are only three references to the American *Instructions* in these ten paragraphs. See Bluntschli, *Das moderne Kriegsrecht*, 11–12. The St. Petersburg Declaration of 1868 prohibited the use of explosive projectiles weighing less than fourteen ounces; I have not seen any of Lieber's comments on this declaration.

tion, enslavement, perfidy, and assassination are all prohibited. And *Instructions* rejects the "wanton devastation of a district." In *A Code*, Lieber had prohibited devastation "for the sake of creating depopulated districts," giving the theological rationale, "since it is the will of our Maker that in the normal state the land shall be tilled and peopled." Because it rejects devastation for this specific end, *A Code* is stronger than the *Instructions*, which only excludes "wanton devastation," i.e., devastation without reason. By contrast, *A Code* appeals to the end of peace. Since the ultimate object of war is peace, and since war is only a temporary interruption of the normal state of affairs, it is not legitimate permanently to sacrifice the normal for the exceptional and transient state. This principle also rules out the Confederate proposal to invade Pennsylvania and set the coal fields on fire, leaving the "bowels of that state in inextinguishable flames for centuries."[92]

But Lieber insisted that this principle did not forbid "stone fleets." In the early years of the Civil War, the Federal navy sank some small sailing vessels loaded with stones to close the Charleston harbor. Some English and French commentators expressed their outrage over these "stone fleets," contending that the ports belong to all mankind for commerce and refuge. Noting that all destruction in war is a loss to all mankind up to a point, Lieber conceded that these "stone fleets" were tragic but stressed that all war is tragic. For him, there were only two questions from the standpoint of the laws of war. "Is the destruction and obstruction greater than necessary; will it endure after the military necessity has ceased?" Drawing upon Bache's views about their short-term effects, Lieber held that the "stone fleets" passed both tests and that they became an issue only because they were novel and so dramatically symbolized the

---

92 *Instructions*, #16; *A Code*, #7. Lieber's revision of *A Code* indicates that Halleck suggested that *permanently* be added before *depopulated districts*. Lieber's marginal note in his revision indicates the historical case that prompted this rule: "I had Louis XIV here in mind." He wanted to lay to waste the entire Palatinate to create a desert between France and Germany. See "Destruction and Obstruction Characterize War."

general destruction of war. In fact, the "stone fleets" failed to close the harbor to blockade runners; when the ships' timbers were destroyed by marine worms, the stones sank in the mud. But if they had been successful, Lieber claimed, their effects would not have persisted so long as to violate his second test.[93]

Section IX of *Instructions* consists of one paragraph, which condemns assassination as a method or means of warfare. Although the rationale is not given in the code, it can be inferred from other Lieber writings. As a boy, Lieber had taken an oath to try to assassinate Napoleon on the grounds that it would prevent much suffering, and he was later imprisoned because the authorities thought that he had been involved in the plot to assassinate August von Kotzebue, a reactionary playwright. But in *Political Ethics*, he repudiated assassination as a violation of the principle of honor and the principle that a harmless enemy should not be killed. In the 1840s, in a discussion of Hugo Grotius' views, Lieber stressed that if the chief of the enemy state represents what is hostile in that state he also represents what is not hostile, e.g., women, children, and private property. Thus, assassination would not be appropriate. Such an argument, of course, would apply only to the head of state, not to generals and others. But any assassination would have harmful effects that would "greatly impede the ultimate end of war— *quod est Pax*."[94]

Although Lieber did not spell out why assassination would probably undermine the possibility of peace, the main reason appears to be the destruction of trust and confidence. General

93 "Destruction and Obstruction Characterize War"; Lieber, "Law and Usages of War," December 17, 1861. Mr. Bache, whose opinion on the effects of the "stone fleets" was important for Lieber's judgment, was probably Alexander Dallas Bache, head of the Coast Survey, who frequently corresponded with Lieber, and who, after reading *A Code*, asked Lieber in a letter (February 25, 1863) whether it would be legitimate to destroy lighthouses and beacons. Lieber wrote on the letter, "Of course all destruction and obstruction is allowed." See also, "The Stone Fleets," in Mark Mayo Boatner III, *The Civil War Dictionary* (New York: David McKay, 1959), 801.

94 *Instructions*, #148; Lieber, *Political Ethics*, Pt. 2, p. 659; "Note on the Law of War," January, 1841, which discusses Grotius.

Halleck identified assassination with "treacherously taking the life of an enemy." When a small group sneaks to an enemy general's headquarters in the night in order to kill him, "it is the disguise and treachery which gives to the deed the character of murder or assassination." Not only is it wrong to commit assassination, but it is wrong to declare an individual an outlaw in order to encourage his assassination or to take advantage of someone's offer to commit such an act.[95]

The prohibition of torture follows from the prohibition of cruelty. Even torture to extract confessions or important secrets is forbidden. It is cruel because it is the infliction of "pain for the sake of pain." It is different from wounding or killing in combat because it is designed to make a harmless captive suffer and feel pain. Of course, its intention may be to gain important and perhaps even indispensable information for a military operation. But since the immediate object is to inflict pain (and not to incapacitate as in combat), even the ultimate object of valuable information is not enough to remove it from the category of cruelty.[96]

Necessity and Retaliation

The relations between the rules and principles of *jus in bello* and necessity and retaliation are intricate and perhaps render impossible any attempt at a systematic and coherent code of the laws of war. James A. Seddon, secretary of war for the Confederacy, vehemently criticized General Orders No. 100 for embodying "two contradictory and opposed systems of what are designated as instructions, and what are selected as established rules and usages of war." "A military commander under this code," Seddon complained, "may pursue a line of conduct in accordance with principles of justice, faith, and honor, or he may justify conduct correspondent with the warfare of the bar-

95   Halleck, *International Law*, 400–401.
96   *Instructions*, #16, #80; Lieber, "Law and Usages of War," December 17, 1861.

barous hordes who overran the Roman Empire."[97] He praised the principles and rules of restraint, while condemning the practices justified by military necessity.

The ambiguities of the appeal to necessity are evident in Number 14 of the *Instructions*, which defines military necessity as "the necessity of those measures which are indispensable for securing the ends of the war, and which are lawful according to the modern law and usages of war." The meaning of the last clause is unclear. Are necessary acts lawful *because* they are indispensable? Or must they be both indispensable and consistent with the laws of war?

The code is an attempt to take account of both the realities of war and moral and legal restraints. Thus, some rules are formulated so that an independent appeal to necessity is superfluous; the rules already represent a balance of military necessity and other considerations. For example, "unnecessary . . . destruction of life is not lawful."[98]

In other instances, the rules incorporate exceptions based on necessity. For example, commanders are urged to announce intentions to bombard a place so that noncombatants can be removed, but because "surprise may be a necessity," a failure to make this announcement is not a violation of the laws of war. The unarmed citizen is "to be spared in person, property, and honor as much as the exigencies of war will admit," and to be "as little disturbed in his private relations as the commander of the hostile troops can afford to grant in the overruling demands of a vigorous war." Protection is the rule; "privation and disturbance of private relations are the exceptions," warranted by military necessity. Strictly private property is acknowledged and protected, and it "can be seized only by way of military necessity, for the support or other benefit of the army of the United States." Although the refusal to give quarter is generally against the law of war, "a commander is permitted to direct his troops to give no quarter in great straits, when his own salva-

97   James A. Seddon to Ould, June 24, 1863, in *Official Records*, Ser. II, Vol. VI, pp. 41–47.
98   *Instructions*, #68.

tion makes it *impossible* to cumber himself with prisoners." An honorable belligerent is guided by signals of protection on hospitals "as much as the contingencies and the necessities of the fight will permit."[99] Thus, numerous statements of *jus in bello* in the *Instructions* already incorporate the necessity to justify conduct different from the general rule.

A different and more significant question is whether rules without exception clauses can be overridden by the imperatives of necessity. The code suggests an affirmative answer: "To save the country is paramount to all other considerations." Yet Number 16 holds that some means can never be necessary or lawful. Military necessity cannot justify cruelty, torture, the use of poison, wanton devastation of a district, and perfidy. Wanton destruction of art is also excluded. The prohibition of assassination elsewhere in the code appears to be absolute, but it is not specifically excluded from those acts that can be justified by military necessity, although it probably comes under the final category, "any act of hostility which makes the return to peace unnecessarily difficult." By definition, cruelty ("the infliction of suffering for the sake of suffering or for revenge") and wanton devastation (that is, devastation without reason) are excluded. They can never be "necessary," and acts that appear to fall under these descriptions are not cruel or wanton if they are "necessary." Much suffering and devastation can be justified as important for the war effort, especially if the criteria of necessity are nowhere defined. Indeed, necessity can

99 *Instructions*, #19, #22, #23, #25, #38, #60, #116; *A Code* allowed a broader interpretation of military necessity in the seizure of private property. Property could be seized "for the support or other benefit of the army *or of the United States.*" *A Code*, #20, my italics. Contrast Halleck's view of prisoners in *International Law*, 439–40. "The extreme case . . . can seldom, if ever, happen; for a general can almost always find some means of disposing of, or securing, his prisoners of war, short of deliberately putting them to death. . . . in the present day, the conduct of any general who should deliberately put his prisoners to death, would be declared infamous, and no possible excuse would remove the stain from his character." Morris Greenspan summarizes the current law of war in his *Soldier's Guide to the Laws of War* (Washington, D.C.: Public Affairs Press, 1969), 23. According to Greenspan, prisoners may not be killed, "even in cases of extreme necessity."

simply become another term for military advantage, for cutting losses, for refusing to take certain risks of losing a battle or the war. Regarding the taking of private property on grounds of military necessity, Lieber observed that "a distinct line can no more be drawn here than on any other practical application of principle." As Lieber responded to the question of whether a victorious general or sea captain is obliged to cease firing the moment a flag of surrender is raised, "these are delicate points; but this does not prove that a dry formula in so many words can settle it. Humanity, a keen feeling of honor must guide; this is vague, but is the application of any principle in high spheres of morality, absolute and not delicate?"[100] In some matters such as perfidy, these difficulties are compounded by the vagueness of the key terms.

As I have already shown, perfidy and treachery are absolutely prohibited, because trust and confidence keep war from degenerating into an internecine conflict and make peace possible. In A Code, which was circulated for criticism, Lieber did not explicitly exclude perfidy from the methods of warfare that can be justified by military necessity. General Halleck suggested that it be distinguished from deception and then excluded. Military necessity "admits of deception, but disclaims acts of perfidy."[101] Even Bynkershoek, the defender of permissive rules in war, excluded perfidy. But there is ambiguity in Lieber's discussion, however, about what counts as treachery or perfidy. Hence the principle may actually be more flexible in relation to military necessity than the code suggests.

While the use of poison, according to Instructions, cannot be "necessary," Lieber elsewhere wavered on this point. Of

100 Instructions, #5, #16, #148, #36; comment on clipping of July, 1863, in "Notes and Clippings Assembled by Lieber as Working Material on the Law of War, 1840–1869," Lieber Papers; note on "Law of War—Surrender. Striking the Flag," July 12, 1864, Eisenhower Library. In the second draft (first manuscript) of A Code, Lieber wrote, "Military necessity allows of all destruction and obstruction, requisite for the speedy obtaining of the end of the war, short of cruelty" (p. 2, my italics).
101 A Code, General Halleck's annotated copy, original in the Eisenhower Library, photostatic copy in the Huntington Library. See Instructions, #16. See also my thorough discussion of perfidy in "Grounds of Obligation."

course, since poisoned arms inflict unnecessary suffering on a combatant who could be disabled without the poison, they cannot be justified, but it might be necessary to poison wells. In his lecture "Law and Usages of War," December 17, 1861, he maintained "that where the question is to preserve the existence as a nation against a ruthless enemy, and when this great object could be really obtained by poisoning wells and by no other means, I cannot see why it would not be lawful to resort to it?" He adds, "Happily the question can arise but very rarely." Although Lieber defended this position only a year before he commenced work on *A Code* and *Instructions*, perhaps his lectures represent a transitional view. While he had earlier permitted the use of poison without any restrictions, he now justified it only under extreme conditions of necessity, and his later code absolutely prohibited it. Another interpretation, perhaps more accurate, is that this tension between the prohibition of the use of poison and military necessity is not even resolved within the *Instructions* despite its strong statement.[102]

If necessity is an uncertain but important qualification of the laws of war, retaliation is the "sternest feature of war." The laws of war impose obligations on both sides, regardless of the justice or injustice of their cause, but do these obligations endure even when the opposing belligerent refuses to respect the *jus in bello*? Some of the enemy lose their protection if they violate the laws of war, but are the obligations mutual and reciprocal in the sense that deliberate and systematic violations by one belligerent releases the other belligerent from them? While these obligations continue in force, necessity may permit the other belligerent to engage in retaliatory measures that would otherwise be illegal. The rationale is that "a belligerent should not be put at a disadvantage because the enemy breaks the rules," and the purpose of retaliation, or "protective retribution," is to secure compliance with the laws of war.[103] In retaliation, then, a belligerent engages in conduct that would ordinarily be illegal in order to stop the opponent's illegal conduct.

102   *Instructions*, #16.
103   *Ibid.*, #27, #28; Sidney D. Bailey, *Prohibitions and Restraints in War* (London: Oxford University Press, 1972), 54. Although Lieber used the term

The precise relation between retaliation and revenge is very important in Lieber's interpretation of the laws of war. "Revenge is passion, and ought never to enter the sphere of public action. Passion always detracts from power." Revenge shows that "a wrong has been felt as wrong not merely as injury." Yet retaliation is "a modified application of the elementary principle in the human soul—resentment of wrong. This principle, like all others, has been given by Providence for wise purposes, and like all others, works evils if it be not modified by equally important principles. All those principles which Providence has laid in our soul for the progress of civilization and for the existence of society, are, because elementary, dangerous if not reined in." Properly modified, this principle is one of the elements in most law: "an eye for an eye" and tit for tat.[104]

Resentment of wrong should be controlled by a procedure of reasoning and by other principles. First of course, there must be an antecedent violation of the laws of war and not merely revulsion about some conduct, but the evidence for such violations does not have to be sufficient to convince a jury. Second, the retaliation must be necessary; it is "the last resort of the law of war." It should, thus, be employed only after "an unsuccessful summons of the enemy to punish the evil-doers." Third, as "protective retribution," not revenge, retaliation must be judged for effectiveness and risk of escalation.[105]

retaliation, most interpreters use the term _reprisals_. J. M. Spaight contends that the "logical supplement to the golden rule which warns us that as we do, so shall we be done by, is the chief motive for the compliance of civilized states with the usages of war." _War Rights on Land_ (London: Macmillan, 1911), 3–4.
104 Lieber to Sumner, January 22, 1865, in Perry (ed.), _Lieber_, 355; "Law and Usages of War," December 17, 1861, and summary in New York _Times_, January 13, 1862, p. 8; note in "Notes and Clippings Assembled by Lieber as Working Material"; Lieber to Halleck, June 2, 1863. For a discussion of _lex talonis_ in Lieber's thought, see Wilson Smith, "Francis Lieber's Moral Philosophy," _Huntington Library Quarterly_, XVIII (August, 1955), 395–408, and Chap. V in Smith, _Professors and Public Ethics_.
105 Lieber to Halleck, August 24, 1863, February 25, 1865; _Instructions_, #28; Lieber to Halleck, April 9, 1864, January 7, 1863; Lieber to the editor of the New York _Times_, "Retaliation on Prisoners of War," December 26, 1864, p. 4; Lieber to Halleck, June 2, January 7, 1863. Both the first and second

Finally, retaliation "has its limits" not only in the principle of proportionality but also in other principles and rules that are more restrictive than an imitative tit for tat. Discussing the Fort Pillow massacre, Lieber insisted to Halleck that retaliation "must be limited both as to persons and as to manner." Yet his discussion of the limit regarding persons is not clear. He did not restrict retaliation to those who committed the deed, for retaliation is not "punishment for a crime committed by the victim; it is a measure of defence and repression in which the opposite party is treated as a unit, as in all international affairs." Indeed, according to *Instructions*, "all prisoners of war are liable to the infliction of retaliatory measures."[106]

The other limit, Lieber insisted, is "one of principle." But upon examination, this principle appears to be little more than the prohibition of cruelty. In the heated debates about retaliatory measures for the Confederate treatment of prisoners of war at Andersonville and elsewhere, a number of Union officials called for retaliation in kind and for the use of former prisoners of war to supervise Confederate prisoners in Union prisons. Lieber joined Senator Charles Sumner and others in urging that retaliation be consistent with the laws of war, especially regarding cruelty. He also insisted that Union people would not, in any case, be able to bring themselves to do what was proposed and that expediency alone should be sufficient to counteract the proposals.[107]

drafts of *A Code* have this sentence: "The highest use of Military Power derived from Martial Necessity is Retaliation." According to *A Code*, #13, retaliation should be resorted to "only as a means of protective retribution, and, moreover, cautiously, justly, and unavoidably; that is, to say, retaliation shall only be resorted to after careful inquiry, not blinded by passion, into the real occurrence, and the character of the misdeeds that may demand retribution, after an unsuccessful summons of the enemy to punish the evil-doers, and without transgressing the bounds of strict retaliation." The last two conditions are omitted from *Instructions*, #27, #28.

106 Lieber to the New York *Times*, December 26, 1864, p. 4; Lieber to Halleck, April 19, 1864; *Instructions*, #59. Contrast the Geneva Conventions of 1949, and see Greenspan, *Soldier's Guide to the Laws of War*, 23.

107 See Charles Sumner's speech, *Treatment of Prisoners of War* (New York: New York Young Men's Republican Union, 1865), which quoted Lieber. This speech was given in the U.S. Senate, January 29, 1865. Also, see Lieber to

In other situations, where death is warranted in retaliation, death is the limit. Even if the enemy scalped or tortured prisoners, the United States could only put prisoners to death in retaliation. Death should be the "protective retribution" for the enslavement of Negro prisoners of war since the United States cannot use enslavement as a retaliatory measure. The reason for this rule is that "personal freedom" is "the highest of earthly goods." Since the code had declared that Negro soldiers are entitled to full rights as prisoners of war, Lieber was incensed when President Lincoln substituted hard labor for death as retaliation for enslavement. Halleck responded that General Orders No. 100 only asserted "the *right* to retaliate for the offense by death" and that this right also includes lesser penalties.[108]

In contrast to necessity, retaliation is subject to more clearly defined procedures and principles that are analogous to the criteria for justifying war. Nevertheless, retaliation also rests on a determination of necessity, and its limits are asserted but not developed. Necessity and retaliation offer civilian and military leaders two ways to adapt the laws of war to changing military conditions. They seem to imply that a belligerent must always be free to employ winning strategies or tactics even in violation of *jus in bello*. But such an implication would not do justice to the other side of Lieber's interpretation of the laws of war: whatever the aims of the war and however it is fought, some obligations toward the enemy continue. Unfortunately, he did not adequately grasp or reconcile these opposing tendencies in the laws of war.

Conclusion

Lieber's most important contribution to civilization has not survived intact and unmarked. Although he consistently praised

Sumner, January 22, 1865, in Perry (ed.), *Lieber*, 355, and Lieber to Halleck, December 21, 1864. Contrast the article "Retaliation in War," *United States Service Magazine* (New York: Charles B. Richardson, 1865) IV, 211–19.
108   Lieber to Halleck, December 21, 1864, August 3, 1863, Halleck to Lieber, August 4, 1863. See also "Notes and Clippings Assembled by Lieber as Working Material."

"Old Hundred" and thought that it covered practically all of the cases that emerged in the Civil War, he also recognized its imperfections. While most subsequent Union policies and actions were consistent with the code, they were rarely based directly on it.[109] Nevertheless, the code helped to secure consistent and uniform conduct in some areas, and it provided an important authority for moderation, especially against claims that rebels have no rights in armed conflict and that retaliation should be imitative. Although it was still enforced by the United States in the Spanish-American War and some of its content and language remain in the United States Army Field Manual, its long-term and permanent significance has been mediated through the various conferences and codes that it inspired and influenced. When interpreters of legal rules confront new situations, often created by new technological developments, they must proceed to a great extent by analogical reasoning, trying to discern the principles and reasons expressed in the rules in order to apply them to new cases. New weapons and means of destruction, as well as altered social, economic, and political conditions that affect the distinctions between different classes of the enemy, necessitate constant attention to *jus in bello*. In addition, Lieber's code was limited to the conduct of armies on *land*.

My task has been to explore Lieber's interpretation of the laws of war through an examination of several themes from the *Instructions* in relation to his experiences and his other discussions of this subject especially in unpublished materials. His method was empirical in its description of the practices and usages of nations, but it was also normative in its scrutiny of these practices in the light of general principles to see if they could be justified. Thus, neither the historical nor the philosophical approach by itself could be adequate for his purposes. General Orders No. 100 has been criticized because it so completely reflects the thought of one man.[110] However, it is this

109   See Frank Freidel, "General Orders 100 and Military Government," 553. Contrast the criticism by Jefferson Davis in *Official Records*, Ser. IV, Vol. II, pp. 1047–48.
110   See Bordwell, *The Law of War Between Belligerents*, 74.

very quality that allows us to study its rules in their philosophical setting. In general Lieber did not view the rules as *ad hoc* but rather based them on his own systematic interpretation of war and international law (although his acceptance of the prohibition against the use of poison may be an exception). His own desires to improve the code, to prepare an annotated edition, and to teach at West Point, were grounded in his conviction that the force of international law is public opinion, which requires an understanding of the reasons for particular rules. Paradoxically, General Orders No. 100 might have been a less significant monument if Lieber had been able to include his reasons. Many of his writings are avoided because of their prolixity, extraneous materials, and confusions. Although General Orders No. 100 is not wholly free of these defects, the requirements of a legal code forced Lieber to be more concise and direct. The discussions with members of the board and others, as well as their written suggestions, undoubtedly improved the code.

Some of its flaws resulted from Lieber's difficulties in organizing his material, although several of the board's changes also adversely affected the organization. Numerous paragraphs should have been put in different places in order to reflect the logic of the prohibitions and guidelines. For example, Numbers 56 and 75 should be together, and Number 66 should follow Number 62. Although better organization would have partially compensated for the omission of some of the reasons, other problems would have remained because of the nature of the laws of war. Many critics have insisted that the laws of war are inherently contradictory because they try to express morality and law in war. Charles Sumner in his stage of "near pacifism" exclaimed: "Laws of war! Law in that which is lawless! order in disorder! rules of wrong! There can be only *one law of war*; that is the great law, which pronounces it unwise, unchristian and unjust. The term, Laws or *Rights* of War, has been referred to the ancient Greeks; but, it is believed, that they are not chargable [sic] with the invention of such a contradictory combination of words." Despite his contention that there is *jus in bello*, Lieber was not fully successful in handling the tensions posed especially but not exclusively by relations between military necessity and the restraints of the laws of war. Neither interpreters of the laws of war nor civil and military officials can avoid these tensions. Unfortunately, Lieber was not very sensitive to them perhaps because he believed that philosophical consistency cannot be expected in the realm of law, particularly international law. For example, he considered *On Perpetual Peace* as one of Kant's "weakest" works because in treating "jural matters," Kant, like so many others, was "led to great inconsistencies by the love of consistency."[111]

Other difficulties in Lieber's interpretation of the laws of war stem from his love of war, rooted in his own experiences, and his moral evaluation of war and its effects. Although he conceded to the pacifists that war stands in need of justification because of the suffering it involves, his love of war and his praise of its moral qualities appeared to weaken this concession. While such an attitude may affect the number and kinds of restraints that one recognizes, it was not as decisive for Lieber as his sympathetic reading of Bynkershoek, who insisted that everything is permitted in war. And yet Lieber rejected the implications of *c'est la guerre*. Although he made everyone in the opposing state an enemy and appeared to admit all modes of destruction, he qualified this general permission by imposing restraints based on obligations toward the enemy that persist in all wars, regardless of the justice of the cause. According to *Instructions*, important "principles of justice, honor and humanity" should restrain military conflict by establishing different obligations toward different classes of the enemy and by excluding certain methods and weapons that cause unnecessary suffering.[112] Finally, however, the general permission may reenter through the back door of military necessity (including retaliation), which may ultimately exclude only cruelty and wanton destruction. As his discussion of poison suggests, Lieber sometimes failed to discern the principles that require certain prohibitions and their relevance to analogous cases.

111   Sumner, *The True Grandeur of Nations*, 17 n; Lieber to Hillard, May 19, 1839.
112   Lieber, "Law and Usages of War," December 17, 1861; *Instructions*, #4.

Nevertheless, "Old Hundred" is the "germinal document for the codification of the laws of land warfare," which, indeed, have "progressed very little beyond the Lieber Code." Ultimately, it is to Lieber, as Richard Baxter notes, "that we probably owe the certainty to which a large proportion of the law of war has been reduced."[113] Such statements by international and military lawyers attest to the significance of Lieber's work. Despite its structural flaws, inconsistencies, and other difficulties, General Orders No. 100, a mixture of textbook and code, as Lieber himself recognized, stands as a monument, a signpost, and an inspiration to constant reflection on morality and law in war.

113 Telford Taylor, Foreword, in Leon Friedman (ed.), *The Law of War*, I, xviii; James G. Garner, "General Order 100 Revisited," 44; Baxter, "The First Modern Codification of the Law of War" (May, 1963), 250.

Chapter Five

The Nature of Conscientious Objection

Individuals and groups have to draw lines. But they may draw their lines at different places. Some may stop at nonresistance and others at nonviolent resistance, while still others find violence acceptable within limits and some can even participate in unrestrained violence. At each line that is drawn persons will invoke moral considerations for not crossing it. Frequently in discourse about why a person stops at one point rather than another, he or she will claim, "My conscience won't let me do it." When a person refuses to cross certain lines (for example, to participate in military service), what is the nature of his appeal to conscience? And how should our society respond to his appeal? In this chapter, I will analyze the nature of appeals to conscience and indicate some issues in public policies regarding conscientious objection. In the next chapter, I will concentrate on public policies toward conscientious objectors to military service.

Unfortunately the phrase *appeals to conscience* is ambiguous. First, it may indicate an appeal to another person's conscience in order to convince him to act in certain ways. Second, it may mean the invocation of one's own conscience to interpret and justify one's conduct to others. Third, it may indicate the invocation of conscience in debates with oneself about the right course of action, conscience being understood as a participant in the debate, a referee, or a final arbiter. Although it is possible to distinguish these three meanings of *appeals to conscience*, they are usually intertwined in our moral discourse. Nevertheless, I shall concentrate on the second meaning, referring to the

165

other two only when it is necessary to fill out the picture.[1] Appeals to conscience in the second sense raise important issues of justification and public policy that can be considered apart from the other meanings of appeals to conscience.

My concern is with what we might call "conscientious objection" (broader than objection to participation in war), or what John Rawls calls "conscientious refusal."[2] What is involved in a person's description and evaluation of his own or others' acts as "conscientious"? What should our public policy be toward those who appeal to their consciences when they violate customs, established expectations, and laws? In suggesting some answers to these questions, I shall focus on the most general and least disputed aspects of the experiences to which we apply the terms *conscience* and *conscientious*, leaving aside many of the issues raised by various philosophical, psychological, sociological, and theological theories of conscience.[3] My phenomenological description of conscience and interpretation of the logic of appeals to conscience (in the second sense) will, of course, provide *elements* of a theory of conscience, but I do not intend to develop such a theory in this discussion. I shall rather examine the phenomena that we express in the language of conscience and related notions and try to determine how these enter into appeals to conscience (in the second sense) before discussing some public policies toward conscientious objection.

1   For aspects of the appeal to another person's conscience, see James F. Childress, *Civil Disobedience and Political Obligation: A Study in Christian Social Ethics*, Yale University Publications in Religion, XVI (New Haven: Yale University Press, 1971) and Childress, "Nonviolent Resistance: Trust and Risk-Taking," *Journal of Religious Ethics*, I (Fall, 1973), 87–112, part of which appears in Chapter 2. For a theological interpretation of the third meaning, see Karl Rahner, *Nature and Grace* (New York: Sheed and Ward, 1964), Chap. 2.
2   John Rawls, *A Theory of Justice* (Cambridge: Harvard University Press, 1971), #56.
3   For a discussion of many of these theories, see Eric Mount, Jr., *Conscience and Responsibility* (Richmond: John Knox Press, 1969). For a broader view of conscience than the one I am developing, see Eleanor Haney, "Conscience and Law," *Dialog*, IX (Autumn, 1970), 284–94.

Three cases of appeals to conscience and related notions are useful points of reference for our discussion. On June 21, 1956, Arthur Miller, the playwright, appeared before the House Committee on Un-American Activities, which was examining the unauthorized use of passports, and he was asked who had been present at meetings with Communist writers in New York City. Here is part of the dialogue:

Mr. Arens: Can you tell us who was there when you walked into the room?

Mr. Miller: Mr. Chairman, I understand the philosophy behind this question and I want you to understand mine. When I say this, I want you to understand that I am not protecting the Communists or the Communist Party. I am trying to, and I will, *protect my sense of myself*. I could not use the name of another person and bring trouble on him. These were writers, poets, as far as I could see, and the life of a writer, despite what it sometimes seems, is pretty tough. I wouldn't make it any tougher for anybody. I ask you not to ask me that question. . . .

Mr. Jackson: May I say that moral scruples, however laudable, do not constitute legal reason for refusing to answer the question. . . .

Mr. Scherer: We do not accept the reason you gave for refusing to answer the question, and . . . if you do not answer . . . you are placing yourself in contempt. . . .

Mr. Miller: All I can say, sir, is that *my conscience* will not permit me to use the name of another person.[4]

On December 29, 1970, Governor Winthrop Rockefeller of Arkansas commuted to life imprisonment the death sentences of the fifteen prisoners then on death row. He said, "I cannot and will not turn my back on life-long Christian teachings and beliefs, merely to let history run out its course on a fallible and

---

4   Eric Bentley (ed.), *Thirty Years of Treason: Excerpts from Hearings Before the House Committee on Un-American Activities, 1938–1968* (New York: Viking Press, 1971), 819–22, my italics. See also Eric Bentley, *Are You Now or Have You Ever Been?* (New York: Harper and Row, 1972). For some of the contemporary discussion of Miller's stand, see the articles by John Steinbeck and Richard Rovere reprinted in Harry Girvetz (ed.), *Contemporary Moral Issues* (2nd ed.; Belmont, Ca.: Wadsworth, 1968), 97–105. In addition to conscience, Miller felt that the question about who was present at meetings with Communist writers was not germane to the issue of the use of passports, the ostensible subject of inquiry.

failing theory of punitive justice." Understanding his decision as "purely personal and philosophical," he insisted that the records of the prisoners were irrelevant to it. He continued, "I am aware that there will be reaction to my decision. However, failing to take this action while it is within my power, *I could not live with myself*."[5]

In late December, 1972, Captain Michael Heck refused to carry out orders to fly more bombing missions in Vietnam. He wrote his parents: "I've taken a very drastic step. I've refused to take part in this war any longer. *I cannot in good conscience* be a part of it." He also said, "I can live with prison easier than I can with taking part in the war." "I would refuse even a ground job supervising the loading of bombs or refueling aircraft. I cannot be a participant . . . *a man has to answer to himself first*."[6]

Conscience is a mode of consciousness and thought about one's own acts and their value or disvalue. It is often retrospective; in being conscious of and thinking about his past acts, an agent's conscience comes into play. It appears primarily as a bad conscience, as the feelings of guilt and shame that accompany this consciousness of one's own acts as wrong or bad. Hannah Arendt insists that "only good people are ever bothered by a bad conscience whereas it is a very rare phenomenon among real criminals. A good conscience does not exist except as the absence of a bad one." Most often the good conscience is described by nouns such as *peace*, *wholeness*, and *integrity*, or by adjectives such as *quiet*, *clear*, *clean*, and *easy*. Job affirmed this peace of the good conscience when he said (using one of the Hebrew words for the experience that we call conscience), "My heart shall not reproach me so long as I live."[7]

When a person appeals to his conscience or describes his act as conscientious, he makes a hypothetical and prospective

5 Reproduced materials for a course in criminal law, Professor Alan Dershowitz's section, Harvard Law School, 1972.
6 *Newsweek*, January 22, 1973, p. 18; Boston *Globe*, January 13, 1973; Steven V. Roberts, "2 Pilots, 2 Wars," *New York Times Magazine*, June 10, 1973.
7 Hannah Arendt, "Thinking and Moral Considerations: A Lecture," *Social Research*, XXXVIII (Autumn 1971), 418; Job 27:6.

claim. He claims that if he were to commit the act in question, he would violate his conscience. This violation would result not only in such unpleasant feelings as guilt or shame or both but also in a fundamental loss of integrity, wholeness, and harmony in the self. He thus makes a prediction about what would happen to him if he were to commit such an act, a prediction based on the imaginative projection of concrete courses of action in the light of his fundamental standards. His appeal to conscience constitutes a motive-statement about his refusal, an indication of why he is doing it. In order to clarify this motive, let us look at the marks of conscience, especially at the feelings of guilt and shame.

Marks of Conscience and Appeals to Conscience

Some of the marks of conscience are implicit in my comments about good and bad consciences. Conscience is personal and subjective; it is a person's consciousness of and reflection on his own acts in relation to his standards of judgment. It is a first-person claim, deriving from standards that he may or may not also apply to the conduct of others. As Hannah Arendt indicates, "When Socrates stated that 'it is better to suffer wrong than to do wrong,' he clearly meant that it was better *for him*, just as it was better for him 'to be in disagreement with multitudes than, being one, to be in disagreement with [himself].' "[8] In the three cases presented above, the agents held that their consciences required certain actions of them. While it is likely that they would have raised moral questions about others who acted differently, it would have been odd, and even absurd, for one of them to have said, "My conscience indicates that you should not do that." In judging others or advising them about their conduct, I may consult my conscience but only in the sense of imagining what I would think and feel if I acted in a certain way. I may then say that someone else ought not to en-

8 Hannah Arendt, *Crises of the Republic* (New York: Harcourt, Brace, Jovanovich, 1972), 62.

gage in that conduct, but I cannot logically justify this admonition by saying "I would have a guilty conscience if he did that." Perhaps I would have a guilty conscience if I failed to warn him, but my reasons for *his* abstention from that conduct must involve more than an appeal to my conscience; they must invoke the moral values, principles, and rules that are determinative for my conscience.[9]

Although a person's appeal to his conscience usually involves an appeal to moral standards, conscience is not itself the standard. It is the mode of consciousness resulting from the application of standards to his conduct. For example, the retrospective bad conscience emerges after the moral judgment about the act. Even in the prospective bad conscience, a matter of the imagination, conscience still comes after the judgment of rightness and wrongness. C. A. Pierce in *Conscience in the New Testament* comments on "conscience" in I Corinthians: "here conscience is to some extent regarded as dependent on an assessment on other grounds of the quality of acts. In this case it is knowledge of the source of the meat eaten that brings on the pain, not the eating of the meat. Even in its negative and limited function, conscience does not so much indicate that an act committed is wrong, as that an act 'known' (by other means, and rightly or wrongly) to be wrong, has been committed."[10]

To appeal to conscience, thus, is not necessarily to assert that moral rightness and wrongness are determined by the need for a good conscience or that moral integrity serves, in effect, as the source and ground of obligation. As Thomas Nagel suggests,

9   For an analysis of two other issues that emerge from the discussion of conscience as personal and subjective—the duality of the self, and the social context and formation of conscience—see H. R. Niebuhr, "The Ego-Alter Dialectic and the Conscience," *Journal of Philosophy*, XLII (1945), 352–59.

10   C. A. Pierce, *Conscience in the New Testament* (London: SCM Press, 1955), 77. But his analysis of contemporary interpretations of conscience, especially in ordinary language, differs from mine, (p. 117). For a view similar to mine, that conscience follows judgment, see Martin McGuire's fine article, "On Conscience," *Journal of Philosophy*, LX (May 9, 1963), 253–63. Also see Gilbert Ryle, "Conscience and Moral Convictions," in Margaret MacDonald (ed.), *Philosophy and Analysis* (Oxford: Basil Blackwell, 1954), 156–65.

"For if by committing murder one sacrifices one's moral purity or integrity, that can only be because there is *already* something wrong with murder. The general reason against committing murder cannot therefore be merely that it makes one an immoral person."[11]

A number of puzzles appear at this point. If conscience emerges after a moral judgment or after the application of moral standards, what does it mean to consult one's conscience, to have a conflict of conscience, and to say "I believe that I ought to do that but my conscience tells me not to." When a person consults his conscience, from the perspective that I am developing, he examines his moral convictions to determine what he really thinks and feels, even reconsidering his values, principles, and rules, their weight, and their relevance to the situation at hand. When he consults his conscience, it will only give him one answer: do what you believe you ought to do. This appeal to conscience (in the third sense of the phrase) is thus only one step in the examination of one's moral convictions.

A "conflict of conscience" appears when a person faces two conflicting moral demands, neither of which can be met without at least partially repudiating the other one. This is a conflict of conscience because there is a firm judgment, right or wrong, that both courses of action are required. Conscience gives conflicting directives because it follows conflicting judgments. Perhaps the agent has misconstrued his situation and the relevant moral standards, and the only way out is to reconsider them. This may also be the situation of a "doubtful conscience," which is unsure about the operative standards and their weight.

More difficult in terms of the perspective that I am developing is the statement, "I believe that this act is right and that I ought to do it, but my conscience prevents me from doing it." What sense can one make of this statement if conscience follows rather than authorizes moral judgments? First, it may be another version of the conflict of conscience situation that I just

11 Thomas Nagel, "War and Massacre," *Philosophy and Public Affairs*, I (Winter, 1972), 132.

described. Second, it may be an example of what John Rawls calls "residue guilt feelings" that persist after a person has changed his moral convictions (e.g., about some "vice" that was prohibited in his earlier religious training). Third, perhaps the situation is closer to that of the doubtful conscience since uncertainty may result from changes in a person's moral convictions so that he is not sure what he now believes. For example, as a person surrenders his pacifism and becomes a defender of justified violence, he may not be able at some points in time to say that he does or does not believe that violence is wrong for him and that his conscience does or does not provide a sanction against his participation in war.[12]

Another important mark of conscience is often overlooked. The appeal to conscience asserts a personal sanction rather than an authority. This mark is frequently overlooked because first-person appeals to conscience most often appear in the explanation of acts that contravene the demands of an established authority such as a religious community or a legal-political order. I shall return to this point later, but now I want to analyze this sanction. J. Glenn Gray in *The Warriors* describes what happens when soldiers discover that they cannot continue obeying certain orders. "Suddenly the soldier feels himself abandoned and cast off from all security. Conscience has isolated him, and its voice is a warning. *If you do this, you will not be at peace with me in the future.*" This threatened "ache of guilt," as Gray describes it, is a fearful sanction for those with an interest in the self and its welfare. In the words of Shakespeare, "It fills a man full of obstacles."[13]

The agents in the three cases mentioned earlier emphasize this personal sanction. They fear the loss of selfhood, integrity, and wholeness in the anticipated judgment of the future self on the present self's acts, and they express this fear in several dramatic ways: "I could not live with myself," "A man has to answer to himself first," or "I must protect my sense of myself."

12   For a similar view, see McGuire, "On Conscience," 262.
13   J. Glenn Gray, *The Warriors: Reflections on Men in Battle* (New York: Harper and Row, 1970), 184–85, my italics; *Richard III*, act 5, sc. 4, line 142.

Others have said, "I could not look at myself in the mirror" or "I could answer it, but if I did, I would hate myself in the morning."[14] Hannah Arendt summarizes the rules or logic of conscience drawn from Socrates. "These are the rules of conscience, and they are—like those Thoreau announced in his essay—entirely negative. They do not say what to do; they say what not to do. They do not spell out certain principles for taking action; they lay down boundaries no act should transgress. They say, *Don't do wrong, for then you will have to live together with a wrongdoer.*"[15]

Furthermore, these dictates of conscience are purely formal, not material. "Let your conscience be your guide." But its advice is formal. "Do what you believe to be right and avoid what you believe to be wrong, *or else.*" Let there be consistency and harmony between belief and action under the threat that inconsistency will undermine integrity and occasion a bad conscience.

This claim about the formal nature of the dictates of conscience may seem at first glance to be contrary to our experiences. Conscience is awakened, consulted, or invoked only when there is some difficulty, some perplexity, or some temptation; retrospectively, it appears when a person has violated some of his standards. This perplexity or temptation is not general but specific. It relates to standards in specific circumstances, whether real or imagined. Conscience thus appears in envisioning (or remembering) a concrete course of action. Yet its admonition remains constant. Do what you believe is right or suffer the consequences. As agents we do not experience conscience as a general and indefinite call to integrity but only as a call to integrity in the face of situations that offer some temptation to depart from standards. The self over time acting

14   Ring Lardner, Jr., before HUAC, October 30, 1947; see Eric Bentley, *Thirty Years of Treason,* 197, 189. For a very interesting discussion of the relation between the widespread use of mirrors and a sense of individuality and selfhood, see Lionel Trilling, *Sincerity and Authenticity* (Cambridge, Mass.: Harvard University Press, 1972).

15   Hannah Arendt, *Crises of the Republic,* 63, my italics.

in real situations and imagining others comes to associate this admonition about integrity with particular moral requirements that it has identified as matters of conscience. Thus conscience, whose warning is formal, appears to have material content because it is experienced only in situations that raise specific moral questions and because the self usually has stable values, principles, and rules that, in part, constitute its character.[16]

I have emphasized the sanction of the loss of integrity, or wholeness, which is closely connected with the feelings of guilt or shame. When a person appeals to his conscience, he indicates his liability to certain feelings that he predicts will result from acting in certain ways. The phrase *bad conscience* especially indicates the feelings of guilt and shame.[17]

It is not fruitful or even possible to distinguish natural and moral feelings in terms of sensations or behavioral manifestations. Rather the distinction is to be found in the type of explanation that is offered for the feelings. When an agent explains why he experiences certain feelings, he will sometimes offer a moral explanation. Moral feelings, then, are those feelings that are explained by moral notions. Both feelings of guilt and feelings of shame are involved in conscience (although we tend to emphasize guilt perhaps because of the Jewish and Christian traditions), but the moral notions that explain them come, roughly, from different parts of morality. As Rawls puts it, "In general, guilt, resentment, and indignation invoke the concept of right, whereas shame, contempt, and derision appeal to the concept of goodness."[18] In the former we have the society's basic morality, its stations, duties, and obligations; in the latter

16   See Peter Fuss, "Conscience," *Ethics*, LXXIV (January, 1964), 111–20, esp. 116–17.

17   In my analysis of these feelings of guilt and shame, I draw on Rawls, *A Theory of Justice* and David A. J. Richards, *A Theory of Reasons for Action* (Oxford: Clarendon Press, 1971). See also, Herbert Morris (ed.), *Shame and Guilt* (Belmont, Ca.: Wadsworth, 1971).

18   Rawls, *A Theory of Justice*, 484. A number of debates (e.g., between the intellectualistic and pragmatic interpretations of conscience) are involved in these matters although I cannot try to resolve them here. See Bernard Wand, "The Content and Function of Conscience," *Journal of Philosophy*, LVIII (Nov. 23, 1961), 765–72.

we have the morality of aspiration, ideals, and supererogation. If an agent feels guilty, he invokes a moral concept of right, expects others to feel resentment and indignation, and can relieve his feelings by acts of reparation or by forgiveness. If he feels shame, he invokes an ideal such as self-control or love, expects others to feel contempt for his shortcomings, and can overcome the feeling of shame for his failures only by improving in the future.

The same act may, of course, evoke both feelings of guilt and shame. Take, for example, the act of yielding to the state's demand that one serve in the armed forces. A person who thinks that a war violates the principles of just war may feel guilty about his involvement in it. But he may also have an image of himself as one who can withstand social pressures, and he may be ashamed that he submitted to family and community pressures to serve in the army. In our earlier cases, Rockefeller's statement seems to put greater emphasis on shame than guilt. His image of himself as a person who acts when he has the opportunity despite social pressures is critical as is his understanding of himself as a Christian, but he also invokes the moral concept of right in his reference to barbarism and a "fallible and failing theory" of punishment.

Occasionally, within a religious framework, one finds another explanation for a feeling that is close to guilt and shame although it is probably distinct from both: impurity or unworthiness particularly vis-à-vis God and whatever else is holy. Basil the Great said, "Killing in war was differentiated by our fathers from murder . . . nevertheless, perhaps it would be well that those whose hands are unclean abstain from communion for three years."[19] His attitude was part of a general aversion to bloodshed.

A person who appeals to his conscience indicates not only that the refused act is prima facie wrong, given his moral convictions, but that it is also actually wrong in these circumstances, at least for him. This apparently trivial observation is very important, for the conscientious agent claims that none of

19   See Roland Bainton, *Christian Attitudes Toward War and Peace* (Nashville: Abingdon Press, 1960), 78.

the available public descriptions, justifications, or excuses for the act will ease the anguish of his conscience if he performs it. First, the appellant to conscience claims that he can find no justification for the act in question, at least none that will satisfy his conscience. Sometimes it is suggested that a moral absolutist should be willing to sacrifice his moral purity for the sake of some greater good. Thomas Nagel rightly indicates that such a notion is incoherent, "For if one were justified in making such a sacrifice (or even morally required to make it), then one would not be sacrificing one's moral integrity by adopting that course: one would be preserving it."[20] At any rate, the appeal to conscience is a denial that such a justification is present. The moral issue, nevertheless, is an important one, especially since it can be argued that in some genuine conflicts of conscience a violation of a moral principle or rule is necessary and justified. But this issue of the assumption of guilt or "dirty hands" is not identical with the issue of a "bad conscience," for the agent may consider his act to be justified (and hence not subversive of his moral integrity), although the violated moral principle still exerts its influence, for example, in the feeling of guilt and in the duty of reparation.

Second, the appellant to conscience claims that he will not be able to forget the act in question if he performs it. Conscience is sometimes depicted as a still, small voice, but it is perhaps more accurate to view it as a voice that is heard only when one is still and quiet, when one, in effect, stops and thinks. Perhaps this is the basis of Goethe's statement, "The actor is always without conscience; only the spectator has a conscience." This inner witness can be avoided if a person continues his activity and never stops to think; then his crimes can be committed with impunity as far as his conscience is concerned.[21] But the

20   Nagel, "War and Massacre," 132–33. R. M. Hare responds to Nagel's point in "Rules of War and Moral Reasoning," *Philosophy and Public Affairs*, I (Winter 1972), 180. See also Michael Walzer's superb discussion of "dirty hands" in "Political Action: The Problem of Dirty Hands," *Philosophy and Public Affairs*, II (Winter, 1973), 160–80.
21   Johann Wolfgang Goethe, "Maximen und Reflexionen," in Ernst Beutler (ed.), *Gedenkausgabe der Werke, Briefe und Gespräche* (Zürich: Artemis Ver-

agent who appeals to his conscience claims that this route is closed, for he will not be able to forget the act in question if he performs it.

Third, he claims that he will not be able to deny that the act is his if he performs it. Sometimes a denial of responsibility for an act is used to silence conscience. Instead of trying to show that the deed, apparently against conscience, is actually justified, one might try to show that it is excused. A more common strategy is to attempt to shift the responsibility for the deed and its consequences to someone else. Many soldiers apparently deny not only legal responsibility but also moral responsibility for their deeds by pointing to their oaths as soldiers and by pleading superior orders. In the traditional understanding of the order of the universe, the king could absolve his subjects of their misdeeds. In Shakespeare's *Henry V* one of the soldiers says, "we know enough if we know we are the King's subjects. If his cause be wrong, our obedience to the king wipes the crime of it out of us."[22] The appellant to conscience insists not only that he will be unable to forget the act in question but that he will also remember and think about it as his own. Even if others do not hold him responsible for it, he still has to answer to himself.

I can amplify this point by reference to a legal case in which the Georgetown University Hospital applied for an order to authorize blood transfusions to save a woman's life although she and her husband, both Jehovah's Witnesses, conscientiously opposed the transfusions, which, they said, would violate the biblical prohibition against consuming blood.[23] The order was granted by Judge J. Skelly Wright, who indicated that both the husband and the wife conceded that court-ordered transfusions

---

lags-AG, 1949), 522 (maxim no. 241). See Shakespeare's *Richard III* and Hannah Arendt's discussion in "Thinking and Moral Considerations," 417–66. Also of interest on this and other matters is Edward Engelberg, *The Unknown Distance: From Consciousness to Conscience, Goethe to Camus* (Cambridge, Mass.: Harvard University Press, 1972).

22 Gray, *The Warriors*, 181–83; *Henry V*, act 4, sc. 1, line 137.

23 *Application of President and Directors of Georgetown College*, 331 F. 2d 1000 (D.C. Cir.), *certiorari* denied, 377 U.S. 978 (1964).

would not be their responsibility although they could not consent to them. Judge Wright was thus able to protect their consciences and to save the woman's life. In most cases of conscientious objection, however, the agents hold that even coercion
does not relieve them of their responsibility.

Having looked at some of the marks of appeals to conscience, we need now to inquire into the *context* of such appeals, when they are made. Such appeals are made only when
there is a need or demand to explain one's past, present, or future acts. Although this demand may emerge either from the
internal dialogue of the self or from the inquiries of other persons ("Why are you doing that?"), I am more concerned with
the public forum. Especially for acts that contravene customary
and conventional expectations and standards, the appeal to
conscience functions as a motive-statement, an explanation,
which may be taken to justify or excuse the act, mitigate its
guilt, or even bring it under a recognized exemption, such as
conscientious objection to participation in war in any form.
R. S. Peters stresses the important feature of the contexts of
such appeals when he says that we seek or ascribe motives only
"when a breach with an established expectation has occurred
and there is need to justify some action."[24]

The agent accepts the demand for explanation because this
is required by his sociality or because he recognizes that a plausible case can be made for a different act on grounds of prudence or morality. In the latter instance he may recognize a conflict between moral claims and other desires, such as the desire
for survival or security, or a conflict between different moral
claims. Such conflict situations emerge with special urgency
when traditional authority structures are losing their power. As
Pierce remarks, "It is clear that *conscience* only came into its
own in the Greek world after the collapse of the city-state. The
close integration of politics with ethics, with the former predominant, was no longer possible: there was no sufficiently

24   R. S. Peters, "Motives and Motivation," *Philosophy*, XXXI (April, 1956),
118.

close authority, external to the individual, effectively to direct conduct. Consequently, as a *pis aller*, men fell back on the internal chastisement of *conscience* as the only authority." A similar historical point can be made about seventeenth-century England and the crisis of authority that Christopher Hill has described as "the world turned upside down" in his book by that title.[25] But even in times of less dramatic social conflict, appeals to conscience are also common.

What are we to make of the appeal to conscience as a motive-statement in this sort of context? In *Human Acts*, Eric D'Arcy offers a helpful analysis of types of motive-statements and their logic. All of them are explanations in terms of the agent's objective for the sake of which he acts. They are offered and ascribed when there is reason to think that the act (X) is good and the motive (M) is bad, or that M is good and X bad. The first type of motive-statement (type 1) is forward looking. It explains an act in terms of its function as a means to an end. The agent says, "What I really want is not the natural accompaniment or outcome of the act X, but the end M to which X is simply a means. I do X for the sake of M." For example, "I am working at this job in order to please my wife." The second type of motive-statement (type 2) shows why a course of action that has "no intrinsic attractiveness, has been in some way rendered an objective worthy of pursuit by some circumstance *not naturally or necessarily connected with it.*" This may be a past circumstance (leading, for example, to acts of revenge, gratitude, or reparation), or a present circumstance (for example, love or a sense of duty). One says, "What I want is indeed the natural outcome or accompaniment of the action; but I want it, not because of its intrinsic attractiveness, but because of its being made worth while by some extrinsic circumstance C. I do X because of C." For example, "I am laying down my life for him out of a sense of gratitude." The third type of motive-statement (type 3) is not properly a motive-statement at all but rather

25 Pierce, *Conscience in the New Testament*, 76; Christopher Hill, *The World Turned Upside Down: Radical Ideas During the English Revolution* (New York: Viking Press, 1972).

functions to deny that any motives other than the natural outcome of the act are present. It asserts that no "ulterior" motives
are at work. For example, "I am caring for my elderly father
simply and solely out of love." Such a statement adds nothing
to an account of the conduct; it only dispels suspicion.[26]

D'Arcy classifies the appeal to conscience as a type 2 motive-statement. To say that a person acted "for conscience' sake"
or out of a sense of duty is to explain his act in terms of an
extrinsic circumstance. It is to say that he acted not because the
action was attractive or because the natural outcome was attractive but because an extrinsic circumstance was operative. Yet
most cases of conscientious refusal are more complex and interesting than D'Arcy's analysis of type 2 suggests. For often, as
in the case of conscientious objection to participation in war,
the act (refusing to fight) and the natural accompaniment or
outcome (avoiding the risks of being killed) are not totally un-
attractive. Indeed, others suspect that precisely this outcome is
sought, and they consider the act to be unworthy, cowardly, or
unfair to others. Hence they are hostile to those who refuse to
serve. Such charges and hostility obviously make the act and
its outcome less attractive to the objector. His appeal to his conscience is designed to dispel suspicion about his motives, not
to indicate, as in type 3, that the natural outcome is the only
motive but to deny that this attractive outcome (not dying) is
the motive of the act (not fighting) and to assert that an extrinsic
circumstance (not killing as required by conscience) is the motive.

If my analysis is correct, the appeal to conscience is also a
motive-statement of type 1, the forward-looking, means-to-end
type (although this terminology is not entirely appropriate). In
appealing to conscience, I indicate that I am trying to preserve
a sense of myself, my wholeness and integrity, my good conscience, and that I cannot preserve these qualities if I submit to
certain requirements of the state or society. While the act of

26   Eric D'Arcy, *Human Acts: An Essay in Their Moral Evaluation* (Oxford:
Clarendon Press, 1963), 158, 155.

obedience or submission is not naturally or necessarily associated with a negative outcome (loss of integrity) for many or
most people, it would have this result in my life. I must avoid
the sanction of a bad conscience. An analysis of Arthur Miller's
refusal to give information to HUAC suggests that his motive-
statement about conscience invokes conscience not only as an
extrinsic present circumstance but also as an end to be attained
or, negatively, a sanction to be avoided.

Against either my approach or D'Arcy's, there is the contention that *conscientious* applies to a person and a procedural
policy of decision making rather than to the motive of acts.
Conscientious refers not only to acts done from a sense of duty
or "for conscience' sake" but also to a person's orientation and
procedural policy when these can be characterized as scrupulous, painstaking, and serious. Although we consider all acts
done from a sense of duty as conscientious, the converse does
not hold. We also consider an act to be conscientious when the
actor has seriously tried to discern his duty by considering the
views of others and by testing his criteria of rightness and
wrongness.[27]

John Llewelyn illustrates the critical point of this position
when he contends that "the conscientious man invokes conscience when he wishes to disclaim the capacity to *justify* an
action and yet reserve the right to deny that the action was un-
considered."[28] Although the Rockefeller statement is somewhat
ambiguous, it seems to be a candidate for such an analysis. His
reasons were "Christian" and "personal and philosophical."
Perhaps he considered them somewhat inappropriate for public policy, or perhaps he thought that others would not find
them convincing. If he had thought that his reasons would be

27 For this second sense of *conscientious* as applying to decision-making
procedures, see Albert R. Jonsen, *Christian Decision and Action* (New York:
Bruce, 1970), and David Little, "A View of Conscience Within the Protestant
Theological Tradition," in William C. Bier, S.J. (ed.), *Conscience: Its Freedom
and Limitations* (New York: Fordham University Press, 1971), 20–28.
28 John E. Llewelyn, "Conscientiousness," *Australasian Journal of Philosophy*, XXXVIII (December, 1970), 221.

acceptable to the people in his state, his appeal to conscience would have been unnecessary. To this extent Llewelyn's point is correct, for then the appeal to conscience would have added nothing but an indication of how deeply Rockefeller felt about reasons that would have been sufficient by themselves. Although Rockefeller appealed to a private framework, he hinted at another social framework of justification when he referred to "barbarism" and "a fallible and failing theory of punitive justice." He also could have drawn on a wide range of arguments against capital punishment, some of which have since been employed to exclude some laws authorizing capital punishment. But even so, I do not think that Rockefeller's invocation of conscience really was a disclaimer of the capacity to justify his act. Moral justification is, as Sidney Hook suggests, "a matter of reasons not of conscience."[29] But the appeal to conscience presupposes justification to oneself if my argument about conscience following judgments of moral worth is correct.

Typically, a person invokes conscience in the course of explaining acts that contravene normal and established expectations and thus require explanation. He invokes conscience not only to indicate that he made his decision "all things considered," including the reassessment of his standards, but also to indicate his motive for acting. Although that motive is, in part, avoidance of a sanction imposed by the self on itself, the sanction comes into play only if there is a judgment of the act in terms that the self accepts. A person's appeal to conscience thus presupposes justification to himself, if not to others.

The agent typically views his appeal to conscience as a last resort to be employed only when he thinks that he has exhausted other arguments for justifying or excusing his conduct. For the appeal to conscience is unnecessary if other reasons are acceptable, and it appears to constitute a cloture of debate. Usually the agent has given up the attempt to convince others of the objective rightness of his act and is content to assert its sub-

29   Sidney Hook, "Social Protest and Civil Disobedience," in Paul Kurtz (ed.), *Moral Problems in Contemporary Society: Essays in Humanistic Ethics* (Englewood Cliffs, N.J.: Prentice-Hall, 1969), 165.

jective rightness, perhaps to secure some positive treatment such as an exemption from ordinary duties. He cannot make an appeal to conscience until he has made a moral judgment because conscience follows judgment, and he does not need to make that appeal if the grounds for the judgment are acceptable to others. (I hardly need to emphasize that these stages are rarely clearly demarcated in actual moral discourse.) And yet if our observations about "consulting one's conscience" and "conscientiousness" are accurate, a person of conscience can never view the case as irrevocably closed. He or she must be willing to reopen it in the light of new evidence.

The Keeper of Conscience: Conscientious Objection and Public Policy

I think that this understanding of conscience and appeals to conscience has several important implications for public policies regarding conscientious objection and refusal. I can only suggest a few of these implications, which revolve around the issue of the "keeper of conscience." In an exchange with Governor Winthrop in the seventeenth century, Anne Hutchinson defended entertaining "saints" in her home by insisting, "That's a matter of conscience, Sir." Governor Winthrop responded, "Your conscience you must keep or it must be kept for you." Anne Hutchinson replied, "Must not I then entertain the saints because I must keep my conscience?" I do not propose to treat this matter of the "keeper of conscience" in terms of a systematic political philosophy that would emphasize the final sovereignty of either the state or the individual. Indeed, my approach suggests that such an ultimate perspective on which of the two authorities, state or conscience, is final, while sometimes helpful and even indispensable, is often the wrong question for public policy. This question is too broad and must be specified in particular areas or particular laws, but it is also the wrong question in some contexts because conscience is more usefully understood not as an authority but as a sanction. When we ask as citizens and legislators, "What ought to be our policy toward conscientious claims for exemptions from laws?" we are asking, "When should (or may) we force a person to choose between the severe personal sanction of conscience and some legal sanction?" This is a question of public policy toward a class of genuine conscientious objectors to some particular law. It is a different question whether any particular individual belongs to that class, that is, whether he is able to pass the threshold test of sincerity.

My procedure will be to utilize a number of principles and distinctions that are mutually consistent, although their coherence in a general political philosophy is not indicated. Many of these principles and distinctions are already at work (although not necessarily decisively) in the liberal, constitutional, democratic polity of the United States—in public policies, for example, and legal decisions—and my concern is to use and criticize some of them rather than to offer a constructive political philosophy as an alternative. Probably this level of discussion is most useful for criticism and direction of public policy.

Obviously, public policy judgments involve balancing several values and principles, but in the area of the protection of conscience, some guidelines for such balancing seem to be possible and appropriate, especially in terms of setting presumptions and burdens of proof. If my analysis of conscience is correct, a state is a better and more desirable one if it puts the presumption in favor of exemption for conscientious objectors (not merely to war). It is prima facie a moral evil to force a person to act against his conscience, although it may often be justified and even necessary. And it is unfair to the conscientious person to give him the alternative of obedience to the law or criminal classification.[30]

---

30 See the arguments by John Mansfield, "Conscientious Objection—1964 Term," in Donald A. Giannella (ed.), *Religion and the Public Order, 1965* (Chicago: University of Chicago Press, 1966); J. Morris Clark, "Guidelines for the Free Exercise Clause," *Harvard Law Review*, LXXXIII (1969), 337, 351; and the exchange between Gerald MacCallum and Hugo Bedau in Norman S. Care and Thomas K. Trelogan (eds.), *Issues in Law and Morality* (Cleveland: Press of Case Western Reserve University, 1973), 141–68.

My proposal can be seen more clearly by a comparison between two traditions in the interpretation of the free exercise of religion. Prior to *Sherbert* v. *Verner*, freedom of religion was seen primarily as the freedom of religious belief; religion was protected from the intentional and direct discrimination of the state. To determine whether the free-exercise clause had been violated, the courts only had to consider the question from the standpoint of the legislators (not the conscientious objectors) to see whether there was a valid secular legislative intent. With *Sherbert* v. *Verner* there was a shift in the interpretation of the free-exercise clause, although all its ramifications are far from clear. A Seventh-Day Adventist in South Carolina was denied state unemployment benefits because she refused to take employment that required her to work on Saturday, her sabbath day, and the Supreme Court held that South Carolina could not "constitutionally apply the eligibility provisions so as to constrain a worker to abandon his religious convictions respecting the day of rest." The decision incorporated action along with belief under the protection of the free-exercise clause, and it also considered incidental effects of secular policies apart from legislative intent. According to this interpretation, it is not enough to see whether there is valid secular intent; the state also has to consider the effects of the law from the standpoint of those who raise conscientious objections. Only in this way can it be determined whether conscience is affected. Furthermore, if conscience is affected, the state has to show that a compelling interest cannot be met in alternative ways to avoid the injury to conscience. That is, once there is evidence that conscience is affected, the state has the burden of proof. It must show its overriding interests in the legislation and policy and the absence of alternative means to achieve its ends. It is not enough to show a compelling interest of a general sort in the regulation. In effect, the state must show a compelling interest in denying the exemption to conscientious objectors. For example, if the possibility of spurious claims threatened to dilute the unemployment compensation fund and disrupt the scheduling of work, the state would have "to demonstrate that no alternative forms of regulation would combat such abuses with-

out infringing First Amendment rights."[31] The point is not that
the state must not discriminate against conscience or intend to
injure it (for this was already accepted), but that the state must
intend that conscience not be injured even to the extent of assuming some burdens and costs to prevent such injury.

This general contention may be illuminated by a closer examination of types of conscientious objection and types of governmental interest. In one type of situation, the state may demand that a person perform some positive action to which he
is conscientiously opposed. For example, it may impose on him
the positive duty of military service. If the conscientious objector refuses to carry it out, should criminal penalties be imposed? Later I will contrast these duties with negative ones—
duties to refrain from certain conduct.[32]

The government has a variety of possible responses short of
applying criminal sanctions (against which my argument has
established a presumption). Its role as teacher and educator
should not be underestimated. But when conscience opposes
these positive duties, the state can often yield without any serious cost; or it can sometimes perform the act for the objector,
thereby accomplishing its end and relieving the objector of the
burden of conscience; or it can impose an alternative duty that
will preserve fairness to other citizens (by preventing economic
and other advantages) while protecting the objector's conscience.

The government can usually yield to conscientious objectors to jury duty, the only other conscription besides the military in the United States, without any serious cost.[33] Scruples
against judging others can simply be accommodated along with

31   For a superb discussion of *Sherbert v. Verner*, 374 U.S. 398 (1963), from
which I have drawn, see Alfred G. Killilea, "Standards for Expanding Freedom of Conscience," *University of Pittsburgh Law Review*, XXXIV (Summer,
1973), 531–55. But contrast *Trans World Airlines, Inc. v. Hardison* 97 S. Ct.
2264 (1977).
32   Although I recognize that this distinction and the related distinction between act and omission are not wholly satisfactory, they serve useful analytic
functions in this essay.
33   See *In re Jenison* 375 U.S. 14 (1963).

numerous existing grounds for exemption, although it may be desirable to ask for alternative service.

Sometimes (e.g., in some medical treatments, inoculations, and tax collection) the government can protect the individual's conscience by performing the act in question for him. In such cases the agent may not consider his conscience violated because he did not consent to the act. An example is the case of the Jehovah's Witnesses whose consciences would not permit them to consent to a blood transfusion although they could live with a court-ordered transfusion. Also, faced with the conscientious refusal to pay taxes for military expenditures, the government may attach the objector's salary or bank account. This obviously achieves the government's end, and it may avoid offense to conscience by eliminating the agent's responsibility. But this removal of responsibility will not work for all conscientious objectors, even in the areas of medical treatment and taxes, for they may view conscience as imposing strict liabilities. It also will not work in some other cases, such as military service, where "the government cannot obtain its ends through the objector without violating his conscience."[34] Regarding inoculations, the government should determine whether its interest in public health and safety really requires that each individual be inoculated, for the unprotected individual may not be a threat to anyone else. My argument is not that conscience should be satisfied in every instance, but that the government should show that it cannot secure its legitimate interests, specific as well as general, by alternative means.

Finally, the government may be able to impose some substitute or alternative service and thus respect conscience. This is especially true of noncombatant or alternative service in the national interest in lieu of military service. Such a requirement not only offers some test of the objector's sincerity, but it also respects the principle of fairness in relation to other citizens by imposing burdens on all who are drafted even if the burdens are not exactly the same. Some cases of conflict between con-

34 Clark, "Guidelines," 348.

science and the law are not susceptible to these approaches; they probably include the refusal to testify in courts of law and the stance of noncooperation with the government in any of its positive requirements, such as registration for the draft.[35]

Several important issues emerge from these cases of conscientious objection to positive legal duties. First, in some instances, there is an important distinction between service and obedience or subjection. In the range of positive duties, a few are clear examples of service, as when individuals are selected for military service or jury duty in order to carry out the law. They then become the law's instruments. Also, there has been a duty to assist the police in the suppression of crime. Some have contended that a refusal of service is not a nullification of the law, although disobedience might be.[36] Thus, the government need not treat conscientious refusals of service and conscientious disobedience in the same way.

Second, the nature of the service is also important, especially since some acts are closer to the core of some religious and moral traditions, as well as personal character, than others, and the state itself may have reasons for encouraging the attitudes reflected in some conscientious refusals: for example, the centrality of pacifism to the historic peace churches and its affinities to dominant attitudes in day-to-day life. It might even be possible to single out military service for special treatment because killing human beings is considered prima facie wrong from practically all moral standpoints.

Third, the question of the number of persons seeking exemption is very important. If the state could not get enough servants for juries and military operations, it could justifiably deny the exemptions. But a better procedure would be to limit the number of exemptions for conscience, determining by means of a lottery who would be exempted and who would be forced to serve or face criminal penalties. There are, however, practical reasons for exempting conscientious objectors from

35 Ibid., 357–58.
36 See Michael Walzer, Obligations: Essays on Disobedience, War, and Citizenship (Cambridge, Mass.: Harvard University Press, 1970), 136.

jury duty and military service, for forced participation may be detrimental to the enterprise as a whole and many would choose jail or exile rather than participate in the military. Pacifist consciences are perhaps protected, in part, because their numbers are more or less predictable, while the number of just-war objectors cannot be estimated in advance of a particular war. Nevertheless, a lottery would be possible for selective objectors as well as for pacifists if the state faced serious shortages of manpower, and it would obviate one of the main difficulties feared by opponents of selective conscientious objection.[37]

Now we can look briefly at conscientious objection to and violation of a negative legal duty, the prohibition of some conduct that the agent considers essential to his religious or moral convictions. Several examples are proselytizing, polygamy, and sacraments involving prohibited substances. The Volstead Act contained an exemption for wine used by churches for communion, and the California Supreme Court has held that the Native American church may use peyote in its religious ceremonies. Again, the state should yield to conscience in matters that do not involve harm to persons outside a consenting moral or religious community (or minors within the community). When the conflict is only between the state and the individual conscience over negative duties, the state's interest in paternalism should be rejected and the state should grant conscience this freedom.

In disputes with individuals who have conscientious scruples about some actions, the liberal state, especially through the courts, usually invokes secondary concepts that appear to be value-neutral. Such concepts (for example, the distinction between belief and action or between private and public) have the virtue of establishing regularity over time and stable expectations—important for any rule of law. But they often obscure the

37 These fears were expressed by the National Advisory Commission on Selective Service, *In Pursuit of Equity: Who Serves When Not all Serve?* (Washington, D.C.: Government Printing Office, 1967), 48–51. John Mansfield also argues for such a lottery, see "Conscientious Objection—1964 Term," 46 n, 73.

real policy question, which involves values: how much room should conscience have and how much freedom and protection should it have in relation to other interests? My argument, grounded in an understanding of conscience as a sanction, is that we should start with the presumption in favor of liberty of conscience, which then forces the state to bear the burden of proof to show that its interests are compelling and can be realized through no other means than a denial of the exemption.

By applying my framework in some detail to public policies toward conscientious objectors to military service, I can trace its implications, connect it to both pacifism and just-war theories, and fill it out by analyzing the distinction between conscientious and nonconscientious objection, the distinction between moral-religious and other forms of conscientious objection, and the test of sincerity.

Chapter Six

Policies Toward Conscientious Objectors to Military Service

One major reason for the shift to the all-volunteer army was the vigorous opposition in the 1960s and early 1970s to conscription into service in a war widely perceived to be unjustified.[1] At that time, to receive an exemption from military service as a conscientious objector, a person had to establish that "by reason of religious training and belief" he was "conscientiously opposed to participation in war in any form." The section on conscientious objectors in the Military Selective Service Act of 1967 read:

Section 6 (j) Conscientious Objectors.—Nothing contained in this title shall be construed to require any person to be subject to combatant training and service in the armed forces of the United States *who, by reason of religious training and belief, is conscientiously opposed to participation in war in any form.* As used in this subsection, the term 'religious training and belief' does not include essentially political, sociological, or philosophical views, or a merely personal moral code. Any person claiming exemption from combatant training and service because of such conscientious objections whose claim is sustained by the local board shall, if he is inducted into the armed forces under this title, be assigned to noncombatant service as defined by the President, or shall, if he is found to be conscientiously opposed to participation in such non-combatant service, in lieu of such induction, be ordered by his local board, subject to such regulations as the President may prescribe, to perform for a period equal to the period prescribed in section 4 (b) such civilian work contributing to the maintenance of the national health, safety, or

1   See the editorial, "How Conscientious Is an Objection?" Washington *Post,* July 14, 1970, Sec. A, p. 14. See also Michael Walzer, *Obligations: Essays on Disobedience, War, and Citizenship* (Cambridge, Mass.: Harvard University Press, 1970), 144.

191

interest as the local board pursuant to Presidential regulations may deem appropriate and any such person who knowingly fails or neglects to obey any such order from his local board shall be deemed, for the purposes of section 12 of this title, to have knowingly failed or neglected to perform a duty required of him under this title.[2]

Three major criteria determined who could be exempted under this section: conscientiousness, pacifism, and religious training and belief. Widespread opposition to the war in Vietnam generated pressure to break down the second and third criteria. Under a steady stream of judicial interpretation (which will be discussed later), the religious requirement was washed away for all practical purposes. But, despite several challenges, the requirement of pacifism remained intact. As society considers the possibility of restoring a draft for military service, it is important to determine *whether* conscientious objectors should be exempted from military service and *who* should be counted as conscientious objectors. I shall address the first question very briefly in order to concentrate on the scope of the conscientious objector provision, particularly whether objectors to particular wars should be exempted along with objectors to all wars.

Two points about my perspective may be useful. First, it is important and necessary to deal with penultimate questions even if we cannot resolve ultimate questions. Thus, I will not try to determine whether the state or conscience should be granted final authority but, rather, what our public policy ought to be toward conscientious objectors to military service. Should we exempt them from some public responsibilities in order to protect them from the sanction of conscience?

Second, I will concentrate on three principles that frequently come into conflict in this area of public policy: respect for persons and their consciences, fairness in procedures and in the distribution of burdens in the society, and utility—the production of a net balance of good over bad consequences. I shall not here defend these principles, which can be supported

2   50 U.S.C. App. #456 (j), my italics.

in various ways.[3] I shall rather assume them to be widely accepted in part because of their frequent invocation in public, legislative, and judicial debates about conscription and conscientious objection. I want to consider their implications for the exemption of conscientious objectors from military service.

Exemption of Conscientious Objectors from Military Service

Although there are good reasons for exempting at least some conscientious objectors from military service, it is difficult to claim a constitutional right for such an exemption. In debates about the Bill of Rights in 1789, James Madison proposed an addition to the Second Amendment: "but no person religiously scrupulous of bearing arms shall be compelled to bear arms in person." In the absence of such a clause, but also in the absence of a clear necessity to determine the issue, the Supreme Court has frequently observed that exemption of conscientious objectors (COs) from military service is a privilege, a matter of legislative grace. What Congress gives, Congress may, of course, take away. But, nevertheless, it may not attach unconstitutional conditions to its privileges.[4]

Pragmatic reasons for exemption of COs, such as the difficulty or impossibility of making adequate soldiers out of people who are conscientiously opposed to fighting, are not unimportant. In addition, it would be very difficult politically to eliminate a privilege that is now expected because it has been extended for so long. Attempts to eliminate it would provoke vigorous opposition not only from the historic peace churches

3 See the discussion of these principles and others in Tom L. Beauchamp and James F. Childress, *Principles of Biomedical Ethics* (New York: Oxford University Press, 1979).

4 *Annals of Congress: The Debates and Proceedings in the United States*, Vol. I (1789), 434, reprinted in Lillian Schlissel (ed.), *Conscience in America: A Documentary History of Conscientious Objection in America, 1757–1967* (New York: E. P. Dutton, 1968), 47; *United States v. Macintosh*, 283 U.S. 605 (1931); *Hamilton v. Regents of University of California*, 293 U.S. 245 (1934); *Sherbert v. Verner*, 374 U.S. 398 (1963).

(Mennonites, Brethren, and Quakers), who were the earliest beneficiaries of this privilege, but also from many other religious and secular groups.[5]

Principled grounds for exemption of COs include respect for conscience and fairness. It is at least prima facie wrong to force a person to act against his conscience, although it may sometimes be justified and even necessary. And it is unfair to the conscientious person to give him the "hard choice" between obedience to the law and criminal classification when this can be avoided. In our tradition and our vision of the free society, "in the forum of conscience, duty to a moral power higher than the state has always been maintained." In addition, the "value of conscientious action" to the community has been recognized by legislators and courts as well as by others.[6]

Arguments against exemption of any COs usually appeal to the unfairness of exempting some people from military service when others have to serve. For this reason, exemption of COs from combatant service is also conjoined with the requirement of either noncombatant service or alternative service for an equal period of time. Such a requirement is an attempt to distribute some of the burdens of conscription more fairly and equitably. The CO has to spend an equal amount of time in service, and his life plan, including his career and his family life, is disrupted. Of course, the risks of injury and death are not equalized. Because COs for the most part are not exposed to such risks, it might even be fair for them to serve for longer periods of time or for less pay.

Consequentialist arguments against an exemption for at least

---

5   For the history of conscientious objection in the United States, see Schlissel (ed.), *Conscience in America*, and *Conscientious Objection*, Selective Service System Special Monograph No. 11 (2 vols.; Washington, D.C.: Government Printing Office, 1950). See also Richard K. MacMaster with Samuel L. Horst and Robert F. Ulle, *Conscience in Crisis: Mennonites and Other Peace Churches in America, 1739–1789*, Studies in Anabaptist and Mennonite History, XX (Scottdale, Pa.: Herald Press, 1979).

6   See *United States* v. *Macintosh*, 283 U.S. 605, 633 (1931) (Hughes, C.J., dissenting), and *Gillette* v. *United States*, 401 U.S. 437 (1971).

some COs sound hollow in view of our society's successful policies in the past. At the very least these policies have been successful in that they have protected many consciences without any apparent damage to the country's military security. Nevertheless, it is appropriate to ask whether a policy of exemption can be maintained without detrimental effects when the criteria of conscientious objection are broadened. Thus, the question of exemption of COs and the question of the scope of that exemption merge. As I have indicated, arguments based on principles of respect for persons and fairness support a policy of exempting (some) COs from military service, even though fairness may also justify and even require the imposition of some other burdens such as noncombatant or alternative service. But consideration of possible or probable consequences may make exemption for a broad range of COs difficult if not impossible.

Religious Training and Belief

Exemption of COs from military service in the United States has generally been limited to religious pacifists. Civil War and World War I exemptions were limited to members of "peace churches." The Selective Service Act of 1917 exempted from combatant duty any registrant who was "found by a local board to be a member of any well-recognized religious sect or organization organized and existing May 18, 1917, and whose then existing creed or principles forbid its members to participate in war in any form, and whose religious convictions are against war or participation therein in accordance with the creed or principles of said religious organizations." The actual administration of the law was more liberal, for the secretary of war, under whose auspices all COs served, ordered that "personal scruples against war" be counted as sufficient for conscientious objection.[7]

7 See Schlissel (ed.), *Conscience in America*, 133, 165, and 171 (the last for the president's 1918 executive order that recognized "religious or other conscientious scruples").

While the Selective Training and Service Act of 1940 did not require church membership, COs had to be opposed to participation in war in any form "by reason of religious training and belief," a criterion subject to widely different interpretations. This criterion was interpreted in broader and broader ways as it moved up the levels of appeal. Its ambiguity also troubled the federal courts. Some federal courts defined it as equivalent to conscience, however informed, while others restricted it to theistic beliefs.[8] In 1948 Congress tried to resolve these conflicting interpretations by sharpening the statute: "Religious training and belief in this connection means an individual's belief in a relation to a Supreme Being involving duties superior to those arising from any human relation, but does not include essentially political, sociological, or philosophical views or a merely personal moral code." In a major decision, U.S. v. Seeger, the Supreme Court held that Congress "was merely clarifying the meaning of religious training and belief so as to embrace all religion," including such modern interpretations as Paul Tillich's and John A. T. Robinson's as well as the ethical culture movement. Thus, according to the Court, the conscription act did not discriminate among forms of religious expression. But the Court went on to construct a test of belief "in a relation to a Supreme Being": "whether a given belief that is sincere and meaningful occupies a place in the life of its possessor parallel to that filled by the orthodox belief in God by one who clearly qualifies for the exemption."[9] According to this "parallel belief" test, what is relevant is not the content of the belief but its place or role or function in the believer's life. It is not necessary to affirm theism.

In 1968 Congress deleted the "Supreme Being" clause, but retained the clause that excluded "essentially political, sociological, or philosophical views or a merely personal moral code" as grounds for exemption. In Welsh v. United States, decided

8   See, for example, the broad definition of the Second Circuit in United States v. Kauten, 133 F.2d 703 (C.A. 2d Cir. 1943) and the narrow interpretation of the Ninth Circuit in Berman v. United States, 156 F.2d 377 (1946).
9   U.S. v. Seeger, 380 U.S. 163 (1965).

under the pre-1968 language because of the date of origin of the case, the Supreme Court held that what is necessary for a registrant's conscientious objection to all war to be "religious" within the meaning of the statute is that

this opposition to war stem from the registrant's moral, ethical, or religious beliefs about what is right and wrong and that these beliefs be held with the strength of traditional religious convictions. . . . If an individual *deeply and sincerely holds beliefs which are purely ethical or moral in source and content* but which nevertheless impose upon him a *duty of conscience* to refrain from participating in any war at any time, those beliefs certainly occupy in the life of that individual 'a place parallel to that filled by . . . God' in traditionally religious persons. Because his beliefs function as a religion in his life, such an individual is as much entitled to a 'religious' conscientious objector exemption under #6 (j) as is someone who derives his conscientious opposition to war from traditional religious convictions.

The conscientious objection provision, according to the Court, "exempts from military service all those whose consciences, spurred by deeply held moral, ethical, or religious beliefs, would give them no rest or peace if they allowed themselves to become a part of the instrument of war." Its exclusionary clause does not rule out COs whose pacifism "is founded to a substantial extent upon considerations of public policy." It does, however, rule out "those whose beliefs are not deeply held and those whose objection to war *does not rest at all* upon moral, ethical, or religious principle but instead *rests solely upon* considerations of polity, pragmatism, or expediency."[10]

Obviously the Court avoided facing the constitutional question as to whether this exemption of COs violated the establishment clause of the First Amendment. Indeed, Justice Harlan, who concurred in the result but filed a separate opinion, contended that while *Seeger* was "a remarkable feat of judicial surgery" because it removed the theistic requirement of the statute, *Welsh* performed "a lobotomy." The *Welsh* decision reinterpreted the statute in order to salvage its constitutionality.

Future legislation should affirm the conclusions of *Seeger*

10 *Welsh v. United States*, 398 U.S. 340 (1970), my italics.

and *Welsh* but should state those conclusions in nonreligious terms. The criterion of "religious training and belief," now rendered almost completely vacuous, should be stated merely as a criterion of moral, ethical, or religious conscientious objection. Respect for conscience should not be limited to respect for "religious" conscience, however liberally defined. The place, function, centrality, and intensity of the belief in the registrant's life are important for defining both conscientious objection and its moral, ethical, or religious bases. How moral, ethical, and religious bases might be distinguished from other bases such as political ones will be considered in relation to conscientious objection to participation in a particular war.

Absolute Pacifism and Selective Conscientious Objection

Another question of scope concerns the range of opposition to participation in war. Should exemption from military service be granted only to those who are conscientiously opposed to participation in any war, or should it also be extended to those who are conscientiously opposed to participation in a particular war? So far our government has only recognized universal or absolute conscientious objectors (UCOs), *i.e.*, those who are pacifists. While *pacifism* has various meanings, I shall define it narrowly for this discussion as opposition to participation in any war. An absolute pacifist, then, is one who is opposed to his or her participation in all wars. Obviously, this is a minimal definition, for most pacifists are also opposed to war and not only to their own participation in it. Likewise, for this discussion, the selective conscientious objector (SCO) is opposed to his or her participation in a particular war but not necessarily in all wars.

Since 1940 conscription legislation has exempted only COs who are opposed to "participation in war in any form," a phrase that also appeared in the 1917 legislation. Although some interpreters have held that "in any form" modifies "participation" rather than "war," such an interpretation makes no sense.

A CO might oppose only combatant duties while being willing to perform noncombatant duties, such as service as a medic. Until the war in Vietnam the requirement of absolute pacifism received little attention, despite the centrality of the just-war tradition in the Roman Catholic and major Protestant denominations, probably in part because it was assumed that government officials, rather than citizens, determine whether or not a particular war is just. Unfortunately, discussions of selective conscientious objection in the 1960s and early 1970s suffered greatly from their entanglement with the war in Vietnam. The policy questions are independent of that particular context, however much it may have stimulated interest in them.

The Supreme Court has consistently upheld this legislative requirement of absolute pacifism for exemption from military service, even while occasionally stretching its meaning. One major challenge came from the Jehovah's Witnesses who, over time, have created many difficulties for the selective service system. They are not strict pacifists. They are not only willing to use force to defend themselves, their families, and their faith; they are also willing to fight in some wars, namely, theocratic wars, such as the battle of Armageddon that Jehovah will conduct. Before 1955 the Justice Department determined that Jehovah's Witnesses claiming exemption from military service solely on the basis of the movement's beliefs would not be recognized as conscientious objectors because they were not "conscientiously opposed to participation in war in any form." In Sicurella v. U.S., the Supreme Court held that Congress "had in mind shooting wars when it referred to participating in war in any form—actual military conflicts between nations of the earth in our time." It also noted that Jehovah has not commanded such a war since biblical times and that no such command was expected in the immediate future. In effect, the Court gave Jehovah's Witnesses the benefit of the doubt.[11]

During the Vietnam era, Black Muslims were frequently denied exemption from military service because they indicated

11   Sicurella v. U.S., 348 U.S. 385 (1955).

that their religion would permit them to fight in some wars, for example, if the United States gave them territory to defend. Thus, the government argued that their objection to the war in Vietnam was political rather than religious and selective rather than universal. In Muhammad Ali's case, the government did not question the religious basis of his opposition, or his sincerity, but his pacifism. In such cases, the defense usually argued that the Black Muslims are similar to the Jehovah's Witnesses in all respects that are relevant for conscientious objector classification.[12]

Apart from these exceptions, SCOs have not been recognized.[13] Whether they should be included in any future exemptions for COs depends on several factors. At the risk of some oversimplification, I will consider the main arguments for and against exemptions for SCOs under three headings: the nature of SCO claims, fairness and respect for persons, and consequences. To a great extent, the last two depend on the first.

The Nature of the SCO's Claims

A major argument against exemption for SCOs is that their "so-called selective pacifism is *essentially a political* question of support or nonsupport of a war and cannot be judged in terms of special moral imperatives. Political opposition to a particular war should be expressed through recognized democratic processes and should claim no special right of exemption from democratic decisions."[14] If this argument is sound, it will obviously provide important premises for the arguments that in-

12 *Clay* v. *United States*, 403 U.S. 698 (1971). This case is discussed in Richard J. Regan, S.J., *Private Conscience and Public Law: The American Experience* (New York: Fordham University Press, 1972), 31, a valuable study of legal decisions regarding conscience.

13 *Gillette* v. *United States*, 401 U.S. 437 (1971), upheld the constitutionality of the restriction of the exemption to UCOs.

14 Report of the National Advisory Commission on Selective Service, *In Pursuit of Equity: Who Serves When Not All Serve?* (Washington, D.C.: Government Printing Office, 1967), 50, hereinafter cited as *In Pursuit of Equity*. See also John A. Rohr, *Prophets Without Honor: Public Policy and the Selective Conscientious Objector* (Nashville: Abingdon Press, 1971).

voke the principles of respect for persons, fairness, and utility. But there are reasons for thinking that it rests on several confusions. In trying to determine whether selective conscientious objection is essentially political, rather than moral, we are interested in the distinction between moral and nonmoral rather than the distinction between moral and immoral. The first distinction concerns the classification of judgments and reasons; the second concerns their evaluation.

Consider the following reasons that a draftee might offer for holding that his participation in a particular war would violate his conscience: (1) all wars are wrong; (2) our aims in this war are unjust; (3) the evil effects of this particular war will probably outweigh its good effects; or (4) this war is wrong because we are directly killing noncombatants. The first reason represents the UCO, who rejects participation in any war. The other three reasons represent possible claims by an objector to a particular war. Are reasons 2–4 essentially political rather than moral?

Several reasons for characterizing selective conscientious objection as essentially political may be rejected without further discussion. The SCO's qualified judgment about war, the complexity of his reasons, and his appeal to the facts of the situation in no way make his position less "moral" than the UCO's.

The subject matter of all four judgments is a governmental policy: war. Thus, we cannot appeal to the subject matter in order to distinguish political and moral. In terms of subject matter, UCOs are just as political as SCOs, for all of them alike make a negative judgment about a governmental policy.

Some opponents would respond that selective conscientious objection is essentially political not because it is a judgment about government policy, but because it is a judgment about *one's own government's policy*.[15] While the UCO condemns all governments for their policies of war, the SCO offers a special condemnation of his own government. But it is logi-

15 Rohr, *Prophets Without Honor*, 143, 148.

cally possible for the SCO to hold that both belligerents are
waging an unjust war (e.g., when two powers are seeking to
expand their territorial influence). Nevertheless, in many cases
(perhaps most) the SCO will hold that his own government's
policies are unjust. This stance does not, however, render his
position essentially political rather than moral.

In order to see why it is not possible to characterize SCOs as
essentially political simply because they make a judgment
about governmental policy, it is useful, as Alan Gewirth suggests, to distinguish the subject matter about which judgments
are made from the nature of those judgments.[16] An agent may
make moral, political, or other kinds of judgments about political matters. Suppose we criticize a president who vetoes a bill.
We might criticize his political act because we believe it is unwise for him to alienate a powerful lobby that could help him
be reelected, or because we believe it is unjust. While the subject matter of the judgments is a political act, the two judgments
are different and have different grounds, one political and one
moral.

In the last several years, philosophers have devoted considerable attention to the (metaethical) distinction between moral
and nonmoral judgments. They have proposed several criteria
of moral judgments. The first three are formal: a moral judgment must be (1) prescriptive, (2) overriding, and (3) universal-
izable. The first and second criteria relate very closely to the
place, function, centrality, and intensity of belief that the Supreme Court has emphasized in analyzing conscientious objection. And it is clear that the SCO's judgment may be both
prescriptive and overriding for him. According to the third
criterion, to be moral, a judgment must be consistent from case
to case; that is, the agent must judge relevantly similar cases in
a similar way. The SCO may hold that he is conscientiously
opposed to participation in war X but not in war Y. According
to the third criterion, his opposition may count as "moral" if he

16   Alan Gewirth, "Reasons and Conscience: The Claims of the Selective
Conscientious Objector," in Virginia Held, Sidney Morgenbesser, and Thomas
Nagel (eds.), *Philosophy, Morality, and International Affairs* (New York: Ox-
ford University Press, 1974), 99.

identifies relevant dissimilarities such as the injustice of X and the justice of Y. A fourth criterion focuses on material content, usually the welfare of others. According to this criterion, a judgment is not moral unless it makes some reference to the welfare of others. Any of the reasons (2–4) offered by the SCO may satisfy this criterion and count as moral in contrast to political.[17]

Some critics of selective conscientious objection have held that consideration of the consequences of a war (as in position 3) is political. They tend to view consequentialist reasons as political and deontological reasons, which hold that there are some standards of right and wrong independent of an act's consequences, as moral. But this distinction between consequentialist reasoning and deontological reasoning will not enable us to differentiate political judgments from moral judgments or even to distinguish SCOs from UCOs. It rather indicates two types of moral reasoning in political and other activities. Even if a government's policies and opponents' judgments are based on consequentialist considerations, they are not necessarily political, rather than moral.

It is not even possible to distinguish UCOs and SCOs in terms of their mode of moral reasoning. While much pacifism (e.g., that of the historic peace churches—Mennonites, Brethren, and Quakers) is deontological, pacifism may be based on judgments about the effects of all wars (e.g., that they produce more evil than good).[18] Conversely, SCOs often oppose a particular war not because of its consequences, but because of its violation of principles of right conduct.

In traditional just-war theory there is an important distinc-

---

17 For a discussion of these formal and material criteria and philosophers who have proposed and opposed them, see James F. Childress, "The Identification of Ethical Principles," *Journal of Religious Ethics*, V (Spring, 1977), 39–68. The terms *moral* and *ethical* are sometimes used interchangeably, but I will distinguish them in the following way: *moral* is closer to practice, whereas *ethical* is closer to *reflective* practice.

18 For a good discussion of the varieties of religious pacifism, see John Howard Yoder, *Nevertheless: The Varieties of Religious Pacifism* (Scottdale, Pa.: Herald Press, 1972).

tion between *jus ad bellum* (the right to go to war) and *jus in bello* (right conduct within war). The former includes such considerations of ends and consequences as just cause and proportionality—considerations appealed to by positions 2 and 3. The latter includes such constraints on conduct as prohibition of treachery and direct attacks on noncombatants. For example, position 4 holds that "This war is wrong because we are directly killing noncombatants." The SCO may object to a particular war because it contravenes *jus ad bellum* or *jus in bello* or both. Either may be a moral objection.[19]

In addition, either may be expressed in a conscientious conviction, a "can't help." As I indicated in Chapter 5, an agent who appeals to his conscience as a motive for his conduct claims that if he acted against certain moral convictions, he would experience a severe personal sanction: guilt and shame and a loss of integrity, wholeness, and unity in the self. John Rohr has argued that selective conscientious objection is not a " 'can't help,' but is based on arguments that are constitutional, political and historical—as well as moral or religious."[20] But this experience of conscience, this "can't help," may be the outcome of processes of moral deliberation. Although a person's appeal to his conscience usually involves an appeal to moral standards, conscience is not itself the standard. It is the mode of consciousness resulting from his application of standards to his conduct. It is not limited to intuitionists who hear voices of

19   Commentators tend to concentrate almost exclusively on one or the other. For example, Alan Gewirth and Carl Cohen tend to characterize selective conscientious objection in terms of *jus ad bellum*, while Paul Ramsey comes close to advocating recognition only of SCOs who appeal to the standards of *jus in bello* articulated in legal codes, treaties, and other such agreements. See Gewirth, "Reasons and Conscience," 89–117; Cohen, "Conscientious Objection," *Ethics*, LXXVIII (July, 1968), 269–79; Ramsey, "Selective Conscientious Objection: Warrants and Reservations," in James Finn (ed.), *A Conflict of Loyalties: The Case for Selective Conscientious Objection* (New York: Pegasus, 1968), 31–77. For another argument for recognition of objection to war crimes as defined by international law, see Donald A. Peppers, "War Crimes and Induction: A Case for Selective Nonconscientious Objection," *Philosophy and Public Affairs*, III (Winter, 1974), 129–66.
20   Rohr, *Prophets Without Honor*, 22. See also *In Pursuit of Equity*, 50.

conscience or to fideists who hear the voice of God. It may result from a complex application of several principles to a set of circumstances. The possibility that the war itself may change, or that the agent's interpretation of the facts may change, in no way alters the moral or conscientious nature of his opposition to the war.

Fairness and Respect for Persons

If there were a sharp distinction between the grounds of selective and universal conscientious objection, such that selective conscientious objection is political and universal conscientious objection is moral, then neither the principle of respect for persons nor the principle of fairness would strongly support exemption for SCOs. But if, as I have argued, both selective and universal conscientious objection may be moral as well as conscientious, these principles support exemption for SCOs as well as for UCOs.

First, at the very least, fairness (or formal justice) requires treating similar cases in a similar way. If both the UCO and the SCO are conscientiously opposed to participation in a war for moral or religious reasons, they are relevantly similar. To exclude the SCO because of the content (such as just-war theory) or the scope (such as viewing killing in some wars as justified) of his moral principles is unjust.[21] Neither the content nor the scope of his principles requires that they be labeled as political rather than moral. As an SCO on moral grounds, he is entitled to treatment similar to that of the UCO. To exempt the UCO while forcing the SCO to serve is to put the SCO at an unfair disadvantage. Others have argued that a policy restricting exemption to UCOs discriminates against citizens in the mainstream of Jewish, Christian, and humanist thought and practice in the West. It affords legal recognition to a "minority" or "sectarian" position (pacifism) while excluding the "consensus" position (just-war theory).[22]

---

21 See Cohen, "Conscientious Objection," 271, 277.
22 *In Pursuit of Equity*, 48–49. This argument, offered by some members of the Commission, was rejected by the majority.

Second, exclusion of the SCO is a denial of equal respect. If respect for persons requires respect for conscientious objection, it cannot be extended to UCOs and denied to SCOs simply because SCOs appeal to principles of just war rather than pacifism. The difference in content or scope does not constitute a warrant for disrespect to SCOs.

But whether these principles are decisive for public policy will depend in part on prediction and assessment of the consequences of broad and narrow policies. Indeed, the difficulties of fairly administering an exemption for SCOs are alleged to create some of its worst consequences.

Consequentialist Arguments

In *Gillette* v. *U.S.*, the Supreme Court held that Congress had valid, neutral, secular reasons to exempt the UCO but not the SCO from military service. The government had offered lines of argument based on (1) the nature of SCO claims (that is, that selective conscientious objection is basically political) and (2) fairness (that the administration of selective conscientious objection would be erratic, uneven, and even unfair). The Court rejected the first line of argument, at least in its narrow sense, emphasizing that selective conscientious objection may be "rooted in religion and conscience" whatever other judgments are involved. But the Court did hold that the nature of selective conscientious objection, in conjunction with the fairness argument, may be held to support the statutory restriction to universal conscientious objection. Bad consequences might arise if SCOs were exempted from military service because such an exemption cannot be fairly administered in view of the "uncertain dimensions" and "indeterminate scope" of the claims of SCOs.

But real dangers . . . might arise if an exemption were made available that in its nature could not be administered fairly and uniformly over the run of relevant fact situations. Should it be thought that those who go to war are chosen unfairly or capriciously, then a mood of bitterness and cynicism might corrode the spirit of public service and the values of willing performance of a citizen's duties that are the very heart of free government. . . . In light of these valid concerns, we conclude that it is supportable for Congress to have decided that the objector to all war—to all killing in war—has a claim that is distinct enough and intense enough to justify special status, while the objector to a particular war does not.[23]

The Court's analysis of policies was undertaken to determine whether Congress had a neutral, secular justification for drawing the lines as it did. In the presence of such a justification, the Court could hold that exclusion of SCOs did not violate either the establishment clause or the free-exercise clause of the First Amendment. But the Court did not imply that Congress "would have acted irrationally or unreasonably had it decided to exempt those who object to particular wars."

Let us examine the debate about consequences more carefully. Although proponents sometimes appeal to the positive consequences of a policy of exempting SCOs, for the most part they try to show that the consequences feared by critics are not probable or terrible, or that they are outweighed by good consequences or relevant principles.

Many of the consequentialist arguments against exemption of SCOs point to possibilities (what could happen) rather than to probabilities (what probably would happen) if selective conscientious objection were recognized. And yet public policy regarding SCOs should be based on probable positive and negative consequences, not mere possibilities. For example, the report of the majority of the National Advisory Commission on Selective Service, used by the Supreme Court in *Gillette* v. *U.S.*, held that "legal recognition of selective pacifism *could* open the doors to a general theory of selective disobedience to law, which *could* quickly tear down the fabric of government" and "*could* be disruptive to the morale and effectiveness of the Armed Forces."[24] We need to determine the probability of such consequences as well as to assess them.

---

23 *Gillette* v. *U.S.*, 401 U.S. 459 (1971). Some of the concerns about fairness mentioned by the Supreme Court would also be applicable to pacifists. The administration of a provision for UCOs might favor the "more articulate, better education, or better counseled," and might favor claims more closely connected to conventional religiosity.

24 *In Pursuit of Equity*, 50 (my italics). See the criticisms by Quentin L. Quade, "Selective Conscientious Objection and Political Obligation," in James Finn (ed.), *A Conflict of Loyalties*, 195–218.

Selective disobedience to law. There are at least two important responses to the claim that legal exemption of SCOs could or would lead to selective disobedience to law. First, if this wedge argument holds for selective conscientious objection, it also holds for universal conscientious objection. Whether the request for an exemption from a law is absolute or selective has no bearing on "selective disobedience to law." After all, to take opposition to the payment of a particular tax—the example used by the National Advisory Commission—many UCOs also oppose the payment of taxes that support the military system, and they, as well as some objectors to the war in Vietnam, refused to pay part of their income taxes and the telephone tax surcharge.

Second, this wedge argument holds for neither selective nor universal conscientious objection. There are important dissimilarities between the legal recognition of selective (and universal) conscientious objection and "selective disobedience to law." In the one case, the government accepts certain reasons for exemption from legal duties; in the other, individuals or groups disobey established legal requirements. And it is not clear why legal recognition of certain reasons for exemption from military service would contribute to disobedience. Indeed, legal recognition of selective conscientious objection would reduce the number of criminal acts in one area; no longer would acts of refusing to participate in a particular war be criminal. SCOs would not have to go underground or into exile. In addition, without their "examples" of disobedience, disobedience to law might decline.

Perhaps opponents of selective conscientious objection do not really fear "selective disobedience to law." They may instead believe that if society recognizes the SCO's claim to exemption from military service, it will be hard-pressed to deny other conscientious claims for exemption, for example, from particular taxes. But several distinctions developed in Chapter 5 are relevant. The first is between service and obedience. Individuals selected for duties of service are the law's instruments; they carry out the law. Such service is different from obedience, or at the very least, it is a special form of obedience. And the government need not treat conscientious refusals of service and (other) conscientious disobedience in the same way. The second distinction concerns the nature of the service, i.e., the kinds of action required. The society could hold that killing in war is such a distinctive and special kind of action that conscientious scruples to its performance should be respected whether they are universal or selective.

Numbers. One widespread fear is that exemption of SCOs could or would allow a de facto referendum by which large numbers of citizens who are eligible for a draft could thwart a national policy arrived at democratically. While this fear should not be ignored or dismissed, it may not be determinative. Several points need attention.

First, in contrast to some supporters of selective conscientious objection, I do not think it is possible to generalize from Britain's lack of serious difficulty with its policy of exempting SCOs particularly because it was under siege during World War II and fighting for its survival against an enemy widely perceived to be evil.[25] All that the British example shows is that selective conscientious objection is sometimes feasible.

Second, the number of SCOs is unpredictable because it depends on the particular war. The number of UCOs is relatively stable and predictable. If the number of SCOs is large because the war is considered by many to be unjust or because the government cannot make its case stronger, then perhaps the war needs reconsideration.

Third, if, however, the state faces an emergency, a situation of necessity, it may justifiably draft both UCOs and SCOs, but it should not distinguish between them if my analysis of the na-

---

25 For generalizations from the British experience, see Gewirth, "Reasons and Conscience," 98, and David Malament, "Selective Conscientious Objection and the *Gillette* Decision," *Philosophy and Public Affairs*, I (Summer, 1972), 383–85. Contrast Quade, "Selective Conscientious Objection and Political Obligation," 205. For a discussion of the British experience, see Denis Hayes, *Challenge of Conscience: The Story of the Conscientious Objectors of 1939–1949* (London: George Allen & Unwin, 1949).

ture of both claims is sound. Instead of denying exemptions for both types of COs, or preferring the UCO over the SCO, a better (in part because fairer) procedure would be to limit the number of exemptions for conscience, determining by means of a lottery who would be exempted and who would be forced to serve or face criminal penalties. This procedure would also be a fairer way to reduce numbers than by restoring the traditional religious requirement.[26] Of course the number would need to be set in a nonarbitrary and noncapricious way.

Morale and effectiveness of the armed forces. The National Advisory Commission contended that "a legal recognition of selective pacifism could be disruptive to the morale and effectiveness of the Armed Forces." How does the commission's report support this contention? First, it holds that "a determination of the justness or unjustness of any war could *only* be made within the context of that war itself."[27] But there is no reason why the SCO cannot make a judgment about *jus ad bellum* and *jus in bello* apart from involvement in that war.

Second, the report somehow supposes that a legal recognition of selective conscientious objection *requires* that each citizen and soldier assume the task of determining whether a particular war is just or unjust. It is alleged that this policy would force "upon the individual the necessity" of making that decision and put "a burden heretofore unknown on the man in uniform and even on the brink of combat." But, in fact, a provision for selective conscientious objection would *permit* individuals to make this determination; it would not *require* them to do so. And even now individual soldiers can be held accountable for

26   Ralph Potter contends that we should restore the religious criterion in order to accommodate SCOs because he believes that we cannot eliminate the religious requirement and the pacifist requirement at the same time. See Potter, "Conscientious Objection to Particular Wars," in Donald A. Giannella (ed.), *Religion and the Public Order*, No. 4 (Ithaca, N.Y.: Cornell University Press, 1968), 44–99. See also Paul Ramsey, "Selective Conscientious Objection," 31–77. For a defense of a lottery, see John Mansfield, "Conscientious Objection—1964 Term," in Donald A. Giannella (ed.), *Religion and the Public Order 1965*, (Chicago: University of Chicago Press, 1966), 46 n, 73.
27   *In Pursuit of Equity*, 50, my italics.

"crimes of war," their actions against the "laws of war" (such as killing innocent people), although not for participation in an "unjust" war. Thus, it is not clear why a provision for selective conscientious objection would have "disastrous" results for the individual soldier, his unit, and "the entire military tradition."[28]

It is possible that the morale of the armed forces would suffer if large numbers of persons eligible for the draft or already drafted claimed to be SCOs. It is hard to fight a war that one's fellow citizens consider unjust. But there is little evidence to support the claim that this difficulty would be increased by the exemption of SCOs, even though more people could avoid military service. Indeed, exemption of SCOs could provide a pressure valve and reduce societal protest about an unpopular war.

The most likely source of a negative effect on the morale and effectiveness of the armed forces, emphasized by the Supreme Court, is the draftee's sense of unfairness in the distribution of the burdens of military service. A draftee might have conscientious objections to a particular war but feel bound by the results of the democratic process. His own resolve, however, might weaken if he perceives that the burdens of service are distributed in an erratic and unfair way. And, the Court continued, erratic and unfair distribution could be expected in view of the "indeterminate scope" of selective conscientious objection. Thus, the Court held, Congress had good reasons (though it would not have acted "irrationally or unreasonably" if it had exempted SCOs) to decide "that the objector to all war—to all killing in war—has a claim that is distinct enough and intense enough to justify special status, while the objector to a particular war does not."[29]

It is difficult to predict with assurance what might occur under a policy of exemption for SCOs. But in view of the important principles involved, the government ought to seek ways to distribute burdens of service equitably while respecting conscientious objection, both universal and selective. If a fair administrative procedure cannot be developed, and if the

28   Ibid.
29   Gillette v. United States, 401 U.S. 437 (1971).

country reaches a state of emergency, universal conscription could, of course, be justified.

Positive consequences of selective conscientious objection. Some proponents of selective conscientious objection appeal not only to the principles of respect for persons and fairness in their attempts to rebut the consequentialist arguments against it but also to the positive effects of excusing SCOs from military service. One such argument is that legal recognition of SCOs would elevate "the level of moral discourse on the uses of force" in the society.[30] Presumably, people would reflect on the criteria of justice of and in war. Although few people would dispute the importance of elevating the level of moral discourse about war, such a consequence would have little weight by itself; it is not a very probable result of exemption of SCOs; and it can be sought in other ways. Furthermore, it is more plausible to hold that a policy of recognizing SCOs would not be feasible without an elevation of the society's moral discourse. This elevation is a presupposition rather than a probable consequence of the recognition of SCOs. Without it some of the consequences that opponents fear may indeed occur. The elevation of the level of moral discourse would include respect for the conscience of the laws, for democratic decision-making, and for the (rebuttable) presumption in favor of compliance.[31]

Another argument also focuses on moral education. It holds that principles or rules such as "Never kill in war" are "almost sure to lead to error through oversimplification; while principles of a more limited scope, while also uncertain, have a far better chance of approximating the truth, if there is one. We do well, therefore, to credit the conscientious man with limited principles, rather than to discredit him because his principles are limited."[32] This, according to Carl Cohen, is a matter not

---

30 *In Pursuit of Equity*, 49 (a minority position). See also Ralph Potter, "Conscientious Objection to Particular Wars."
31 Paul Ramsey, "Selective Conscientious Objection," 35, and John Courtney Murray, S.J., "War and Conscience," in Finn (ed.), *A Conflict of Loyalties*, 19–30.
32 Cohen, "Conscientious Objection," 277.

only of justice but of wisdom. This argument is risky, however, because it introduces the question of truth and falsity into the determination of whether COs should be excused from social duties. The SCO should be exempted not because his reasons are more likely to be true (because more limited or qualified), but because the principles of respect for persons and fairness support such a policy. (I will return to the question of truth and falsity in the final section.)

In summary, while the positive consequences sometimes adduced for excusing SCOs from military service are tenuous, other arguments are more compelling. First, the principle of respect for persons supports recognition of the conscience of the selective objector as well as the universal objector. Second, because the UCO and the SCO are relevantly similar, it is unfair to excuse the UCO without also excusing the SCO. Both of these arguments hinge on the nature of the SCO's judgment and reasons. Like universal objection, selective objection may be based on religious and moral principles and may be genuinely conscientious. Although the SCO's opposition is more complex and is based, in part, on the facts of a particular war, it is not necessarily or solely political. Finally, most of the negative consequences of exemption of SCOs from military service that critics anticipate are not very probable, and the critics' claims often rest on conceptual confusions. When conjoined with an analysis of the nature of the claims of SCOs, the principles of respect for persons and fairness support governmental efforts to develop a mechanism to obviate the difficulties of administering a provision for selective conscientious objection in a fair and equitable way. If such efforts fail and serious problems develop for the armed forces or if the government faces an emergency in war, it may be forced to override the claims of COs.

The pragmatic consideration (especially the hopelessness of making an adequate soldier out of the CO) applies to both the UCO and the SCO. Forced participation probably would be detrimental to the war effort, and many would choose jail or exile rather than military service, as they did during the war in Vietnam. Few opponents of selective conscientious objection ever deal explicitly with this consideration either (a) because they believe that the negative consequences of exempting SCOs, for the war and for the society, would outweigh the negative consequences of not exempting them or (b) because they believe that SCOs are at best political objectors and at worst slackers and that, consequently, the threat of imprisonment for noncompliance would be sufficient to make them adequate combatants. I tried to answer (a) in this section and (b) in the discussion of the nature of SCO claims, but I will also touch on (b) in the next section.

Conscientiousness and Sincerity

At least in this century, the third criterion of conscientious objection has been conscientiousness. Determination of conscientiousness or of sincerity in claiming conscientiousness is easier, of course, if the other two traditional criteria, pacifism and religious training and belief, are employed. Indeed, pacifism and a narrow interpretation of religious training and belief can provide objective tests of conscientious objection. Because I have proposed eliminating both of these criteria, determination of conscientiousness hinges on subjective considerations. The task is not to determine the truth or falsity of the beliefs in question, but only to determine that they are truly and deeply held.

Even the "erroneous conscience," based on moral or religious beliefs, also merits protection. After all, from the standpoint of the government, universal conscientious objection represents an "erroneous conscience." An "erroneous conscience" may be mistaken in terms of its moral or religious principles or its interpretation of the factual situation to which it applies its principles. And there may be an interest in trying to distinguish the "factual" and "moral" errors of universal or selective conscientious objection perhaps in order to deny an exemption to the CO whose position presupposes mistakes about factual matters. For example, an SCO may be mistaken in his belief that his country is systematically killing innocent civilians. Even if some factual mistakes may, in principle, disqualify a CO's position, it is not easy or even possible to disentangle the factual and ethical components of a position. Finally, the primary consideration in conscientiousness is not the truth or falsity of the moral belief but its sincerity.

Whether a conscientious objection policy that emphasizes such subjective considerations can be administered evenly and fairly is, as we have seen, a very important consideration in its adoption. Sorting out the genuine and spurious claims of conscientious objection will be a difficult administrative task. In this section, I will not make proposals about procedures (e.g., local boards, appeals boards, and judicial review), which also need careful attention. Instead, I will make a few observations about tests of sincerity of claims of conscientious objection.

Why not accept the potential CO at his word? Why not accept without question his claim to be a CO on moral, ethical, or religious grounds? A major reason is that exemption from military service because of conscientious objection imposes greater burdens on others, some of whom have to serve in the COs' places and bear greater risks of injury and death. Thus, it is important to have some tests of sincerity because COs gain or are thought to gain some advantage over others by not serving as combatants in military service. And the principle of respect for persons does not require respect for the insincere conscience.

Earlier I contended that, because of the principles of fairness and respect for persons, the government should bear the burden of proof that the class of COs should not be exempted from military service. Nevertheless, the individual who claims to be a member of that class of COs should bear the burden of proof that he really holds the convictions in question and that he holds them deeply and intensely. He should bear the burden of proof because he may be presumed to have an interest in avoiding the risks of injury and death in military service. Sincerity is a threshold question to be answered by the objector. But the objector's burden of proof should not be heavy. He should not have to establish his sincerity beyond a reasonable doubt. To establish that the preponderance of the evidence is on his side should be sufficient.

There are complex motivations for requests for exemption from military service. For example, a person may want both to avoid the risks of injury and death and to avoid participation in what he believes to be immoral killing. But then the question is: How can we determine whether "conscientious objection" on moral, ethical or religious grounds is primary or dominant in the objector's motives for requesting exemption from military service? What is the weight or significance of his motive of conscience compared to his other motives? For example, we may wonder whether his conscience is necessary or sufficient for his opposition to participation in a war. As C. D. Broad has suggested, an objector's conscience may be (1) necessary and sufficient, (2) necessary but not sufficient, (3) sufficient but not necessary, or (4) neither necessary nor sufficient for his opposition to participation in war.[33] Objectors in the last category should not qualify for exemption because conscience does not play a significant role in their action, but objectors in the first category should qualify for exemption because, whatever their other motives, they would not have objected to participation if their conscience had not been involved, and their conscience would have driven them to opposition even if other motives (such as fear) had been absent.

But (2) and (3), perhaps the most common, are the most difficult. Suppose conscience is necessary but not sufficient. Both conscience and fear are an agent's motives, but neither one is strong enough to drive him to seek an exemption, while both together are strong enough. Is this conscientious objection? Or suppose that conscience is sufficient but not necessary. In such a case, conscience by itself is strong enough to lead the agent to request an exemption, but his fear is also strong enough. Where conscience is sufficient but not necessary, exemption is warranted, but whether exemption is warranted for the person

33   C. D. Broad, "Conscience and Conscientious Action," in Joel Feinberg (ed.), *Moral Concepts* (New York: Oxford University Press, 1970), 74–79.

whose conscience is necessary but not sufficient would depend on its centrality and strength in his claim.

Even apart from self-deception and intentional deception of others, a person can rarely be sure that his action is conscientious, as C. D. Broad has insisted, because to determine the necessity and sufficiency of certain motives a person has to ask what he or she would do if certain actual motives, such as fear, were absent. We cannot know the answer to that question with any certainty even when we examine our own conduct, much less the conduct of others. For this reason, Broad argued against the British exemption of COs in World War II and, in another context, contended that the death penalty ought to be applied to COs.[34] Such a penalty would presumably provide a clear and definite test of sincerity. Others have suggested imprisonment or a severe tax or even confiscation of the CO's property.[35] Such proposals may help us distinguish those who would only have some "pinpricks" of conscience if they had to serve in the military from those "whose consciences, spurred by deeply held moral, ethical, or religious beliefs, would give them no rest or peace if they allowed themselves to become a part of an instrument of war."[36] But they go too far. It is unfair to impose such hard choices on conscience when they can be avoided. Furthermore, the society loses the service that the CO can provide in other ways. Alternative service not only (partially) satisfies the principle of fairness but also provides one test of sincerity because it reduces (though it does not eliminate) the advantages that the CO might gain.

In addition to such obvious tests as demeanor and credibility, one major test of sincerity is *consistency*. Its application is, of course, easier in the case of the UCO than in the case of the

---

34 C. D. Broad, "Ought We To Fight for Our Country in the Next War?" in Broad, *Ethics and the History of Philosophy* (London: Routledge & Kegan Paul, 1952), 232–43.

35 An internal Selective Service report, prepared by Donald Gurvitz, but not accepted by Selective Service. See George C. Wilson, "Conscientious Objector Problem Seen," Washington *Post*, March 27, 1980, Sec. A, p. 13.

36 *Welsh v. United States*, 398 U.S. 340 (1970)

SCO, at least in part because the pacifist's commitments often entail a way of life, a vocation, that reflects his outlook. But even for the UCO certain popular questions (such as "What would you do if your grandmother were attacked?") are irrelevant to his conscientious objection to participation in war. The courts have indicated that such hypothetical questions are irrelevant because they presuppose that pacifism (as objection to participation in war in any form) necessarily precludes killing in all settings. For example, a person can be a UCO and support abortion, euthanasia, and killing in self-defense in some circumstances.[37] Nevertheless, some questions can be useful in determining consistency, for example, questions about different wars. However, consistency cannot be so defined as to rule out "Damascus Road conversions," nor, projected into the future, can it require absolute certainty about unchangeability.

Most tests focus on the authority, power, or strength of the convictions for the registrant, but some also focus on the process by which the convictions were formed. For example, the traditional requirement of "religious training and belief" was usually interpreted to include both training and belief, not training or belief. Nevertheless, the Court tended to concentrate on belief, not training. After *Welsh*, however, a memorandum from the director of the Selective Service held that to "find that a registrant's moral and ethical beliefs are against participation in war in any form and are held with the strength of traditional religious convictions, the local board should consider the *nature and history of the process by which he acquired such beliefs.* The registrant must demonstrate that his ethical or moral convictions were gained through training, study, contemplation, or other activity, comparable in rigor and dedication to the processes by which traditional religious convictions are formulated."[38] Of course, this is one way to hold onto and to interpret the exclusion of a "merely personal moral code." At the

37   See *Goldstein* v. *Middendorf*, 535 F. 2d 1339 (1976).
38   The same point and much of the same language appears in the 1980 proposed revisions in the Selective Service Regulations. See *Federal Register*, XLIV, No. 234 (December 3, 1980), 80138.

same time, the director of Selective Service indicated that claimants of conscientious objection should have consulted "wise men." The danger is that the process of conscience formation will be interpreted in categories that are excessively rationalistic and academic and that favor more articulate and educated applicants.[39]

In conclusion, because of the principles of respect for persons and fairness, as well as practical realities, exemption of some COs is morally appropriate and perhaps even morally (though not constitutionally) mandatory. Such principles also indicate that the scope of the CO exemption should be broad. It should include moral and ethical as well as religious objectors, and selective objectors as well as universal objectors. A major part of my argument established that selective objectors may be conscientiously opposed to participation in a particular war on moral, ethical, or religious grounds. Their position and its grounds are not necessarily or merely political. Furthermore, the possible or probable negative consequences of exempting SCOs from military service have been exaggerated. It is possible to devise mechanisms to avoid some of them, and in view of the importance of the principles involved, such mechanisms should be sought, particularly in order to determine the sincerity of claims of conscientious objection.

---

39 In this discussion, I have concentrated on whether and which COs should be exempted from military service. I have not included conscientious refusals to register for a draft. For an examination of some ethical issues in the government's response to draft evasion, desertion, civil disobedience, and war crimes after they have occurred, see James F. Childress, "The Amnesty Argument," Cross Currents, XXIII (Fall, 1973), 310–28.

Index

Randall Library – UNCW

NXWW

BT736.2 .C53
Childress / Moral responsibility in conflicts : es

3049002782473